THE QUILTWEAR BOOK

To our grandmother,
Erma Daly

THE QUILTWEAR BOOK

Country-Quilted Garments that Work 9 to 5–and Beyond

DIANE E. HERBORT & SUSAN GREENHUT

EPM
PUBLICATIONS, INC

Library of Congress Cataloging-in-Publication Data

Herbort, Diane.
The quiltwear book : country-quilted garments that work 9 to 5—and beyond / Diane Herbort and Susan Greenhut.
p. cm.
ISBN 0-939009-11-0
1. Clothing and dress. 2. Quilting. I. Greenhut, Susan.
II. Title.
TT560.H48 1988
746.9′2—dc19

EPM Publications, Inc., 1003 Turkey Run Road,
McLean, Virginia 22101

Printed in the United States of America

All drawings by Diane Herbort

Cover and book design by Tom Huestis

Cover and garment photography by Steve Payne
Frontispiece photographs by Lise Metzger

CONTENTS

PERHAPS WE SHOULD HAVE CALLED THIS "THE QUILTWHERE? BOOK"

Looking back at this book, we find it nice to see all the garments safe and sound and together in one place. Finally. That's because lately these quilts have gone more places than we'll ever go.

When the idea of doing this book became a signed and sealed contractual obligation, we realized that we had a big problem. We had only five months to construct 16 garments. Fortunately, a cavalry of quilters, fabric companies and sympathetic supporters came to our rescue. From the woolen mills of New Hampshire, and the silk importers of California, to the garment district of Manhattan, we wheeled and dealed and tap danced to get the dressmaker quality natural fibers that we believe are so important to these designs.

In a crunch, something that's supposed to be a labor of love can quickly become an overwhelming chore. So to keep quality and detailing at the level where it belongs, we packed up some of our half-completed projects and sent them down to Texas for a bit of sun, wide open spaces, and the handiwork of some very finicky quilters. In the San Antonio area, Beverly Orbello, Rose Bailey and Susan Stone calmly pieced, appliqued and quilted so that back home in New York and Virginia we could be free to panic over other things.

Even when it seemed that we weren't getting anywhere, our garments were going places. At one point, some of them crossed the Mason-Dixon Line into Yankee Maryland, where Coleen Walters, Jackie Isbell and others quilted, hemmed and set in lots of zippers.

By then, our quiltwear collection was a seasoned traveler. Regular trips to New York became old hat. At the drop of an Amtrack ticket, our garments called on megabucks publishers and visited with the editors at *McCall's Needlework and Crafts Magazine*. So when it came time to photograph the collection, a simple New York fashion shoot was definitely not exotic enough. Instead, we went to the heart of quilting country, the mountains of West Virginia.

In Cabin Creek, West Virginia, a tiny "holler" on the Kanawha River, we met with Judy Parcell and Bonnie Masters, who were then the co-directors of Cabin Creek Quilts, a nonprofit co-operative company of professional quilters and other folk artists. At Cabin Creek, we found that our Seventh Avenue-style garments and the Co-op's more country-style quilts often matched up patch-for-patch. As a result, the Cabin Creek Quilters offered their quilts for our layouts and their services as fashion models for our book.

The week of the photography session, our entire road show, which by now consisted of 16 half-completed garments, a crate of sewing supplies, a jet lagged Viking sewing machine, and several suitcases of blouses, belts, scarves and shoes, arranged to meet the quilters in downtown Charleston, West Virginia. At photographer Steve Payne's cheerful studio, a converted Victorian home just a few blocks from the state capitol, we held what may well be the world's first "modeling bee": two days of nonstop fittings, alterations, make-up sessions and shouts of "Perfect! Now move your left foot two more inches to my left."

Our wardrobe of quilted clothing has certainly been around, but there are a lot more places that we'd like it to go. Such as to the office. To a night at the symphony. To tea at the Ritz. Anywhere you'd wear a tailored suit or a simple silk dress. That's because the garments in this book are designed to go places where other quilted garments may not be appropriate.

Most quiltwear collections tend towards one of two extremes. First there's the casual sportswear look: loose-fitting vests and toggle-closed mandarin collared jackets. Clothing that is good looking and comfortable, but often too casual to wear to the office.

On the other extreme are quilted garments that are too dramatic or self-consciously artistic for real life. We're talking about coats with eye-catching three dimensional landscapes, or evening jackets that are beautiful, but too dressy for most evening occasions. Some of the quiltwear projects that we've seen have so much drop dead chic, only a six-foot-tall Oscar nominee could carry them off. These rather impractical garments are politely referred to as "artwear". We find that too often, the real art lies in finding an occasion to wear them.

That's why Diane has designed this collection of quilted and appliqued clothing. They are garments that you'll want to make, then be able to wear anywhere you go in the course of a real-life day or informal evening.

So pick a project and plunge in. Make your garment as shown, or be creative and see where inspiration takes you. Either way, these garments are all such experienced travelers, you can depend on going far with them.

PART 1
THE BASICS

1
MATERIAL PLEASURES

This is the chapter in which we become crusaders. We're crusading to change the way people think. We want quilters to start thinking like dressmakers. And we want dressmakers to think more like quilters. Here's why: For the garments in this book to work, you have to choose your fabrics very carefully. They have to drape properly. They have to be well suited for the handling that often comes with piecing and applique. And as long as you're going to all this trouble, you'll want your work to last. So your fabric has to be durable.

Unfortunately, the fabrics that have always been your favorites may not be right for the projects in this book. You may do better trying something new or, more specifically, new to your way of thinking. We've found that many quilters tend to stick with their tried-and-true cotton broadcloth. At a fabric store they'll head straight for the calicos, barely stirring the air over a display of silk shantung. People like this are certainly limiting themselves creatively, but more important, they're guilty of not thinking like dressmakers. Crisp cottons don't always drape flatteringly over the body. So if you're making an applique-embellished dress, you're better off thinking like a dressmaker and choosing a fabric that's flattering to the human figure. Perhaps a Thai silk or a lightweight flannel.

Home sewers have a different problem. Being adventurous and trying new fabrics isn't one of them. That's part of the fun of sewing. But before starting a quilt-inspired garment, a sewer needs to spend some time thinking about fabric as a quilter would. Your fabric has to be more than just washable and not wrinkle too much. You have to be able to manhandle it. For example, a linen blend that would work well for a suit would be a disaster for a suit with patchwork detailing. That's because a loose or nubby weave will ravel or stretch during piecing. And a blend that makes a skirt wrinkleproof might also pill after a while. That may be acceptable for an ordinary suit, but if you're going to spend extra time piecing and appliqueing a garment, you'll certainly want a fiber that will look good many years later.

A GUIDE TO QUILTWEAR FABRICS

Patchwork, applique, and quilting may have a reputation as homespun arts, but the fabrics you use can be as highfalutin' as you can imagine. The garments in this book are made from 100% silk, wool, rayon, cotton, plus a few remarkable manmades. Because you may never have tried piecing and applique with these fabrics, we've included some special notes about these materials. In the listing, you may see a few fabrics that are hard to find where you live. To help you gain access to more fabric types and in the widest variety of colors and weights, there is a list in the Appendix of mail-order companies. We've bought fabrics from these companies and have been happy with their selections, prices and service. There are still other reliable mail-order houses and fabric clubs whose advertisements appear in craft, fiber and sewing magazines.

Cottons and Cotton Blends

In general, 100% cotton broadcloth is the easiest fabric to sew. It has good body and is comfortable to wear. Some 100% cottons have a wrinkle-resistant finish. If you like cotton blends because they're easier to care for, you might want to take a look at these treated cottons.

Among quilting purists, blends are still considered taboo. At Cabin Creek Quilts, all quilt tops are constructed from 100% cotton. There's a reason for that. When a top is made from a blend, the polyester batting tends to migrate up through it. On a light-colored quilt, this might never be noticed, but on dark tones, fiber migration can look like a coating of white fuzz. So even though Cabin Creek offers its customers a choice, the quilters themselves prefer pure cotton for tops and backing.

In clothing, blends have the annoying habit of pilling along areas of wear and tear like cuffs, collars, elbows and skirt backs. On the pro side, blends are easy to care for. They rarely wrinkle. Blends also tend to be available in a wider variety of colors and prints.

100% Cotton Quilt Fabric. This is the cotton broadcloth quilters know and love. It's widely available in a huge number of solid colors and prints. It's durable, absorbent and comfortable.

Pima Cotton. This fine-grade cotton is named for Pima, Arizona, where the plant was first grown. It was derived from Egyptian cotton plants, which, for hundreds of years, provided the finest cotton available. Pima cotton is found in many different weaves. Broadcloth, lawn, sateen or pique are just some of the varieties. The long, fine fibers of pima cotton make for soft, silky, lustrous and strong fabric, fabric that is more expensive than ordinary cotton. Because of its quality and premium price, pima cotton is considered a high fashion fabric and is often found in the most current prints and colors. In the same fine category (although not necessarily from the pima plant), are fabrics labeled "Italian cotton" or "Imported" cotton. Liberty®

prints and Stylecrest are brand names for fine dressweight cottons. If you find something labeled "Egyptian Cotton", take a close look. Due to changes in agriculture and trade, cotton grown and woven in Egypt is now such a rarity here that your "find" is most likely an "Egyptian-type" cotton.

Featherweight Corduroy. This lightweight 100% cotton corduroy is very soft and has tiny pinwales. For an interesting variation of textures, combine featherweight corduroy with cotton broadcloth, silk noil or woolens of similar weight.

Cotton Blends. Most sewers are quite familiar with cotton/polyester blends and getting acquainted with the newer cotton/rayon blends. The rayon content gives the fabric a softer drape. Cotton/linen blends have much of the feel of linen, but tend to wrinkle and ravel less than pure linen. Cotton/silk blends benefit from the luster of silk, and are generally less expensive than pure silk.

"Novelty" Cottons. Innovative suppliers and new-to-these-shores imports are making it possible to find many interesting new cottons. Watch for Guatemalan handwovens, fancy jacquard weaves, and textured Japanese cottons. Also look for fabrics that you may have pegged only as craft fabrics: Indonesian batiks or your own tie dyed and stenciled cottons.

Rayon

Rayon is a fiber that's made from cellulose, a chemical derived from the cell walls of cotton, hemp, wood or other plants. Unlike other plant fibers, rayon must undergo a lengthy chemical process before it can be spun. First a pile of wood chips is broken down into a cellulose "soup". Then, in a process that somewhat resembles the manufacturing of polyester, this cellulose solution is forced through a plate pierced with tiny holes. The result is a stream of long, thin plastic-like filaments. Often the threads are spun and woven to mimic the texture of other plant fibers like cotton and silk.

Some people consider rayon to be a natural fiber, because it's derived from plant sources. Others argue that it's a synthetic, a fiber that's manufactured from plant-derived chemicals. You decide. But whatever you call it, get to know it.

Rayon may look and feel like other fibers, but it often behaves differently. Always pre-shrink washable rayon before sewing. Some weaves shrink quite a bit. Others become much softer after one washing. Rayon fibers are weakest when wet, so handle gently and give the fabric lots of support when you hang it to dry.

"Acetate®", "Avril®" or "Viscose®" in a fabric name all refer to rayon. Sometimes the word rayon appears on the label with these words, sometimes not. The final woven fabric can be anything from a soft, smooth broadcloth to a dressy, drapable crepe. Here are some of the rayon fabrics we like and use regularly:

Rayon Faille or **Moire Faille**. Faille (pronounced "file") is a fabric with horizontal ribs running from selvage to selvage. It can be very lightweight and similar to crepe (tissue faille), or a very heavy suiting. We like to use medium-weight faille. Unlike many dressy-looking fabrics, it is very easy to sew and has a surprising softness and drape. Faille works well for simple piecing and machine applique. It's great for crazy quilting or evening looks.

Moire faille ("watered silk") is a shimmery evening-look fabric. Its distinctive water marked pattern is set into the fabric by a heat process. It does water-spot, but rayon watered silk, unlike *silk* watered silk is not instantly ruined when it comes into contact with water.

Rayon Brocade. Brocade is a medium-to-heavy-weight fabric interwoven with a raised design. This design may be of different colors or just a different texture from the background. Rayon brocades are usually softer than polyester brocades and less expensive than silk. All brocades ravel fairly easily but, with care, adapt well to piecing or machine applique techniques. Rayon brocade and faille should be dry cleaned.

Rayon or Wool Challis. (Pronounced "shallie") is a soft, lightweight fabric with either a plain or twill weave. Plain weave challis is most often seen as a scarf fabric with a dark toned ground overprinted with bright, bold flowers. The name for this fabric comes from an Indian word which means "soft". Both rayon and wool challis are light enough to be practically seasonless, and are wrinkle resistant.

Challis is a bit too soft for piecing by any but the most advanced quilters, but is good for hand applique. Challis quilts beautifully and can be used for both the outer and backing layers of quilted garments.

Wool

Anyone who's fallen in love with Amish quilts can understand why wool is an excellent choice for all quilting techniques. Wool is a joy to sew. It stitches up nicely and has that wonderful quality of forgiveness that enables you to ease extra fabric into a seam, or rip and try again. This is an especially desirable quality if you are setting in a jacket sleeve or trying to match the points of a pieced block.

Wool comes in a multitude of weights, weaves and finishes. For the outfits in this book, look for closely woven, light-to-medium weight wool fabric.

Wool is wrinkle resistant, wears well and needs little embellishment to look sophisticated and businesslike. It's the perfect choice for quiltwear.

Wool Flannel. This plain or twill-weave fabric has a soft, slightly napped surface. It does not ravel easily, which makes it ideal for piecing and applique. Flannel comes in various weights, but the medium and light weights work best for the garments in this book. When choosing fabric, don't feel you have to limit yourself to solids.

Even beginners can have good results with heathers, pinstripes, herringbones or plaid flannels.

Wool Suiting. Suiting is similar to flannel but with a smoother, harder finish, which lets it tailor beautifully. It's used most often for men's suits, so the color choice is usually limited to conservative grays, browns and blues. Suitings ravel more easily than wool flannel, but they can be used for simple strip-pieced designs.

Wool Gabardine. This is a firm, twill-woven fabric that has a fine diagonal weave on the front and is plain on the back. Gabardine is a strong, long-wearing fabric, but it ravels easily. We recommend it only for piecing designs that can be completed with minimal handling; log cabin or nine-patch blocks are the safest choices.

Washable Wool. This can be almost any weave, but washable wool flannel is the most popular. Washable wool is a blend of wool and polyester or wool and nylon. The second fiber prevents the wool from shrinking. Good quality washable wool looks, feels and sews like 100% wool.

Wool Tweed. Tweed is a fabric woven from yarns of two or more colors. A tweed can be a plaid, check, herringbone or have many flecks of other colors. Most tweeds are too loosely woven to piece, applique or quilt, but you might try a closely-woven, medium weight tweed. Be sure to pre-shrink tweeds well, especially authentic handwoven Harris Tweed.

Wool Crepe. A soft, lightweight, fabric woven from yarn that has been twisted after spinning. This twist gives wool crepe its special texture. Very drapable. Suitable for dresses, skirts, blouses, lined slacks.

Silk

Silk is a natural fiber that many of us have never sewn or worn, partly because of its reputation as an expensive luxury fabric. Silk is absorbent, strong and drapable, and comes in an almost infinite variety of weights and weaves. Silk accepts dye like no other fiber. This gives those who sew a choice of colors ranging from gentle, lustrous pastels, to the glowing intensity of the brightest, deepest jewel tones.

With the advent of easy-care synthetic fabrics, silk gained a reputation for being expensive and hard to care for. Some of that is beginning to change. New sources for silk are making the silk market more competitive. As a result, silk fabrics and clothing are becoming available at a wider range of prices. Also, with the price of cotton steadily creeping up each year, the price difference is no longer so dramatic. Most important about silk, nothing compares with its elegant, seasonless look and feel.

Contrary to the labels in many store-bought garments, silk can be washed. Just be sure to pre-wash your fabric before you cut. (Washing instructions are given at the end of the chapter). Of course, you may still prefer to dry clean your completed garment. That's fine, especially if it is something like a jacket with interfacings, linings, shoulder pads, etc. However, a silk skirt or dress will benefit from an occasional hand washing to restore and refresh the fibers. The only thing to remember is to wash silk only when you have time to stick around and iron it. It should be ironed while still slightly damp. A spray bottle won't do, because silk dries so quickly. Lightweight silk can be ready to iron in half an hour or less. Medium-weight silks may take a couple of hours to get to that just-damp stage. Always use a warm, dry iron, and press from the reverse side.

Some of the better polyesters do a good job of recreating the look and hand of silk. You may be interested in trying them. Their lower price and easy care certainly make them an attractive option for dresses and blouses. Most often silk-look synthetics can be hand quilted or machine appliqued with beautiful results. However, because of their permanent press finish, a bit more skill is required to piece or hand applique these fabrics. Try a swatch first.

Silk Broadcloth. A plain-woven medium-weight fabric with extremely fine crosswise ribs. Silk broadcloth can be quilted or appliqued. A bit more skill may be required to use it in patchwork, but the results are stunning. This a good fabric for dresses, summer-weight skirts, or quilted vests and jackets.

China Silk. A plain-woven fabric that is lighter and less durable than broadcloth . It is most often used as the lining in jackets, skirts or dresses of silk or wool. China silk can be used for applique, but broadcloth is a better choice for a garment body.

Silk Noil. Noil refers to the shorter waste fibers from the inner part of a silk cocoon. Noil's texture is more nubby and the woven fabric has a duller finish than most silks. Plain weave silk noil does not "read" as a dressy fabric. However, it resists raveling, sews easily and is ideal for all the different techniques used in this book. Plain weave noil is a good fabric for all skill levels.

Noil can also be woven into jacquard weaves with floral or geometric designs; leno weaves with " striped " openwork areas; and twills with fine diagonal ridges. All of these novelty weave noils ravel a bit more than plain weave noil. The twill weave also tends to stretch and be less stable. We recommend that these novelty weaves be used for simple piecing only, or for a garment body with the complex piecing or applique work done in a plain-weave noil.

Crepe de Chine. A fine, plain-woven fabric made from silk yarns that have been twisted after spinning. Soft, lustrous crepe de chine is one of the most widely available types of silk. We find it a bit too fragile for piecing, although experienced sewers might wish to try simple hand or machine piecing. Silk crepe works well for lovely, delicate hand applique. Consider it also for a blouse to coordinate with a silk noil skirt or wool gabardine suit.

Shantung. This is a medium-weight fabric with irregular slubs running horizontally across the fabric. The slubs are formed by doupioni silk, which comes from two silk cocoons that grew together and formed uneven, irregular fibers. This is an elegant fabric with more body and texture than crepe de chine or broadcloth. Accomplished quilters might want to try simple hand piecing or strip piecing, but we wouldn't recommend shantung for a first-time piecing project. Shantung looks quite beautiful when hand appliqued or hand quilted.

Thai Silk. This crisp, medium-weight silk has very noticeable horizontal slubs. It is often woven with the warp threads a different color from the weft, giving the finished fabric an iridescent look. This dressy fabric sews easily, but ravels a bit. Thai silk can be pieced or appliqued with moderate ease. Expert quilters may want to try quilting Thai silk, a technique that brings out the beautiful variations in the fabric's color and texture.

Fabrics with Nap

Velvet, velveteen, corduroy and Ultrasuede® are all napped fabrics. They all have surface fibers that face in one direction. Determining which end is up (or down) then following that direction is a very important consideration in designing and sewing with napped fabrics. The same piece of fabric can look quite a bit lighter or darker depending on whether the nap faces up or down. For that reason, it's necessary to be consistent and cut every garment piece with the nap always running in the same direction. When making patchwork from napped fabrics, your templates and each cut piece must be positioned and marked so that the nap runs correctly on every piece of the finished patchwork. It takes some planning, and occasionally some ripping, and is not a task for beginners.

Velvet. Velvet has a plain or twill-weave back and a thick pile surface. In the factory, two pieces of velvet are woven at the same time so that the pile is sandwiched between the two layers. After the two lengths of fabric leave the loom, a knife splits the pile, creating two separate pieces of velvet.

Velvet can be woven from silk, cotton, rayon, or a combination of any two fibers. We especially like J.B. Martin Co's Matinee® Velvet which has a thick cotton pile woven into a rayon back. It can be machine washed and dried. We did so before sewing and noticed that the fabric seemed to become even softer and more lustrous. The thick cotton pile resists crushing, making this an ideal velvet to use as a base for machine applique. Quilting brings out the fabric's texture and depth of color. We don't recommend velvet for piecing as the thick nap can be a headache when matching up points and seams.

Velveteen. This is similar to velvet, but with a shorter pile. Velveteen is usually cotton or a cotton blend and, unlike velvet, is woven one layer at a time. While not as luxurious as velvet, it can be pieced or used as the background fabric for machine applique. The shorter pile makes it easier to hand quilt than velvet.

Ultrasuede®, Facile® and Caress®. Ultrasuede® is the Skinner Corporation's nonwoven synthetic that looks and feels like real suede. Facile® is a lighter weight version of the original Ultrasuede®. It's remarkably light and drapable. Caress® is even lighter and softer than Facile®, much like chamois. All of these fabrics are quite expensive, but they begin to look less costly when compared to real suede. Laying out a pattern on real suede can be a time-consuming and costly process. Because pattern pieces do not always fit on irregularly shaped skins, a great deal of wasted areas can accumulate. Cleaning is another consideration in choosing between suede and Ultrasuede®. Suede is expensive and often inconvenient to clean. Eventually, the cost of cleaning a suede garment can surpass the cost of the garment itself. Ultrasuede® and Facile® are machine washable and dryable.

We especially like Facile® and Caress®. Their lighter weight and soft drape make them more appropriate for quilt-oriented techniques. They can be quilted by hand or machine, although hand quilting can be tough on the fingers. Both are easy to hand applique because their nonwoven nature makes turned-under seam allowances unnecessary. Neither fabric ravels or frays. Experienced piecers can create stunning patchwork in Facile® or Caress®, although simple patchwork designs are often the best choice. As with any napped fabric, the direction of the nap must be correct on each patch.

Preparing Your Fabrics

Always pre-shrink your fabric, as well as any interfacing or interlinings. Pre-washing is usually unnecessary, although we do recommend it for silk (see below). To pre-shrink most washable fabrics (cottons and cotton blends, rayon and rayon blends) run them through a warm water rinse, followed by a spin cycle. Then toss into the dryer. Do similar groups of colors together—all light prints or all medium-to-dark greens, for example.

You need to check the rinse water to see if it has become strongly colored. If so, you might want to rinse again. Many deep-colored fabrics are over-saturated with dye. The color in the first rinse water may be "over dye". After the initial rinse, the fabric should be colorfast. Still, some colors are notoriously unstable, especially bright pinks, deep reds and purples. Try adding white vinegar or salt water to the second rinse, and let it soak for 30 minutes, then rinse until the water is clear. Once in a while we all get a hopeless case. A red print that continues to bleed after seven washings isn't worth using. Go out and get a new piece of fabric.

As said above, we recommend pre-washing most solid-color silks, even if you intend to dry clean the finished garment. We washed every single piece of silk used for the garments in this book and they all came out beautifully. Cut a small test swatch and try soaking it before you do the entire piece. Some silks have less body after washing, while others may become stiffer. A swatch will also warn you if a fabric will bleed significantly.

Silks should be pre-washed by hand. Fill a basin with warm water and add a very small amount of mild detergent. Dunk the fabric and let it sit for a couple of minutes. Most silks will lose a little dye the first time or two that they are washed. To help set the color, add white vinegar to the rinse water (one tablespoon to a quart of water) each time you wash silk. Then rinse until the water is clear. Handle silk gently while it is wet. Blot it in a towel, then hang to dry. Press with a warm iron while the silk is still damp.

All wool needs to be pre-shrunk. Wool blends which are labeled "washable wool" can be run through the washer and dryer as described above.

Pure wool must be pre-shrunk by steaming. One way to do this is to take the yardage to the dry cleaners and ask them to "sponge and shrink" the fabric. You can also pre-shrink wool yourself. Fill your iron with distilled water, then heat the iron until it steams freely. Lay a section of the wool in a single layer on the ironing board and slowly pass the steaming iron over it. Don't set the iron directly on the fabric, keep it an inch above the fabric. Use the "surge" button on your iron if you have one, and let the steam force its way down into the wool. Work slowly and be sure to steam every inch of the fabric. Sometimes you can actually tell that the fabric has shrunk a bit. Allow each steamed section to cool down and dry before you reposition the yardage and proceed to the next section.

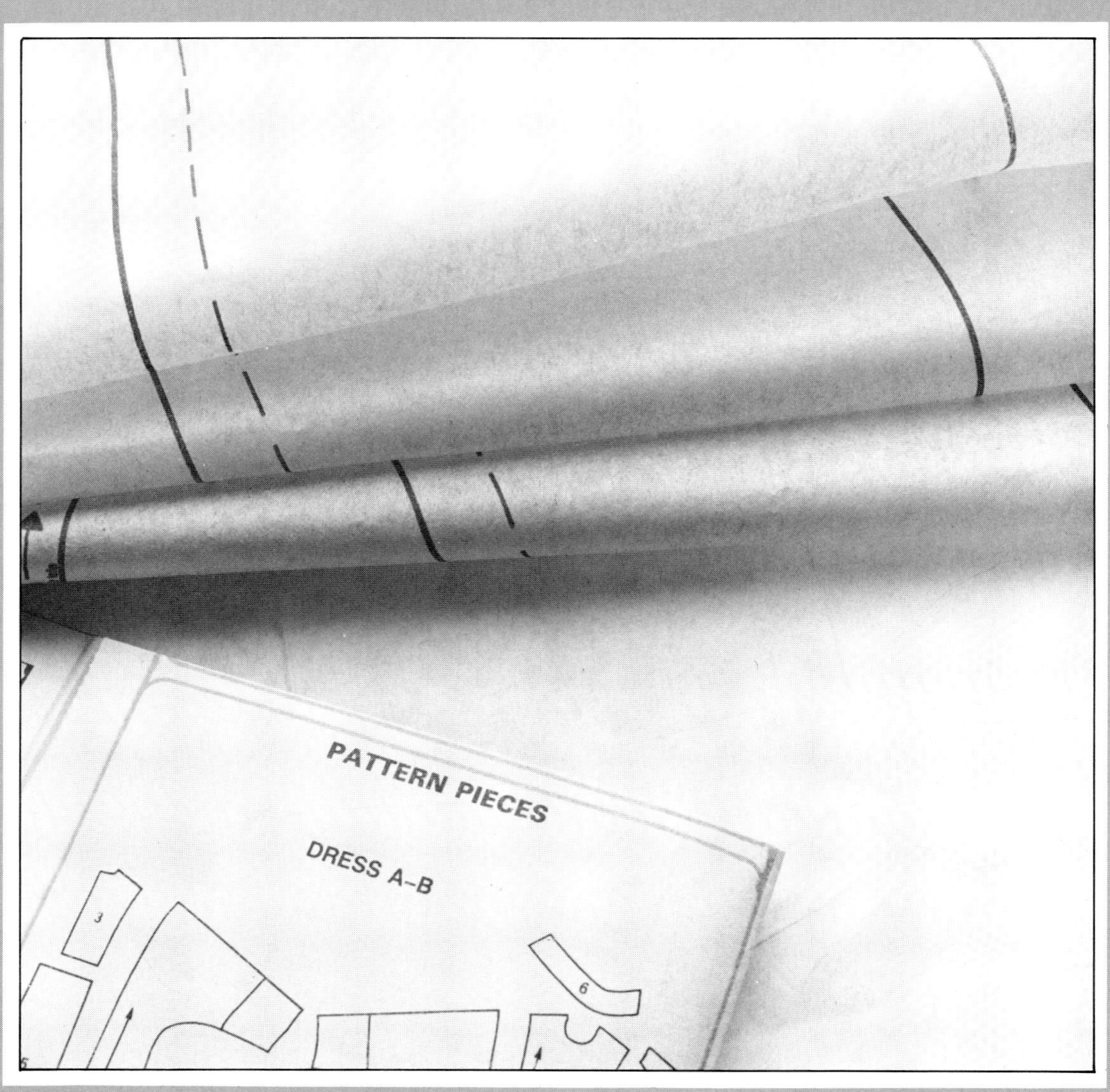
PATTERN PIECES
DRESS A-B

2 CHOOSING AN APPROPRIATE PATTERN

If you've been sewing for a long time, you probably have lots of patterns that have been used only once. And only two or three that you use quite often. For most sewers those old reliables usually include a simple skirt, a pants pattern precisely marked for the proper fit, and perhaps a classic jacket or dress. These are patterns you've made to fit, and have learned to adapt to any project that comes along.

The same principle applies to the garments in this book. Every project is based on one of four commercial patterns: A gathered skirt. A bolero vest. A tailored "Chanel style" jacket. And a yoked dress. We can't tell you which specific pattern numbers to buy because the numbers change too often, but these classic styles appear month after month in virtually every pattern book.

Though we don't give numbers we can provide some guidelines that will help you choose a suitable pattern. The most important thing to remember when shopping for a pattern for quiltwear is to keep it simple. Complicated darts and seam lines interfere with the flow of a patchwork band or an appliqued motif. Also, the simple lines of classic styles will remain in style for years—a worthwhile consideration when you're putting extra time and effort into quilting, piecing or appliqueing a garment.

To be more specific, here is what to look for when choosing each of the basic patterns.

All of the outfits in this book can be made from these four basic pattern styles.

The Basic Dress

Plain, round neckline

Natural shoulder line

Back zipper

Dress body gathered into plain yoke
Avoid: Collars. Darts or princess seams. Shaped yokes.
When choosing a basic dress pattern, in addition to considering the pattern's adaptability to your specific project, it is important to decide early on how you plan to wear the finished garment. Will you wear the dress belted or unbelted? And with what style of shoe—heels or flats? Anything that changes the length of your dress affects the placement of your border motif.

Yes

Avoid

The Basic Jacket

Collarless

"Chanel" styling

Hip length or shorter

Straight sleeves
Avoid: Princess seams or long darts. Side panels. Lapels.
Even after you've chosen your jacket pattern, you'll want to stop periodically and see if you need to make adjustments. After you've cut and basted your muslin, try it on. Check the fit. You many want to add or eliminate back or bust line darts. Also, you'll want to see if the motif you've chosen is right for your height and figure. To check, draw the design, in color, directly on your muslin. Try it on with the blouse you plan to wear with the finished suit.

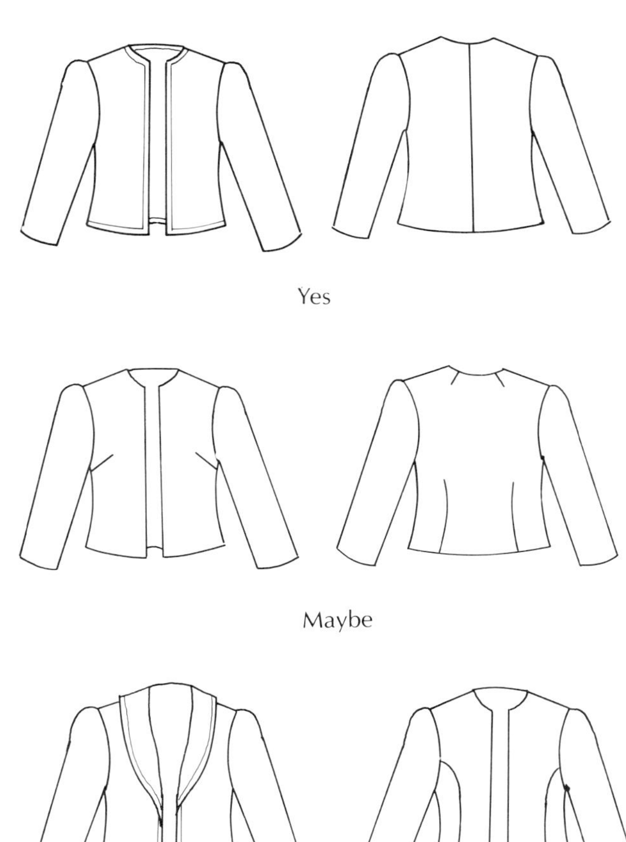

The Basic Vest

Simple styling—2 main pattern pieces

Lined to the edge, could be made reversible

Waist length

Curved front

Open front or frog closure
Avoid: Side panels. Complicated seams or darts.

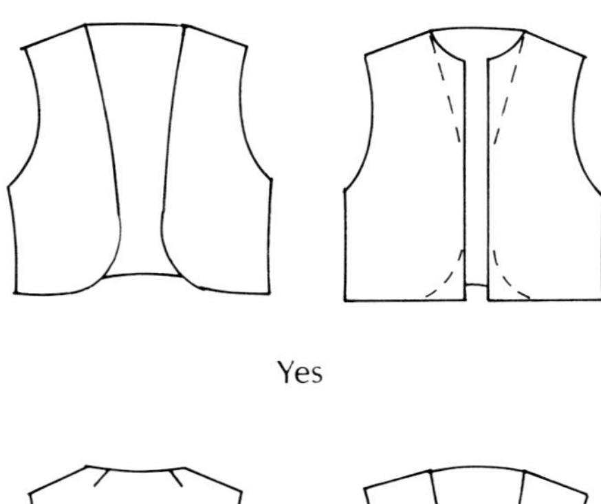

Yes

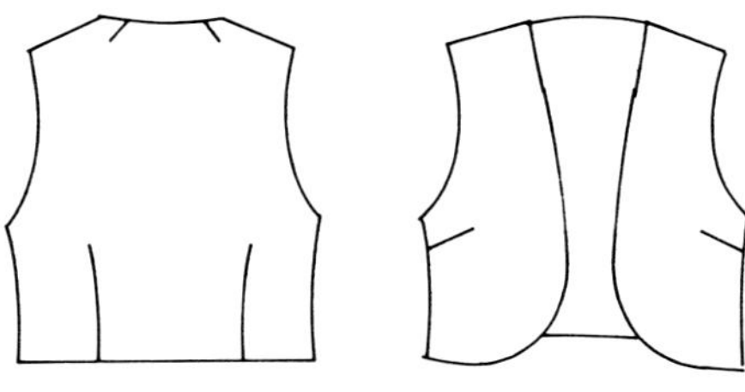

Maybe

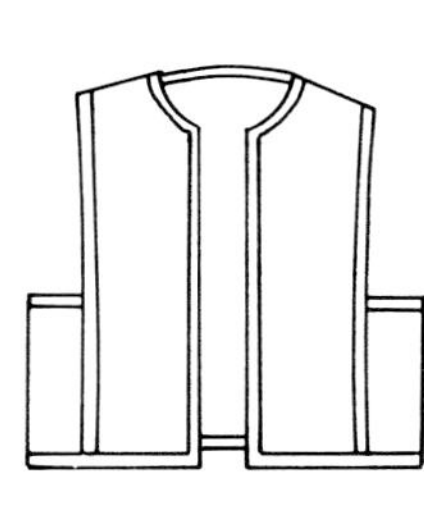

Avoid

The Basic Skirt

Pattern says: "suitable for border prints"

Completely straight across the bottom edge

Gathers or soft pleats at waistband
Avoid: Gored skirts. A-line skirts. Any skirt with a curved hem.

All the skirt projects in this book call for either a 60″ or 64″ width at the finished hemline. Commercial patterns tend to fall somewhere in this ballpark and can easily be adapted to the exact 60″ or 64″ measurement you need. The instructions for adjusting a skirt hem width are in Chapter 3.

Even though your pattern is fine, you may need to make adjustments because of the fabric. Heavy woolens or velvets can sometimes look too bulky after they've been gathered into a waistband. Eliminating excess fullness must be done carefully so as to retain a right angle along the bottom edge. For instructions in how to do this, see Chapter 3.

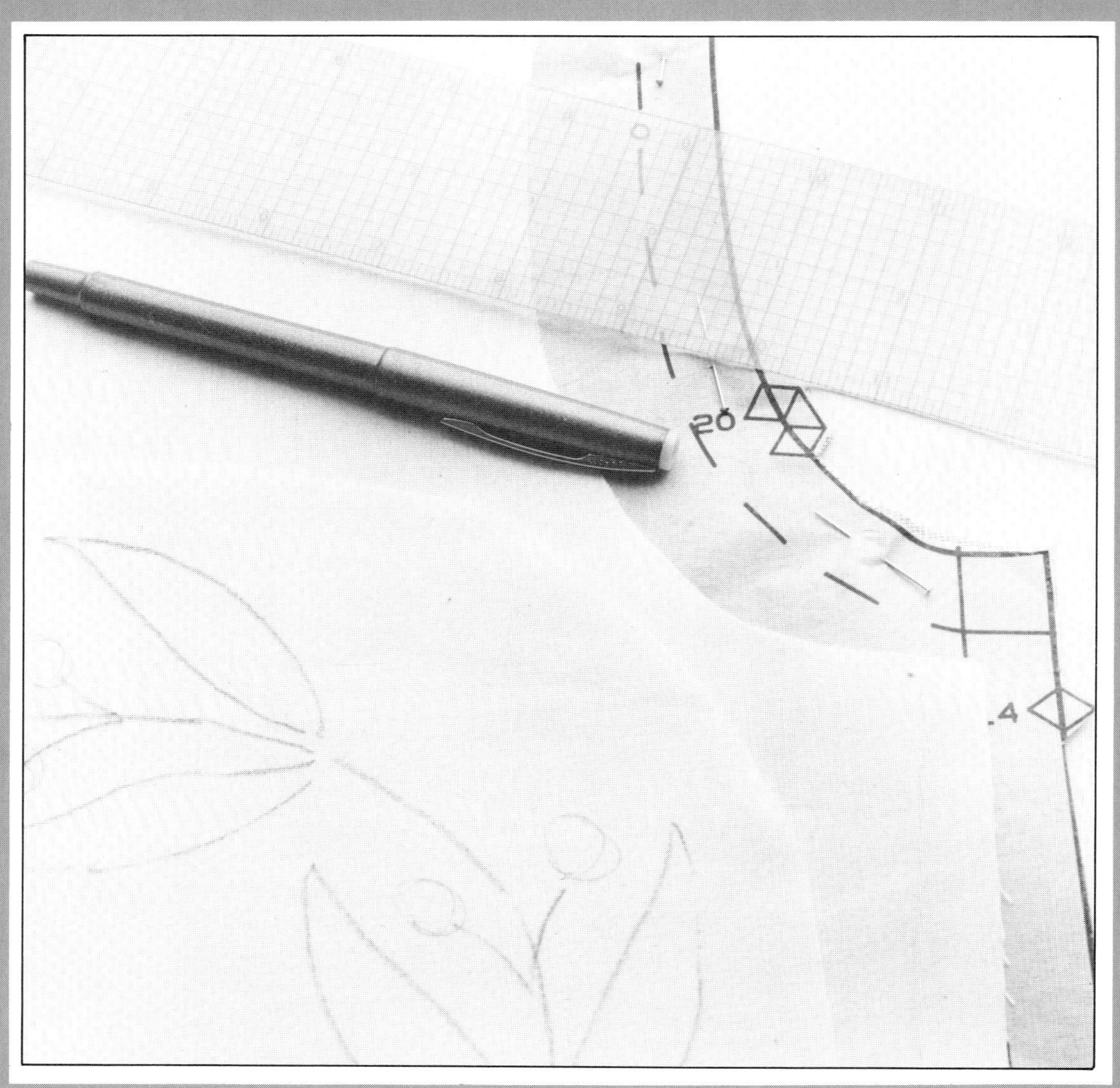
20

3
HOW TO CUSTOMIZE A COMMERCIAL PATTERN

Once you've selected the commercial pattern you plan to use as the foundation for your garment, it will be time to think about customizing that pattern. This means to measure, mark, adapt and redraw your pattern until it fits two very important criteria: your body and your quiltwear project.

Some of the projects in this book will require little, if any, pattern adjustment. At most, it will just be a matter of checking to see if your commercial pattern can accommodate the shape and size of a specific design motif. Some of these details you can work out with a ruler and pencil. Others won't be clearly apparent until you have basted and tried on a test muslin.

Why make a muslin? It's the professional way to sew. Also the safest. In fact, if you're spending more than $30 on material, it's sheer madness not to. So don't cheat.

A certain amount of time and effort are involved in making a muslin, fitting it, and drawing the final pattern. Please don't be tempted to skip these steps. Here's why:

- A muslin is a lot like a scratch pad. Your alterations and adjustments can be worked out here, first. The muslin is your only chance to make sure that all the piecing, applique and quilting designs flow smoothly around the garment, with no obvious breaks or incorrectly matched seams.

- Once you've perfected the basic garment pattern, it can be used again and again. Having done much of the pre-planning, your next project will go much faster.

- The fitting and design preparation involved in making a muslin guarantees that your fit and style are right, freeing you to concentrate on and enjoy the business of piecing, applique and quilting.

Basic steps for adapting and fitting your commercial pattern

CHANGE THE PATTERN. Begin by marking any structural changes on the commercial pattern. These would include such steps as lowering a dress yoke or adding a yoke seam to a plain dress pattern, narrowing or widening a skirt or dress at the hem, or curving the front edge of a vest.

CUT AND FIT THE MUSLIN. Cut out and machine baste a muslin version of your pattern, including one sleeve. You can use cotton muslin or any other medium weight fabric for this. Light-colored solids are best because you'll want to mark the muslin and draw in your applique and patchwork motifs.

Try on the muslin. Check for fit. Also watch for the scale of your design. Does this design fit you? Make any necessary alterations, marking directly on the muslin. Determine the finished length of your garment. Mark hem line.

Transfer all your alterations onto the paper pattern. In most cases, you won't have to take the basted muslin apart to do this. Keep the muslin. You'll need it later.

Trace the new improved copy of your pattern onto patternmaking cloth.

Don't cut it out yet.

DRAW OUT THE PIECING, applique and quilting designs. Refer to the project chapter for these elements. Trace the full size patterns onto artist's tracing paper.

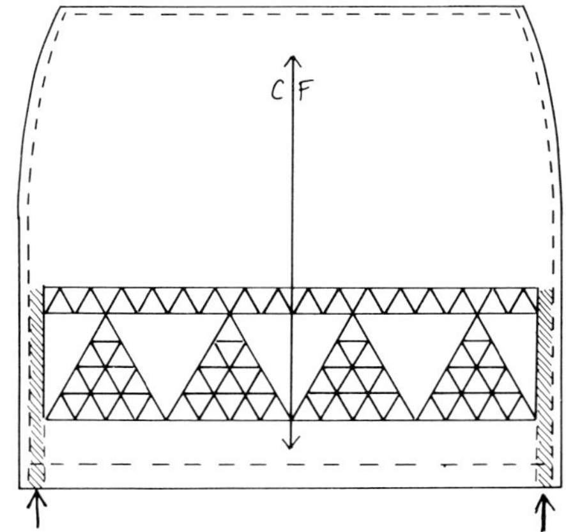

ADJUST THE GARMENT PATTERN or piecing/applique design. Lay the piecing/applique design over the basic garment pattern. Correctly align any check points such as center, front, back, side seams or hems.

Sometimes, a piecing/applique design won't fit exactly right on your garment as it is originally drawn. For example, a row of patchwork blocks may not come out exactly right at your side seams. The chapter on each particular garment tells how to adjust such "misfits".

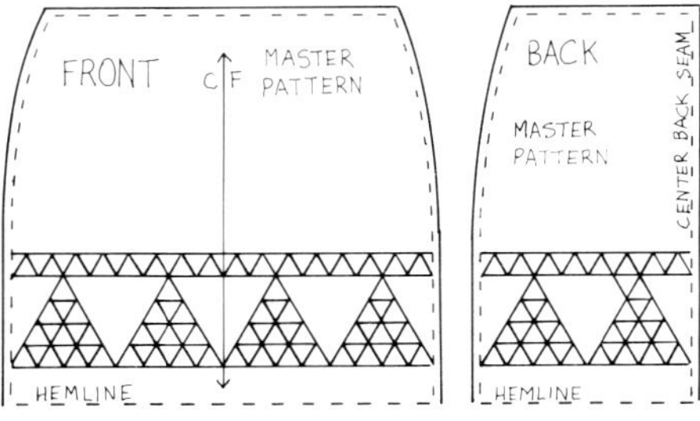

DRAW THE PIECING/APPLIQUE design on the basic garment pattern. Once you have corrected or adjusted the piecing/applique design, slip it *under* the garment pattern that has now been drawn on patternmaking cloth. Line it up correctly and trace it onto the pattern. Write all information on this pattern such as the name of the design, size and any special notations about color placement. This is your completed master pattern. Since you won't want to cut this pattern up when you cut out your fabric, it is necessary to make a copy of each pattern section, adding seam allowances. The copy will be your working pattern.

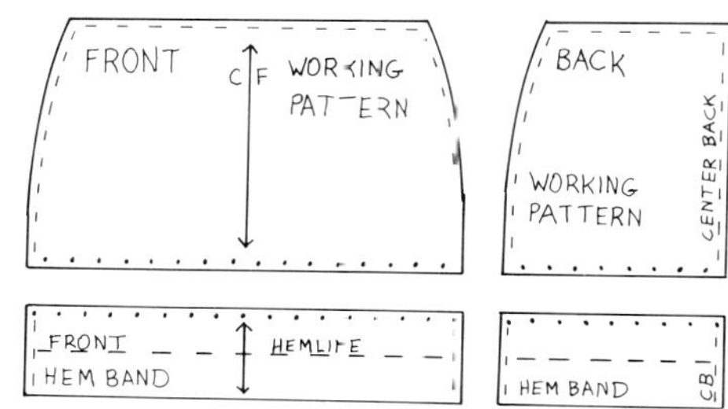

This step is required only for pieced designs: Separate the individual units of each garment. For example, the Sawtooth Border Jacket front illustrated here has a gray jacket body, two rows of pieced sawtooth blocks, and two red borders which will be mitered together.

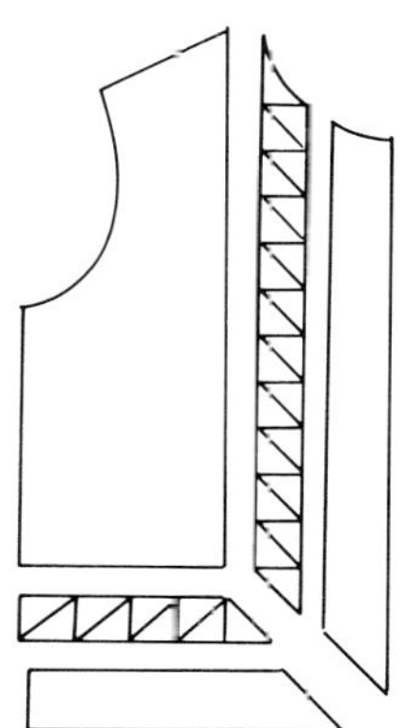

The pattern for the triangle that makes the sawtooth rows is included in the chapter for the Sawtooth Border Suit, so you won't have to redraw those borders. However, the gray jacket body and two red border units must be redrawn. Lay another piece of patternmaking cloth on top of your master pattern. Trace the separate units of your pieced garments, leaving a little space between each unit. Add seam allowances and label each unit.

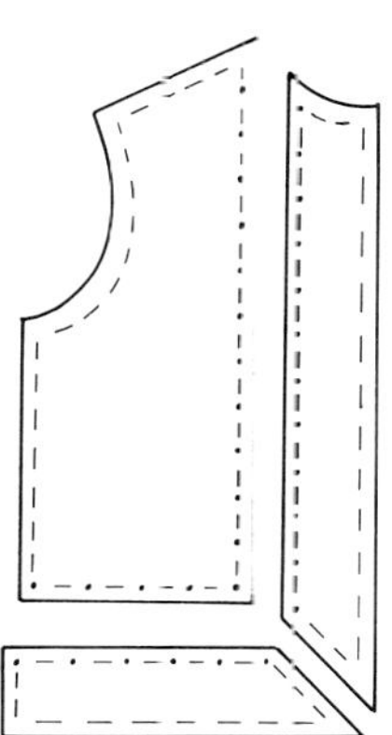

Remember, most parts of a garment, such as sleeves, jacket backs and back yokes are not embellished and require few steps to complete. For these pieces, all you have to do is alter the muslin, mark any changes, and trace a copy on patternmaking cloth.

Your pattern is now ready to use. And reuse.

How to add or subtract skirt hemline width

All the skirts in this book are based on a bottom edge width of either 60″ or 64″. Chances are you will need to adapt your commercial pattern to match this exactly. In the individual chapters for each project, you will find instructions for narrowing or widening a skirt or dress pattern to fit a specific hemline motif. As a general rule, here is what you do to add or subtract skirt width: redraft your pattern (using patternmaking cloth) and add or remove fullness from the *center front fold* or *center back seam*. Do not work from the side seams.

Remember that the amount you add or subtract from one pattern piece will eventually be *doubled* in the final project. Try to distribute any added width equally between the front and back pieces.

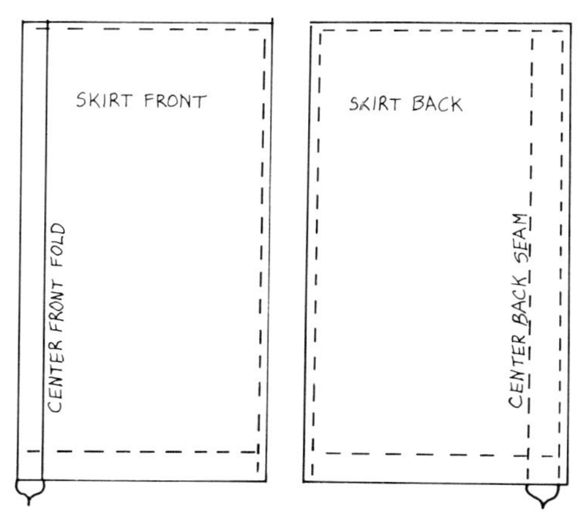

Add or Subtract

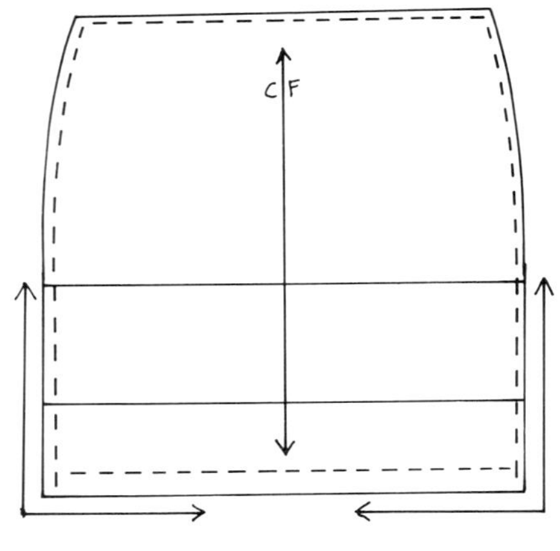

Taking waistline fullness out of a gathered skirt

Eliminating fullness from the waistline and hip area of a gathered skirt is quite easy—*if* you remember to leave room for any pieced or quilted bands along the bottom third of the skirt. Your hemline must remain a straight line and all vertical seams must remain at right angles to the hem at least as far as the top of your finished border motif.

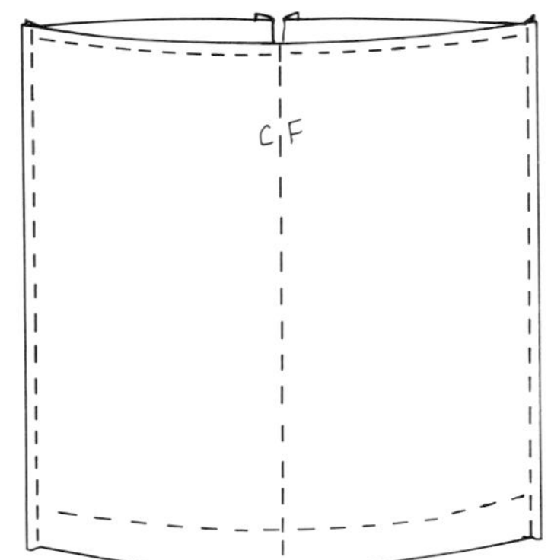

START BY TRANSFERRING your basic skirt pattern to muslin fabric, including seam and hem allowances. Cut, then pin the muslin skirt together. Machine baste *only* the center back seam. Press open.

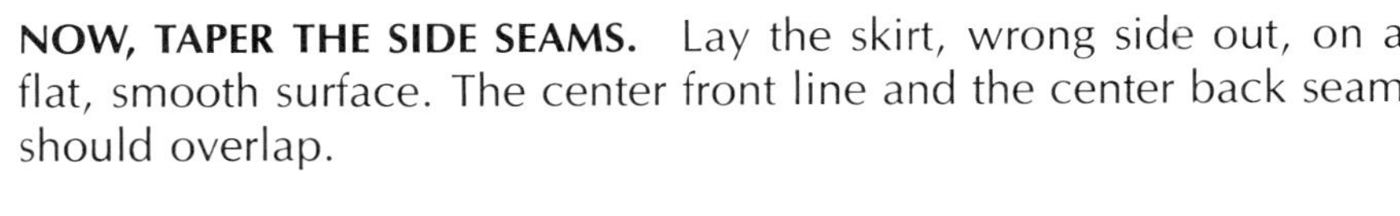

NOW, TAPER THE SIDE SEAMS. Lay the skirt, wrong side out, on a flat, smooth surface. The center front line and the center back seam should overlap.

IF YOU ARE GOING TO BE ADDING any pieced or horizontal bands to your skirt, estimate their position and mark directly on the muslin.

NOW, WORKING WITH A PENCIL, begin sketching in your tapering. This should begin at least five or six inches above the top edge of your border motif. Keep in mind that whatever fullness you take away from *one* skirt side front, will eventually be multiplied by *four*. For example, if you take 1¼″ from one side front seam, by the time you're done, you will have subtracted a full 6″ from the entire skirt. Don't try to take more than 10″ from a skirt.

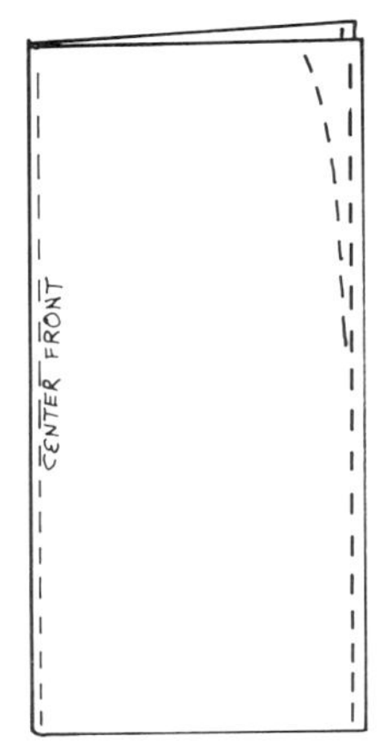

PIN ONE SIDE into a new tapered seam line. Start with an almost unnoticeable angle. You can use a slight curve over the hip line if the skirt will be constructed in a fairly soft and drapable fabric. Complete marking your new curve with a pencil.

FOLD THE SKIRT along the center front. Line up the two side seams. Trace the curve onto the other side.

ASSEMBLE YOUR MUSLIN SKIRT. Machine baste the seams, trimming away all excess seam allowance. Gather the skirt onto the muslin waistband. Try on.

MAKE A MASTER PATTERN. Once your skirt fits, you will have to partly disassemble it to make a pattern. Rip carefully, because we suggest putting the muslin back together afterwards. This will come in very handy for figuring out the placement of patchwork bands or panels. They can be pinned to the muslin or drawn on with water-erasable pen, then erased for another use.

To make a master pattern, draw your original rectangular skirt front and one back half onto a length of patternmaking cloth. Include seam allowances and hems.

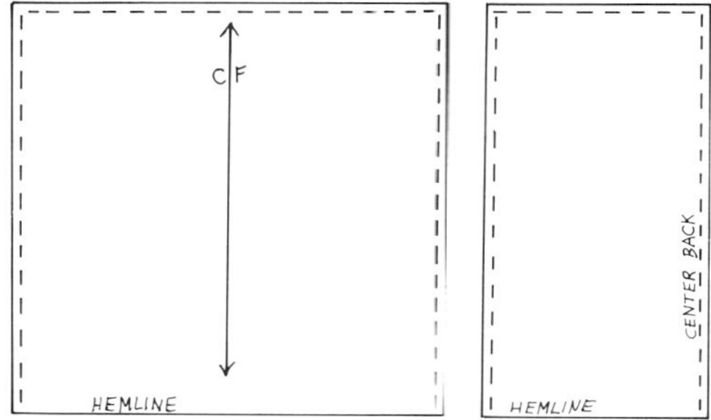

Next, lay the muslin skirt front under the pattern, aligning center front and all other seams. Trace the tapered side seam onto the pattern. Trace only one side, and only one seam. You don't need your muslin any more than this for making the pattern.

Working with this first tapered seam, trace your remaining seams, the other half of the front and the side seam on the back section. Add a notch to the first seam, then trace this mark onto all other seams. Add seam and hem allowances to the skirt front and back. Redraw the waistband including seam allowances.

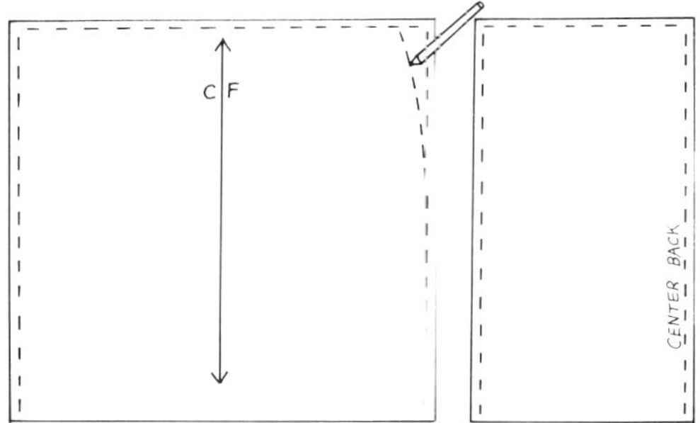

After fitting and tapering, this is what your basic skirt pattern will look like.

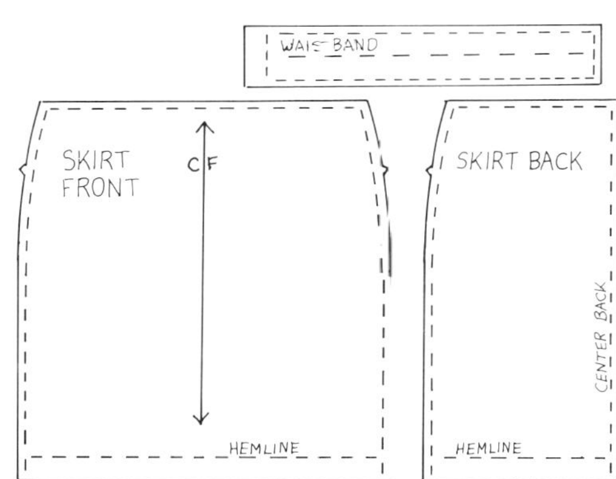

Yoke adjustments

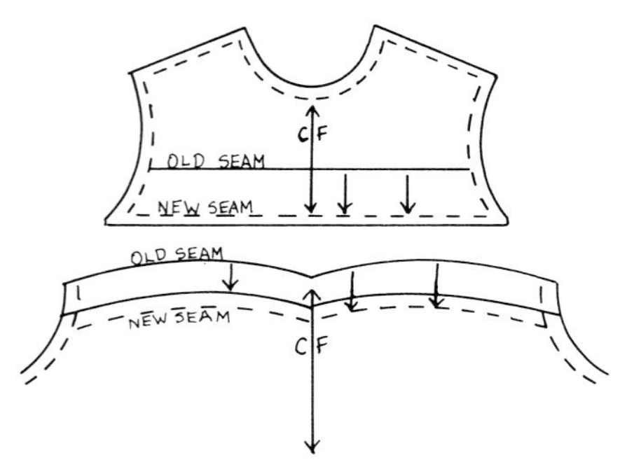

If your instructions call for a yoke that's deeper than the one shown on your pattern, you will need to lengthen the yoke. To do this, start by *adding* the extra length you need to the area below the old seam allowance. As you make these adjustments, be sure that your armhole length does not change. Trace in the underarm seam, transferring it from the dress skirt to the dress yoke. Next, *subtract* an equal amount from the dress skirt. Add seam allowances and notches.

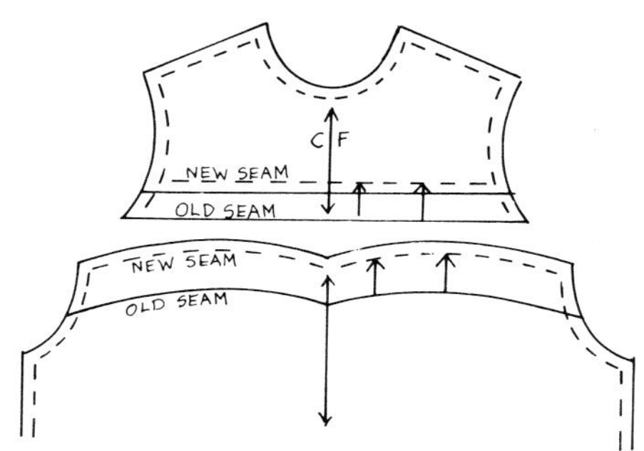

To make a yoke narrower you reverse the above process. Subtract from the yoke length. Add an equal amount to the dress skirt. Measure carefully to be sure the armhole length does not change.

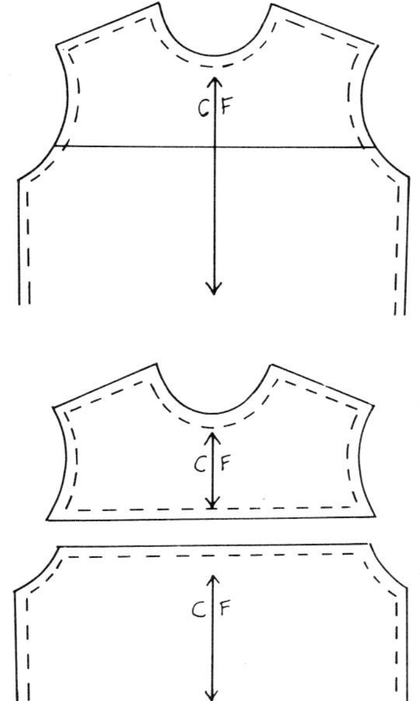

To create a yoke, start by taking the measurements of the yoke you need for your project. Working with these measurements, draw a line across your yoke-less pattern. Cut pattern apart, or redraw as separate yoke and skirt pieces. Next add seam allowances to both pieces. It's up to you whether or not to create a back yoke.

How to curve a "squared" vest pattern

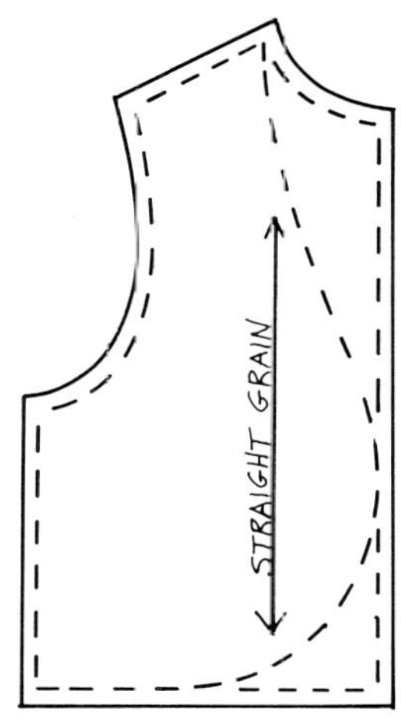

Use a French curve or a flexible curve. With pencil on pattern, work with the seam line, *not* the cutting line. Carefully round off any straight edges or points at the neck and hem. To see if your new curve is correct, cut out a muslin, eliminating the seam allowances on the front edge. Pin it together and try on. Expect to have to perfect your curve slowly, by trial and error.

SIZE 8
FRONT

4
ASSEMBLING A VEST

The instructions in this book call for two different construction methods for the final assembly of a vest. Either method is fine for some of the garments. In a few cases, one method is definitely preferable and we explain why. You may be familiar with both methods from previous sewing projects.

THE "TURN THROUGH THE SHOULDERS" METHOD

WHEN TO USE. When a design must be carefully matched up at the side seams. Also when the side seams have to be sewn together early in order to allow an applique or other piece of trim to fall across the seam line.

TECHNIQUE. Mark and cut out the vest, lining and batting.

Baste the vest and batting pieces together. Treat these two layers as though they were a single unit.

Sew the vest fronts and back together at the side seams. Trim away the batting in each side seam allowance. Trim vest fabric at side seams to ¼″.

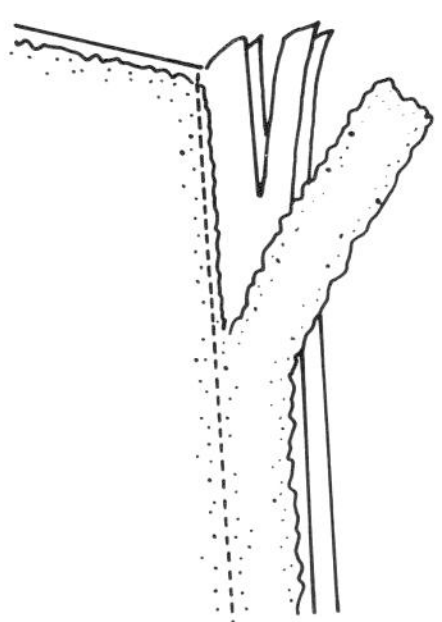

Sew the lining together at the side seams. Press seams open. Trim seam allowances to ¼″.

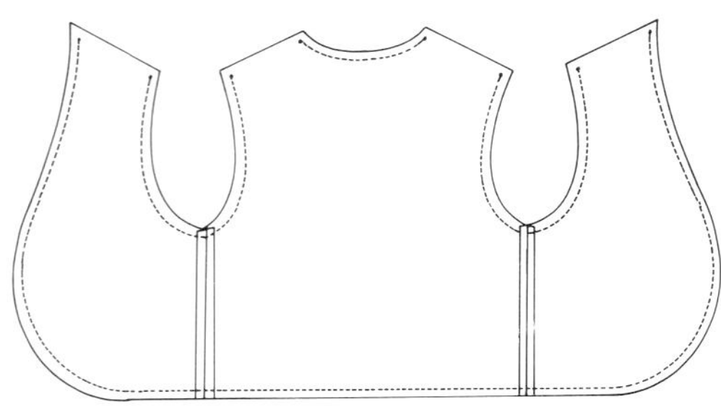

Lay the lining over the vest, right sides together. Pin. Measure all four shoulder seams to be sure they are the same length and will match when joined. Sew vest and lining together along all seams *except* the shoulders.

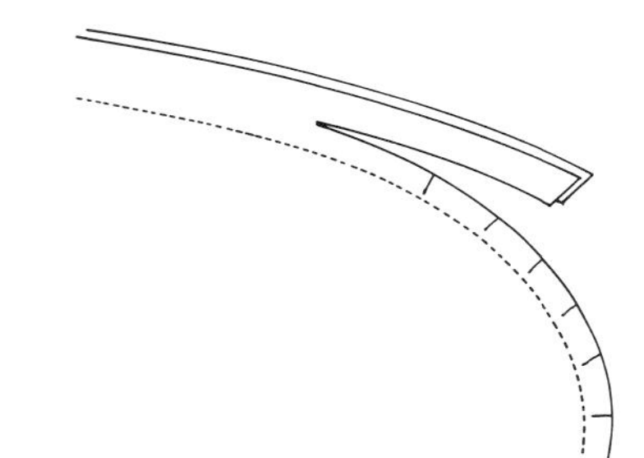

At seam lines, trim the batting away right down to the seams. Trim fabric seam allowances to ¼″. Clip curves.

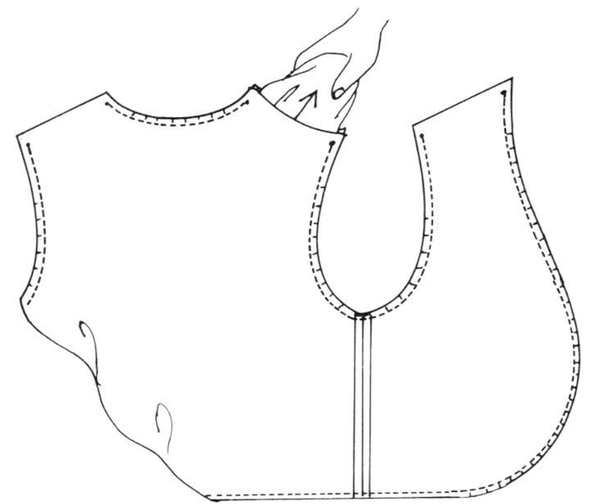

Reach inside one of the shoulder openings and grab hold of the vest. Pull the entire vest right side out through the opening.

Carefully press the edges of the vest, making sure that the lining does not show from the outside.

Pin the outer vest together at the shoulders. Sew by machine.

Turn the lining shoulder seams to the inside. Pin. Blind stitch by hand.

Baste all layers together for quilting.

THE "TURN THROUGH THE SIDE SEAMS" METHOD

WHEN TO USE. Any time you are not restricted by a wraparound motif. Or when an applique or trim does not fall across a side seam.

We find this method to be easier than turning a vest through the shoulders. There is more room to manipulate when pulling the vest through the larger side seam opening. The final seam to be sewn is also longer and easier to sew.

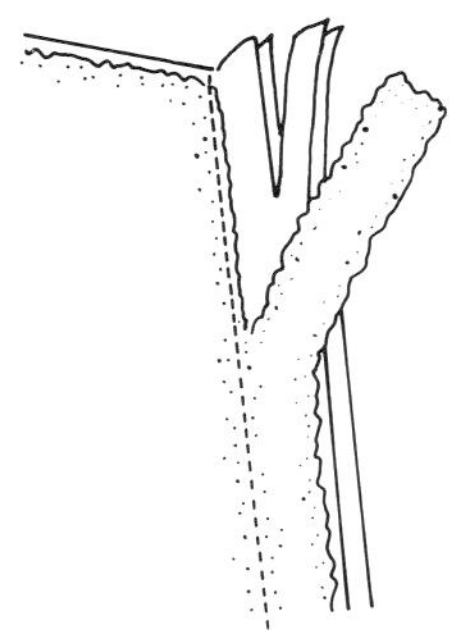

TECHNIQUE. Mark and cut out the vest, lining and batting.

Baste the vest and batting pieces together. From this point on, treat the two layers as if they were one single layer of fabric.

Trim the batting out of the shoulder seams, trimming all the way down to the seam line. Trim the vest shoulder seam allowances to ¼″. Press seams open.

Sew the lining together at the shoulders. Press seams open. Trim seam allowances to 1/4".

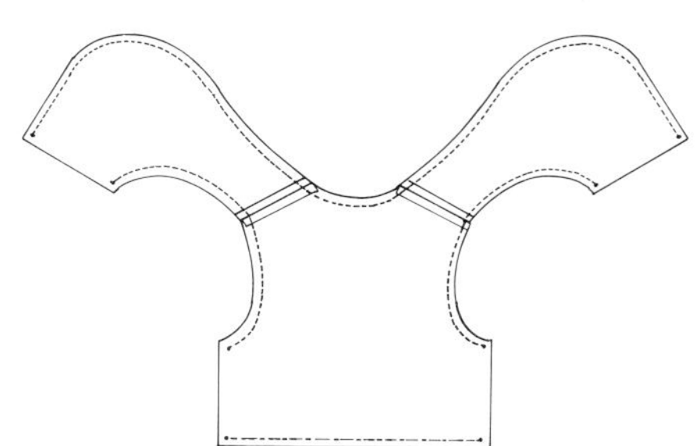

Lay the lining over the vest, right sides facing. Pin this three layer sandwich together. Measure the length of each side from armhole to hemline to make sure that all seam lines are the same length and will meet perfectly when the final side seams are joined.

Sew around the armholes, along the vest fronts and along the back hem. Leave all side seams open. Trim batting down to the seam lines. Trim vest and lining to 1/4". Clip curves.

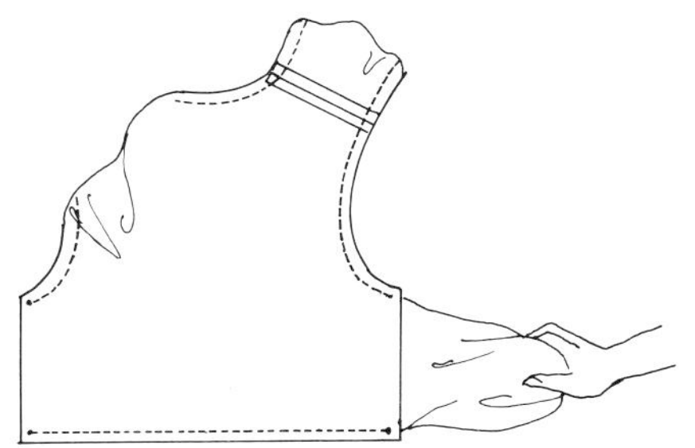

Reach into one of the back side seams and take hold of one of the vest fronts. Begin pulling. Pull everything through the same opening. When vest is right side out, press all sewn edges.

Sew the vest fronts and backs together along each side seam. Trim away the batting. Trim vest fabric to 1/4". Fold the back lining over the front lining and blind stitch in place.

SETTING TRIM INTO A SEAM. These directions apply to lace, piping, cording or braid. When selecting your trim, be sure to choose something that will lie flat when sewn around a curve.

Sew the vest together at either the shoulders or side seams. Pin the trim along the seam lines. The trim should face in, *away* from the seam line. Baste in place. Continue assembling the vest according to regular instructions.

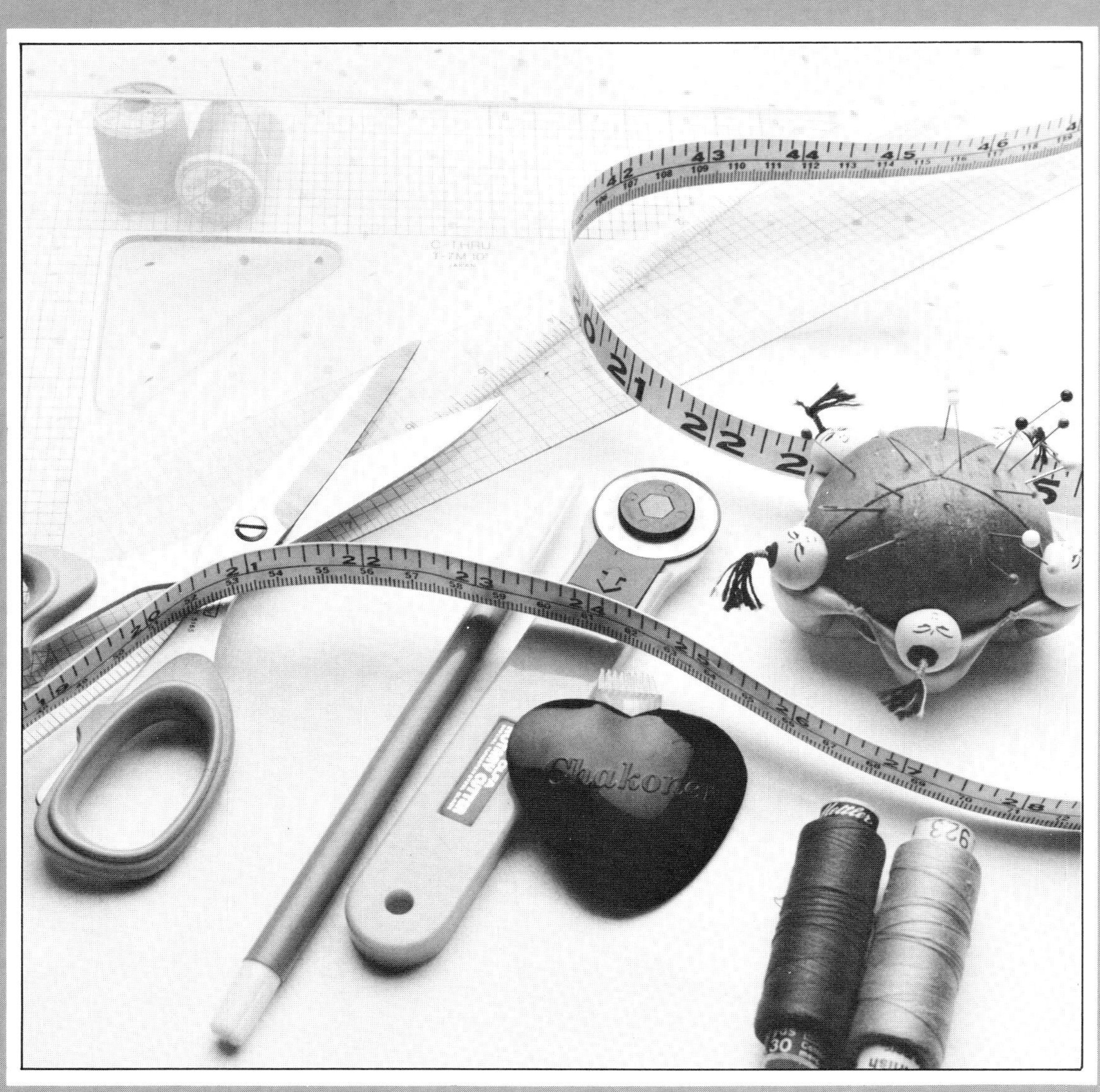

5
SEWING AND PATTERN MAKING SUPPLIES

Do not skimp on the quality of your supplies. Precision tools and sewing aids will make your work faster, more accurate and much more enjoyable. Some of the supplies we recommend aren't really sewing supplies. Some are artist's supplies or drafting equipment. You may find them better built and even cheaper than the supplies sold in many fabric stores. In the case of something like measuring tools, you may never have to spend a dime to get exactly what you need. Unused or unappreciated tools are fair game; so make friends with a retired engineer or a halfhearted drafting student, and borrow shamelessly.

GRAPH PAPER. Eight squares per inch is the best, but ¼″ graph paper will do. Be sure it is accurate. Some dime store versions are not! You will need a tablet of 8½″ x 11″ graph paper, plus a few larger sheets. The large sheets can be purchased individually or in tablets at art or office supply stores.

ARTIST'S TRACING PAPER. Tablets are available in sizes ranging from 9″ x 12″ to 21″ x 27″. The largest size sheets are big enough to trace an entire vest back. You should have two (preferably three) different sizes of tracing paper on hand. That way you won't have to waste a large sheet of paper when tracing a small applique. Look for "parchment" or "regular" weight, not "vellum" weight, which is too heavy and too costly.

PATTERNMAKING CLOTH. This looks like nonwoven interfacing and is available plain or with a grid of red dots or blue lines marking every inch. Beware! Use these markings only to line up your center fronts or some other main line, then go back and measure, using a right angle for all other lines. Patternmaking cloth is usually found in the interfacing section of a fabric store. We especially like the red-dotted Pattern Tracing Cloth® manufactured by Staple Sewing Aids and Pellon's blue-lined Tru Grid® brand. Both of these are easy to draw and write on.

MEASURING DEVICES. A yardstick, ruler and tape measure are essential. Your yardstick should be smooth and unwarped. As to rulers, we prefer an 18″ see-through ruler that is printed with a grid of ⅛″ lines. This ruler makes it easy to mark rows of parallel lines and also to add seam allowances to patterns. You'll need a tape measure. Check to make sure yours is accurate, especially at the ends. If your tape measure is frayed, crumpled and old enough to remember where it was the day Neil Armstrong walked on the moon, accept the inevitable and buy a new one.

ANGLES AND CURVES. Even the steadiest freehand drawer sometimes needs extra help when marking seamlines and cutting lines, or when transferring markings from one source to another.

T Squares	Useful for determining grain line, and for marking straight line alterations. A good T-square hooks onto the edge of a table or tablet of paper.
Dressmaker's or Carpenter's angle	This is an L-shaped piece of metal that looks like two metal rulers welded together at a right angle. Great for squaring off long lines on paper patterns or muslin. The tool's length helps keep your work from shifting or stretching.
Right angle triangle	For smaller pieces, performs many of the functions of a dressmaker's angle. Useful for marking crisp corners on quilt blocks.
French curve	A J-shaped tool that is useful for drawing and redrawing curved areas. Useful when designing or altering armholes, necklines, and princess seams.
Dressmaker's curve	Much like a French curve, but longer. Useful for longer, more gradual curves. Looks like a hockey stick.
Flexible curve	A piece of wire encased in rubber, useful for creating or copying a curve. To transfer a curve from one source to another, simply bend the curve to match the shape you want, set the bent rubber line onto your paper or muslin, then trace along the curved edge with a pencil.

COMPASS. For creating circles or marking parallel lines. Dime store compasses are not very accurate and tend to self-destruct quickly. Good compasses can be found in art and engineering supply stores. The alternative is a plastic ruler with holes drilled down the center at quarter-inch intervals. Plastic rulers are available in many quilt shops.

TEMPLATE PLASTIC. This is thin, stiff, transparent plastic that can be cut with scissors, then marked with a china marker or felt tip pen. Clear plastic templates are durable and their points don't wear down, even with repeated use. They're time savers and can do a lot to increase your accuracy. The see- through view on each template makes it easy to find the grain of your fabric and you can draw the position of plaid lines or a floral motif directly on each template.

Look for template plastic in quilt shops and plastic supply stores. If you can't find what you need, "Shrinky Dink", found in toy and hobby stores, makes a good substitute. This is a heat-sensitive plastic material that shrinks and hardens in the oven. The translucent plastic sheets can be cut into template shapes.

ROTARY CUTTER AND MAT. A rotary cutter is a wheeled knife that looks like a pizza cutter and can slice several layers of fabric at once. This can be a big timesaver, especially when preparing fabrics for strip-pieced designs. Even one layer of fabric can be cut quicker with a rotary cutter than with scissors.

A novice will probably start by using a rotary cutter to cut long strips, but with a little practice, you'll find yourself using it to cut other patchwork shapes and garment pattern pieces. The only disadvantage to this tool is that it can't cut around sharp curves. We highly recommend it for delicate or slippery fabrics such as crepe de chine, shantung and many polyester "silkies" that are very difficult to cut accurately with even the sharpest scissors.

A self-sealing mat is a necessity for use with a rotary cutter. It protects your work surface and helps keep the cutter blade sharp.

SCISSORS. Ideally, you should have three pairs: paper, fabric and applique scissors.

No one buys paper scissors. Good fabric scissors become paper scissors. Sometimes a pair of fabric scissors are honorably retired: more likely they are demoted after family members have used them too often to cut everything but fabric. Accept this annoying reality and your life will be calmer. When you catch your nearest and dearest using your good shears to cut shag carpeting or the dog's toenails, try to find comfort in the fact that you've acquired a new pair of paper scissors.

Fabric scissors should be a good heavy pair of dressmaker's shears, 8" to 10" long and the very best quality you can afford. Treat them right and they will last a lifetime. When shopping for scissors, insist on a test drive. Take scraps of different fabrics to the store and try the scissors before you buy.

Every now and then, treat your good scissors to a trip to the knife grinder. Contrary to popular opinion, knife grinders have not gone the way of streetcar conductors. They're out there, although they tend to spend a lot of time sharpening lawn mower blades. A good grinder sends a blade over as many as seven stones until the edge is hairsplittingly sharp. The before-and-after difference is quite dramatic. Many fabric stores schedule regular visits from a scissors grinder. Watch for their ads.

Be sure to put your name or initials on all your scissors. They all look alike at classes and quilting bees. At home, find a good hiding place for your best shears.

Applique scissors should be 5″ to 6″ long, with sharp points. Diane uses haircutting scissors, which are lightweight and very sharp. They accurately cut the smallest shapes and clip easily into corners. Don't expect your applique scissors to cut through several layers of heavy fabric, however. Their purpose is to cut one (or at best, two) layers of fabric easily and accurately.

MARKING INSTRUMENTS. You will need regular lead pencils and fine felt tip pens for tracing designs, graphing blocks and drawing full-size patterns. The lead pencils can be used to mark piecing, applique and quilting designs on most fabrics.

To mark dark fabrics, try a white chalk dressmaker's marking pencil, the kind with a brush on the end. For greater accuracy, try one of the new fine-lined chalk markers, such as the heart-shaped Chakoner® Marker. This type of marker doesn't work like a chalk pencil. Instead, a wheel dispenses a fine powdered line on the fabric. This is more accurate because the fabric doesn't bunch or stretch as it moves along the surface.

Certain types of pens are sold as fabric marking pens. Their ink is labeled "water erasable". Be skeptical about this. Mark, then rinse a test swatch. Even if the ink does wash out, you should remember that heat can permanently set some brands of water erasable ink. So avoid hot irons and hot water until the ink is completely removed. Except for muslins, which are expendable, we don't recommend the use of water erasable ink at all.

Chalk and lead pencil are relatively easy to remove. A soaking in plain water is usually enough. If that doesn't do it, add some mild soap powder. Do not use detergent. After a sudsy soak, rinse repeatedly, then air dry.

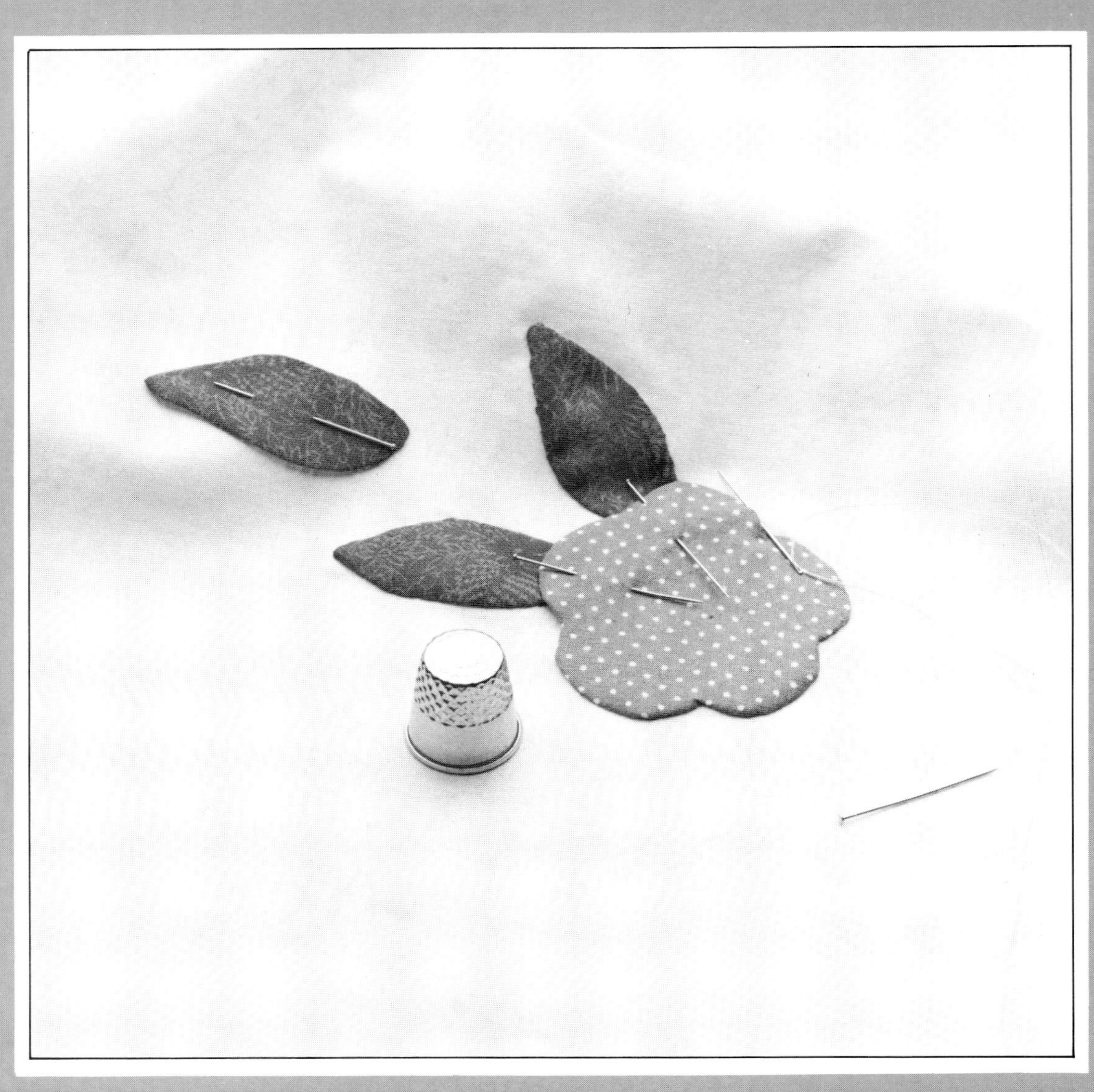

6
APPLIQUE TECHNIQUES

A teddy bear face on a child's bib overalls. An heirloom Baltimore Album Quilt. Betsy Ross's "Star Spangled Banner". Different versions of the age-old technique of applique.

As detailed and artistic as it looks, there's nothing really complicated about applique. Quite simply, applique means cutting out pieces of one fabric and applying them to the surface of another. The real challenge comes with planning your design, picking your fabrics and choosing the best technique for pulling it all together.

If you've never done applique before, an article of clothing is a good place to start. First-time projects are best kept down to size, and clothing offers a good opportunity to experiment with different colors and fabrics. Once you get started, you'll quickly see how, with relatively little effort, applique can turn a simple dress, vest or jacket into something unique and quite spectacular.

In this chapter, we cover basic applique techniques, choosing the correct fabrics, making patterns, marking and cutting fabrics and the business of doing applique both by hand and by machine. This information applies to any of the appliqued garments in this book, and you can also use it to help you embellish clothes that are in your closet right now. Perhaps to make a faded denim shirt look like new again. Or to "customize" a pair of overalls. Or to turn an unwelcome hand-me-down into a little girl's favorite dress.

MACHINE APPLIQUE VS. HAND APPLIQUE

Sometimes it's hard to make a choice. To understand, take a look at the Baltimore Bride's Vests in the photograph on the back cover. Both are from the same applique pattern. The only difference is in the fabrics and the applique techniques. The white vest is 100%

cotton, finished with hand applique and hand quilting. The green vest has moire faille flowers machine appliqued onto velvet. As you can see, the vests are both very pretty, and also very different.

The hand appliqued vest has that classic "heirloom" look. It sends out lovely messages: that you spent a lot of time, care and love on a very special project. It also says that you plan to keep this garment around for a long time. Hand work tends to look delicate, even when bright or bold colors are used.

The green vest makes a bold, fresh statement. It looks new and classic at the same time. Even when you're working with soft fabrics in pastel colors, machine applique tends to look stronger and more well-defined than hand applique. It may give off more of a sportswear than a dressy look. For everyday wear, this can be a good choice.

In addition to your choice of looks other factors are important in deciding which applique technique would be best for a particular project. Fabric can make a big difference. For extremely delicate or sheer fabrics, hand stitching will not only look more appropriate, but give you more control. Heavier fabrics or fabrics that ravel easily work and look better when machine appliqued. A soft, drapey dress made of satin-back crepe calls for hand appliqued crepe de chine flowers. On the other hand, a wool herringbone tweed jumper with appliques of nubby tweeds and novelty weaves *must* be machine appliqued; the fabrics would ravel and fight back if you tried to hand sew them.

How you plan to clean a garment is another consideration. If a garment is going to get lots of wear and tear, you'll probably want to toss it in the washing machine. Machine applique is durable enough to survive the toughest Maytag. It can take a lot of abuse without falling apart, so it's great for children's wear. Hand applique is a bit more delicate and is often reserved for special occasion clothes that are hand washed or dry cleaned.

Time is another consideration. Hand applique takes longer. But it's also a lot like knitting or embroidery in that you can take your work with you. Machine applique goes a bit faster, which can be helpful if you're working on a holiday gift, or in some other kind of hurry.

Finally, there's the matter of personal taste. Some people simply prefer to stitch their appliques by hand. Others, by machine. Diane leans toward machine work. "It's more like drawing," she says. Try both, and see what you think.

MACHINE APPLIQUE

A glance through this chapter should make one thing quickly apparent. We've devoted a lot more space to machine applique than hand applique. There are three reasons for this emphasis:

First, as a teacher, Diane has found that people tend to be less familiar with machine applique than with hand applique. There seems to be a real need for an in-depth look at this useful technique.

Another reason we've devoted more time to machine applique is that the instructions in this book are somewhat different from those in many other applique books. The method described here is based on techniques Diane learned while working in the garment trade.

Finally, an emphasis on machine applique is the most sensible way we can find to organize some simple but rather lengthy step-by-step instructions. The preparation steps for machine applique and hand applique are basically the same. So rather than repeat our ourselves, we've integrated into this one chapter all of the instructions for applique preparation.

Supplies

ZIGZAG SEWING MACHINE. Any kind, plain or fancy, that will form a close, even satin stitch.

APPLIQUE FOOT. or clear plastic machine embroidery foot. See the instruction book for your sewing machine. An applique foot has a wide space between the toes that allows for good visibility, plus a channel at the bottom to accommodate the ridge of stitches. A machine embroidery foot allows you to see through onto your fabric, and has marks that indicate the center, left, and right edges of the widest stitch.

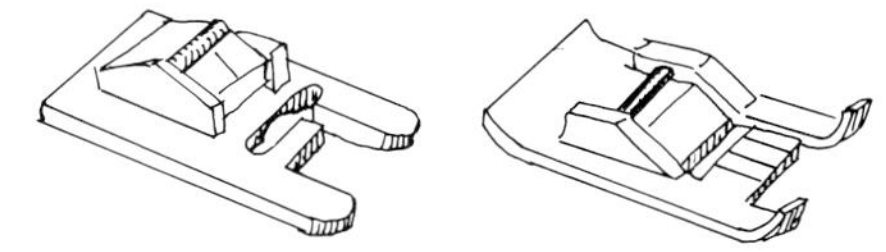

TRACING PAPER. Available at any art supply store. This is for making perforated patterns. Try to use a size that is big enough to hold your entire design motif.

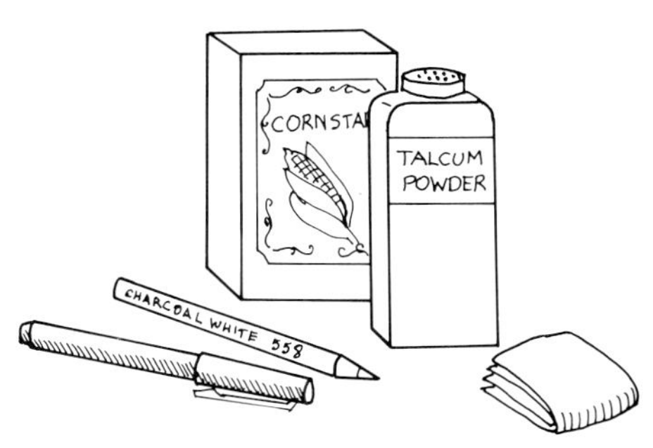

BLACK FELT TIP PEN, lead pencil and white chalk pencil. The pen is for marking patterns, the pencils, for marking fabrics.

CORNSTARCH OR TALCUM POWDER, ground cinnamon or fireplace ashes. These are the ingredients for homemade stamping powder.

SCRAP OF FELT. To pat ("pounce") stamping powder onto a perforated pattern.

FUSIBLE WEBBING. Stitch Witchery® and Fine Fuse® are brand names for fusible webbing. Also available are paper-backed fusing materials (such as Wonder Under®). A glue stick is a handy substitute. Some people like to use Teflon Pressing Sheets (optional) when fusing appliques.

PRESSING CLOTH or sheets of typing paper. To protect your iron from fusible webbing.

WHITE FREEZER PAPER. From the grocery store. Used to stabilize your background fabric during machine applique process.

SEWING THREAD, silk thread or machine embroidery thread. Whichever works best for your fabric and your machine's satin stitch setting.

Fabrics for Machine Applique

Anything goes. Almost any fabric can be used for machine applique. As a general rule, though, your applique fabric should be equal to or lighter in weight than the background fabric. Plain cotton broadcloth is the easiest for a first time project. Besides being easy to handle, cotton broadcloth allows you to get a feel of how your sewing machine performs, and lets you get some good experience at sewing around curves. Cotton also is forgiving. You can stitch, rip and resew without leaving permanent marks.

Here is a list of fabrics, broken down into recommended skill levels. If a fabric is not on the " beginner " list, most likely that's because it's heavy or bulky or slippery, and you're best off doing a few sample swatches until you feel comfortable working with the fabric. Also, some fabrics may not work well with your machine. You'd be well advised to buy a small amount of fabric and test out your idea before you make a major time and financial commitment.

Beginner Fabrics

Cotton broadcloth

Poly/cotton dress fabrics

Cotton denim

Plain-woven wool, such as flannel

Silk noil

Wool crepe

Intermediate Fabrics

Satin (polyester or silk)

Moire faille (usually rayon or polyester)

Taffeta (polyester or silk)

Brocade (silk, rayon or polyester)

Silk broadcloth

Advanced Fabrics

This category includes anything that has a nap that could mar or flatten. Nap can complicate your design planning too. Delicate fabrics can be a problem if they are difficult to press onto the background. You may get some "strike through", where the fusible web bleeds through to the right side. Fusible web is especially likely to strike through on delicate, lightweight or loosely woven fabrics. Some of the fabrics in this category are hard to sew; your machine may have trouble traveling over them. A start-to-finish test swatch can prevent unpleasant surprises.

Ultrasuede® or Facile®

Velveteen and velvet

Corduroy

Chiffon (silk or polyester)

Crepe de chine (silk or polyester)

Fake fur

Anything that ravels easily

Anything with lots of texture

Preparing and Tracing the Applique Pattern

First, trace your applique and quilting motifs onto sheets of tracing paper. Now you're ready to transfer these motifs onto fabric.

If you are working with white or pastel-colored fabrics, you can use the easiest marking method of all:

1. Slip your tracing paper drawings under the fabric.
2. Tape into place, with the paper under the fabric.
3. Using a light table or an improvised substitute, trace the design directly onto the fabric with a Colerase pencil (it will wash out).

That's one way to transfer an applique design onto fabric. Another way is called "pouncing" or stamping.

Making and Pouncing a Perforated Pattern

This is a technique that's been in use about as long as people have been doing embroidery. In the textile industry, pouncing is still the preferred method for temporarily marking fabric. It's accurate. The marks brush off easily. And it works on any fabric, no matter what the color, weight or texture.

Pouncing (which means to mark or treat a surface with a powder) involves poking tiny holes along the lines of an applique pattern. This perforated pattern is laid over the fabric to be marked. Then, powder is patted into the holes of the pattern. When the pattern is lifted away, all that remains on the fabric is a line of dots that's clear enough to accurately show your motif.

Once you've learned to pounce, you can turn just about anything into an applique design. That's how Kewpie Dolls, Campbell Kids, and Dick Tracy characters landed on quilts in the 1930s. Quilters simply pounced old magazine ads and comic strips. Today, it's still possible to sift through old magazines at flea markets and find advertisements outlined with pin pricks. Quite often, the design would be a flower from a soap or perfume ad.

In the 1880s Kate Greenaway figures were taken from *Ladies Home Journal* , *Butterick's Magazine* or *The Delineator*. These same magazines carried advertisements for perforated patterns. A woman could buy flower patterns, drawings of children, animals, also patriotic drawings. They were printed on paper, ready to be perforated. At that time, pounce could be purchased in any dry goods store, in wet or dry form. The type to be used wet came in a bottle to which water was added at home. The solution was similar to watercolor paint. Wet pounce was most popular for embroidery designs. Dry pouncing powder could be purchased in a tin can or a shaker device. A variety of colors were available. Many women made their own powder by mixing cornstarch or talcum with a small amount of cinnamon, wood ash or powdered charcoal. It's just as easy to do the same today.

How to Make a Perforated Pattern

Trace all the applique designs you need for your garments onto tracing paper. Use a black felt tip pen. Be sure to use regular weight artist's tracing paper, not "vellum" weight which is heavier and makes perforations that are sharp-edged and tend to catch on the fabric to be marked.

Flip the pattern over and write "perforate from this side" on the back side of the paper. Do this immediately, lest you forget. The holes must be poked from the back side of the paper. That way, the perforations face up and can catch the powder.

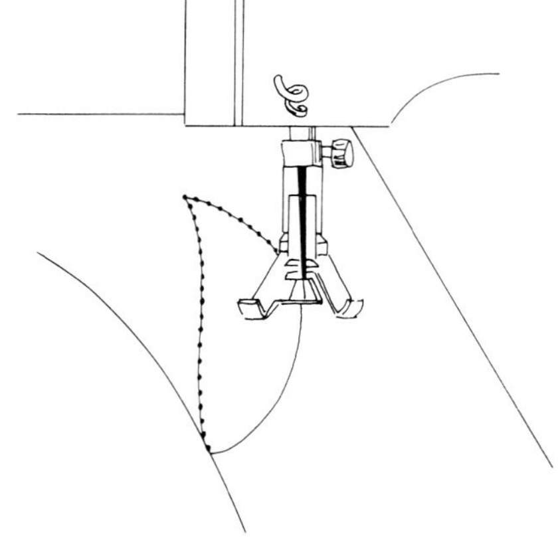

With an unthreaded sewing machine, "draw" along the design lines. Or lay the pattern on a towel or several layers of felt and poke along the lines with a needle or pin.

Lay the perforated pattern on the background fabric with the holes facing up. (They should feel like braille). Weight the pattern securely on the fabric. If there's any shifting during marking, you may have to start over.

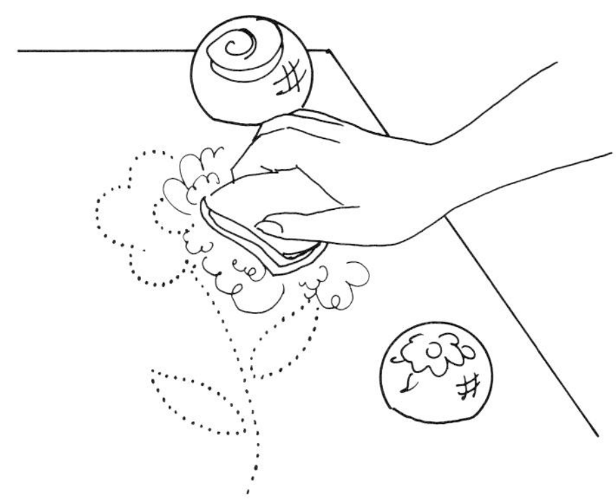

Using an old felt eraser or a wadded-up felt scrap, pat the powder through the holes. Peek under a corner of the pattern to see if the image is clear. Go back wherever it's necessary, then carefully remove the paper pattern. Repeat until all motifs are marked.

Cut Out the Appliques

Before you cut, you have to decide *how* to applique each piece. Take a close look at your design. Think of it as a three-dimensional painting with two, three, sometimes four overlapping layers. Portions of some of the pieces are tucked behind or laid in front of other pieces.

When two shapes touch or overlap, one must have a seam allowance or underlap. In most cases, the underlap is added to the shape closest to the background. Underlaps are *not* included in the patterns shown in this book. You have to draw them in yourself. To help you remember when and where to allow for an underlap, make notes on your tracing paper patterns. Simply draw an under lap extension onto the appropriate applique pieces, using a dotted line.

Later, after you have stamped your appliques, before cutting anything out, go back and draw underlaps onto each applique as required. Since this portion will be hidden, you can draw directly on the fabric. Use a white chalk or black lead pencil.

How to Place and Secure Each Applique on the Background Fabric

There are several methods for securing appliques to a background in preparation for satin stitching. Which method you use will be determined by the fabrics you're working with and the type of garment you're making:

PIN AND BASTE. Pin each applique into position. Hand- or machine-baste around each shape with long straight stitches. If the basting is sewn only 1⁄16″ from the edge, you can zigzag right over it. **Advantages**: Results in soft, supple lightweight appliques. Especially good for delicate fabrics such as chiffon, voile, lightweight silks. **Disadvantages**: Fabrics may not lie flat while being pinned or basted. Appliques can shift or the edges can fray during basting. Fabrics may pucker during zigzagging.

GLUE AND BASTE. Using a toothpick or wooden match end, sparingly apply glue stick to the smaller shapes and any points of fabric. For larger pieces, you can dab glue directly from the stick. Allow the glue to dry thoroughly before sewing. For a medium weight cotton, this could take as long as 40 minutes. After gluing, add a few basting stitches just to be sure, especially on napped fabrics like velvet or corduroy. **Advantages**: Glue washes out. This method is especially good for fabrics like velveteen or corduroy, the nap of which might be crushed by press-basting. **Disadvantages**: Too much glue can gum up a sewing machine needle. Glue does not always hold as well as other methods. Gluing can also cause some fabrics to fray or crumble, especially velveteen.

PRESS-BASTE. This is the technique Diane recommends, and uses 90% of the time. Press-basting almost guarantees that there will be no shifting, puckering, bubbling or stretching of appliques. It's especially good for very elaborate applique designs with lots of tiny pieces. There are three methods for press-basting.

THE FIRST METHOD uses a paper-backed fusible web product such as Pellon's Wonder Under®. Following the manufacturer's directions, press the paper onto the wrong side of the fabric. Mark and cut out the appliques, then peel off the paper. You now have appliques with a thin coating of fusible web on the back. Position the appliques on the background fabric, then press with a warm iron to adhere them. As you can see, paper-backed fusibles are a big time saver. The fusing keeps the edges of cut appliques from ravelling during handling. The drawback is that fusibles tend to slightly stiffen the appliques. This is okay for a vest or a yoke, but could interfere with the drape of a gathered skirt or dress. Since the entire applique is fused to the background, any hand quilting must be stitched through all layers of fabric.

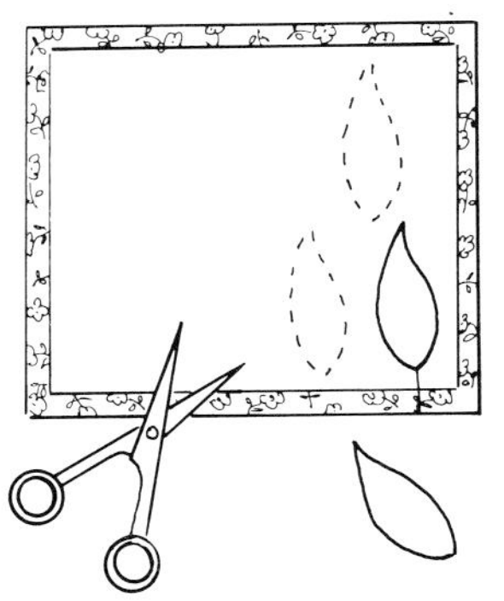

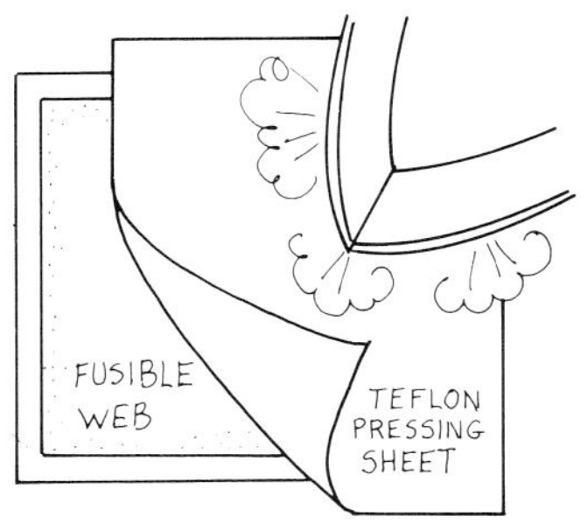

THE SECOND METHOD is similar to the first, but uses by-the-yard fusible webbing such as Stitch Witchery® or Fine Fuse®, and a reusable Teflon pressing sheet. Place the applique fabric face down on the ironing board, then place a piece of fusible web on top of the fabric. Position the Teflon pressing sheet over both, then press with a warm iron. Allow it to cool, then peel off the pressing sheet. The fusible web now coats the back of the fabric. Mark, cut out, and position the appliques, then press to adhere them to the background. Because by-the-yard fusible web is slightly thicker than paper-backed webs, your appliques will turn out a bit stiffer. There is also the chance that the web may bleed through thin fabrics, so make a test swatch first.

THE THIRD METHOD uses fusible web alone, so it's a bit more time consuming. Start by cutting out all your appliques. Then position each applique on the background fabric. Next, cut small, narrow bits of fusible web. Position these bits of web under each applique, along the edges. A pair of tweezers will be helpful for slipping the web into place. Press carefully. The big advantage to this method is that only the edges are fused. This allows you to cut away the background fabric behind each applique if you intend to hand quilt your project later.

Prepare to Sew

Stabilize your fabric before you sew. This step is absolutely essential for lightweight or slippery fabrics and is a good idea for any fabric. Iron a piece of white freezer paper to the back of your design area. Use a dry iron, set at permanent press. The waxy coating on the paper will adhere to your fabric, not permanently, just through the sewing process. If the freezer paper should come loose before you finish sewing, simple re-iron as needed.

ADJUST YOUR SEWING MACHINE. Make sure your needle is sharp and the correct size for your thread and fabric. If you can't remember how old your current needle is, insert a new one now. Change to an applique foot or clear plastic embroidery foot. With a regular foot, you won't be able to see your stitching.

Thread both the top and bobbin with the same weight and color of thread. Loosen the upper thread tension. On most machines this would mean loosening the tension to the buttonhole symbol or even looser.

Find the proper stitch length and width. Your zigzag or satin stitch should be about ⅛" wide, with the stitches close enough to smoothly and neatly cover the edge of an applique. The stitches should not be so close that they pile up and jam the machine. Diane works on a Viking which has settings from 0 to 4. She usually sets the stitch width at 2½, the stitch length at ½.

Always work a test swatch. This should be cut from your final fabrics, glued or press-basted into place, then stabilized the same as the rest of your project. Practice on this swatch, adjusting for thread tensions, stitch length and width and thread color.

ANALYZE THE DESIGN. Look at your design and plan out your stitching order. Notice how the shapes overlap. Begin with the shapes farthest in the back and work your way to the front.

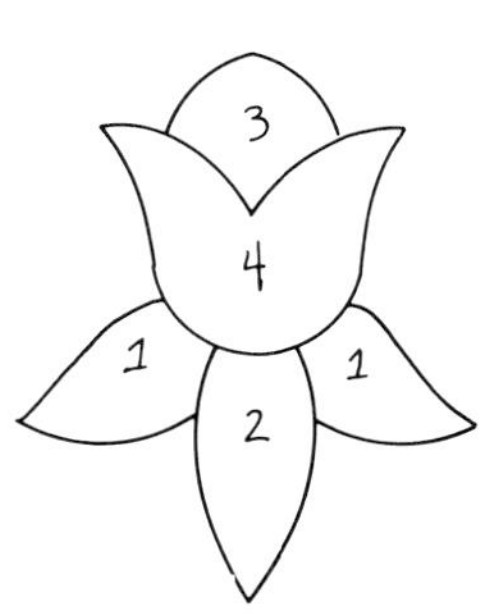

Most of your starting and stopping points will be covered by subsequent lines of satin stitch, eliminating the need to tie off most thread ends.

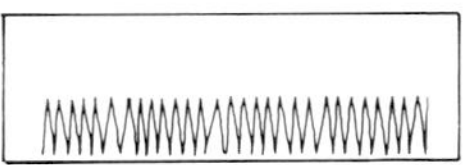

Too close: could fray

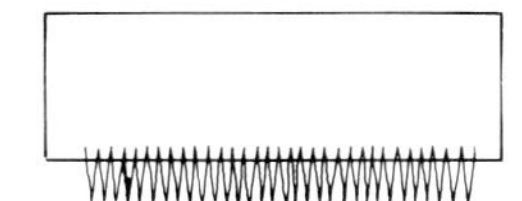

Too far out: could pull loose

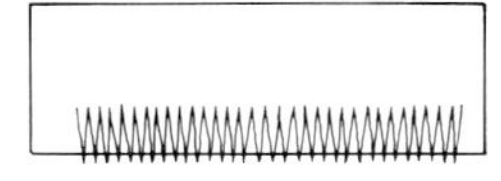

Just right

SEW THE APPLIQUES. Zigzag along the edge of each applique. The outside edge of your satin stitch should extend just one or two threads beyond the edge of the applique. Let the machine sew at its own pace. Pushing or pulling the fabric through will cause skipped or bunched-up stitches. Let the feed dog do its job.

Leave a 2″ tail of thread at the beginning and end of each line of stitches. Clip off those ends that will be covered with additional rows of stitching. Pull all other loose threads to the back and either tie off or thread into a needle and bury in the stitches.

Make sure your satin stitches both cover the edges and anchor the appliques.

Clean Curves, Crisp Corners and Perfect Points

SEWING AROUND CURVES. The secret to smooth, pucker-free applique is to *sew straight* always, even around a curve. If you don't, you can distort your shapes, and leave pulls and bubbles in the finished applique. Follow these directions for perfect curves:

1. Start by sewing the first few stitches, just until you need to change the angle in order to go around the curve.
2. Stop with the needle *in* the fabric, *on the outside edge* of the curve.
3. Lift the presser foot. Pivot the fabric slightly.
4. Lower the presser foot. Sew a few more stitches.
5. Stop. Pivot. Sew.
6. Repeat these steps, inching your way around a few stitches at a time until the curve is completed.

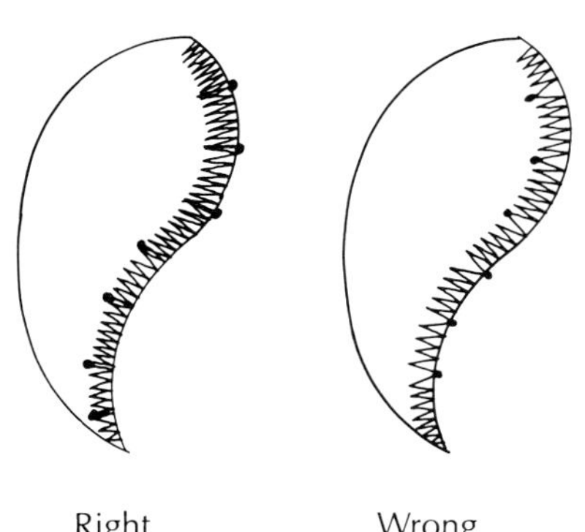

Right Wrong

SEWING SHARP POINTS. For leaves and petals, not only do you have to pivot a turn, you also have to taper your stitches to a sharp, smooth point. Be sure to work a test swatch before you try the real thing.

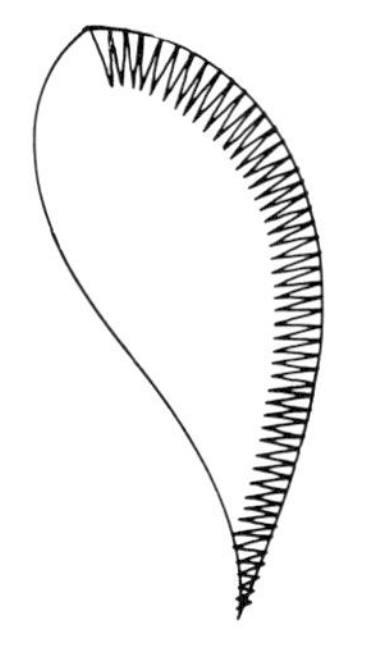

1. As you approach the apex of a point, decrease your stitch width adjustment. If the point is very sharp, you will need to enclose both raw edges of the point at the same time.

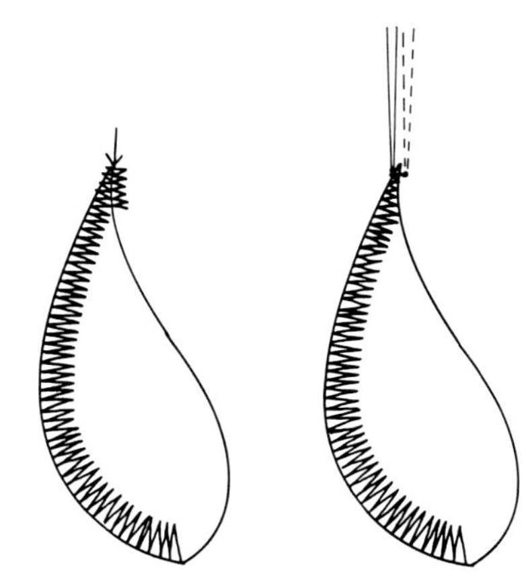

2. At the very tip of the point, you will need to turn by pivoting. With the needle in the fabric at the end of the point, pivot the fabric until you get it into position to stitch down the other side of the point.

3. Adjust your needle position before you continue sewing. This is important because if you simply resume stitching, the first few stitches will land too far off to one side, giving you a very wide and messy point. Do this instead: After you pivot, lower the presser foot. Then raise the needle out of the fabric. Raise the presser foot again and scoot the fabric over just ⅛″—just enough so that the needle will be closer to the point again. Now continue sewing, gradually increasing the stitch width back to normal.

HAND APPLIQUE

Fabrics

The best fabrics for hand applique are made from natural fibers, closely and evenly woven. They should not ravel or fray easily. When shopping, look for fabrics that form a nice crisp edge when turned under, then stay turned. Avoid fabrics that are too stiff, too thick, too loosely woven or too textured.

Though 100% natural fibers are best for appliques, they are not always the best choice for an entire garment. Imagine a 100% linen suit. Now imagine the wrinkles. That's where a blend makes sense. It's important to shop around. Some natural fiber/manmade blends may work better than others, particularly some silk/polyester and wool/polyester blends. Another alternative is to use 100% natural fibers for your appliques, and a blend for your foundation fabric.

Designing an appliqued garment is very different from designing an appliqued bedcover. The applique and background fabrics can be quite different from one another. A dress or jacket body can be cut from material that would be inappropriate for the appliques themselves—too heavy or too easily raveled. The only rule is to overlay the background fabric with appliques cut from a light enough, stable enough weave. With clothing, you have another creative freedom. You can work with fabrics that would be highly impractical for bedcovers. Since you'll probably be dry cleaning or hand washing your appliqued garment, use this cleaning liability as an opportunity to work with rich, elaborate silks or velvets.

Tools

THREAD. Your thread color should exactly match your applique fabrics. Sometimes you can't be sure if you have a perfect match until you've sewn a test swatch. Regular cotton-wrapped polyester sewing thread works fine. Some people like to use the finer weight machine embroidery thread that is manufactured by DMC, Dual Duty (J.P. Coats) and Metrosene. Try fine silk sewing thread if you plan to applique with silk broadcloth.

NEEDLES. Use either hand sewing needles, size 7 to 9, or quilting needles known as "Betweens", sizes 7 to 12. Hand sewing needles have elongated eyes. Quilting needles are short with round eyes. The fine ones (sizes 10 to 12) are tiny and very sharp, wonderful for stitching delicate silk fabrics, but difficult to thread.

PINS. Use only fine silk pins that pierce the fabric smoothly without snagging. They should allow the fabric to lie flat.

SCISSORS. A small, sharp pair with pointed-tip blades are essential for cutting out appliques.

FRAY CHECK®. This commercial product is a liquid that helps prevent fraying while handling cut fabric. It can be very helpful when struggling with tiny points or sharp inward corners. Before using, be sure to test for colorfastness on a scrap of applique fabric.

Getting ready to hand applique

The only difference between hand applique and machine applique is the addition of seam allowances and the final stitching method. The tools and techniques for pattern preparation, fabric marking and cutting, and shaping the applique motifs are exactly the same. Trim away all the built-up layers and background fabric behind the appliques if you plan to hand quilt them later.

For step-by-step instructions, refer to the earlier portions of this chapter.

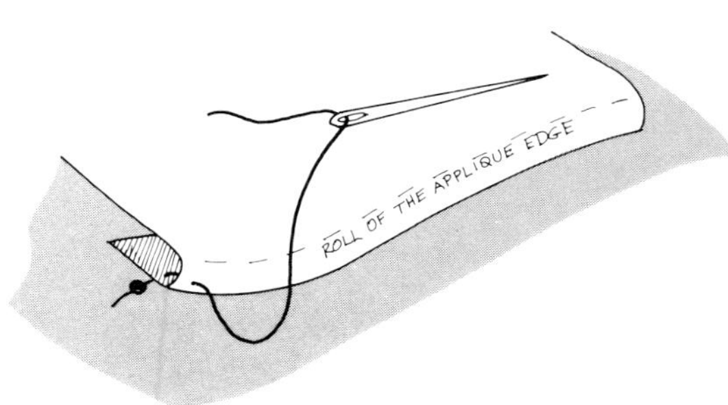

WORKING THE BLIND STITCH. The blind stitch is the basic stitch for all hand applique. For the neatest results, stitches should be evenly spaced, 1/8" or less in length, and as invisible as possible. For perfect results, follow these three steps:

1. Thread a needle with a fairly short length of thread (18" to 22"). Any longer could lead to knotting and snarling. Knot the thread. Insert the needle in the fabric, coming up through the background fabric, then out through the edge of the applique.

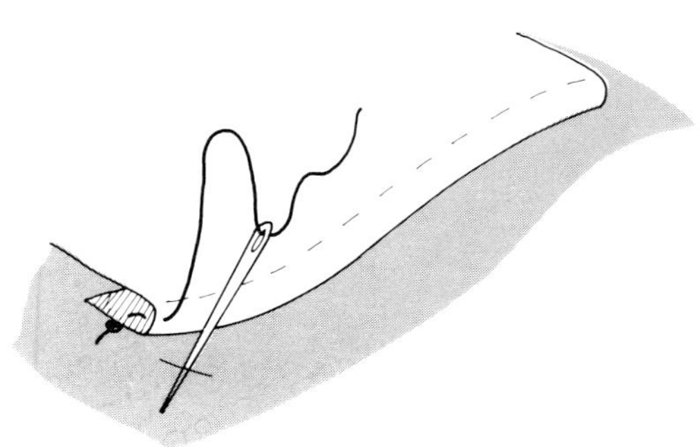

2. Push the needle into the background fabric right next to the place where the thread came up out of the fold. Pull the thread down through the background fabric. The stitch should be partly hidden by the roll of the fabric edge.

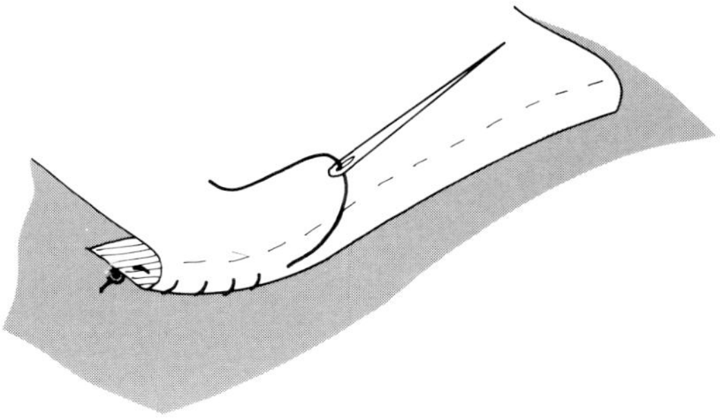

3. Push the needle up through the fold of the applique about $\frac{1}{8}$" from the first stitch. Continue along the edge of the applique, taking tiny, even stitches. Stitch firmly, but not so tight as to pucker the fabric.

7
QUILTING

One of the first decisions you need to make when planning a pieced or appliqued garment is whether to use quilting. Quilting, with its soft peaks and valleys, adds an extra dimension to your finished work. It can also give a too-plain outfit enough extra detailing to become truly unique.

However, quilting is not always practical for clothing. A wool suit that is to be worn all day in an overheated office certainly does not need the extra insulation that comes with quilt batting. We did not quilt any of our wool suit jackets. If the same designs had been interpreted in silk or cotton, a thin layer of filler could have been used. In fact, quilting would have added the proper amount of suit-weight body that otherwise might have been missing from the completed garment.

For an in-between project, in which quilting would look good but wouldn't be wanted for extra warmth, you can omit the batting entirely. You simply quilt the outer shell and the lining together. Your finished work will not have the same qualities of a regular three-layer quilt sandwich, so try to sample first to see if this is the final look you want. Empty quilting like this is also a good compromise for the sleeves of a quilted suit jacket.

When designing with quilting, start by using filler only where it is absolutely necessary; where the quilting stitches will go. For example, if your quilting design will be placed at the end of a sleeve or on a 10″ wide skirt border, put batting only in those areas. This cuts down on bulk and unwanted warmth.

In most cases, interfacing can and should be eliminated from sections of garments which will include filler. Interfacing is difficult to quilt through. Also, the combined effect of quilting stitches and filler will usually reinforce and stabilize your garment enough to make interfacing unnecessary.

Be extra sure to run a line of machine stitching along necklines, armholes, center fronts or any other areas which would normally be interfaced or might have a tendency to stretch out of shape with handling.

A quilted garment is rarely *entirely* quilted. In these garments, only the shaded areas are quilted. A thin layer of batting interlines only these quilted sections.

What kind of filler?

It is best to use a very thin filler in clothing. Most of us don't need any extra bulk added to our bodies. We want only enough thickness to add dimension to the quilting stitches. For that reason, soft cotton flannel or cotton jersey knit is a good choice for a quilted garment. Be sure to pre-wash and pre-shrink either fabric beforehand.

Diane is not a big fan of the many types of "fleece" available for quilting. They are often too dense and have too much body to allow garments to drape softly. On the plus side these fillers are widely available and work both for hand quilting and machine quilting.

If you're concerned about bulk, look for a batting that can be split. Many 100% polyester batts can be carefully peeled apart to halve their thickness. We've also had good results in splitting Fairfield's Cotton Classic batt which is 80% cotton and 20% polyester. After splitting, position your batting so that the smoother bonded side faces outward on your garment and the fuzzier, "peeled" side faces the lining.

You might want to try silk batting, especially if your garment is silk. Silk batting does not come in flat sheets like cotton or polyester batting. It comes in a cocoon-like wad that must be cut, then fluffed out to form flat yardage. The results are well worth the extra work. Silk batting is almost weightless. It drapes more softly and fluidly than any other kind of filler. Check the resource index in the back of this book for information on where to purchase silk batting.

Marking quilt designs on garment fabrics

In general, the same techniques used for marking applique designs apply to marking quilting designs. These techniques are covered in Chapter 6, "Applique Techniques". If your garment is pieced or appliqued first, and then quilted, mark your quilting design immediately after this piecing and applique work is completed. Do it before the 3-layer quilt sandwich is assembled and before sewing any garment seams.

To mark your quilting lines, use a fine lead pencil. A mechanical pencil is good. If a lead pencil doesn't work, try an erasable colored pencil. We've had some luck with a brand called Colorase®. We especially like the silver pencil. It shows up on lots of backgrounds. As with any "washable" pen or pencil, be suspicious about that adjective. Do a test swatch first to see if the marking is completely washable, and check what happens when it's exposed to the heat and steam of ironing.

When marking the lines and curves of your quilting pattern, use your dressmaker's marking tools. Not only will they help keep long lines even and accurate, they'll help keep the fabric from shifting and stretching under the pressure of your marking tool. Long, straight quilting lines do not need to be pencil-marked at all. Instead, mark these lines with quarter-inch wide drafting tape. Quilt alongside the tape, then peel off when your work is completed.

Assembling and quilting a garment

Most garments must be completely or partly assembled before they can be quilted. Only rarely can a garment be quilted before it has been completed. A garment where only a small, separate section needs to be quilted is an example; or perhaps a vest with bound edges that do not have to be turned. Before assembling your garment, decide which of these three assembly-and-quilting methods is best for your project:

QUILTING AFTER ASSEMBLY. After all piecing or applique is completed, mark the quilting design directly on the fabric, then assemble the garment. Now you're ready to quilt. This method most often requires quilting in the hand, without a hoop, especially on small, curved areas such as the upper vest shoulders. If you prefer to work with a hoop, baste cloth strips to the edges of your work so you have some extra fabric to fit into the hoop. Make sure you baste securely. A skirt is an easy project for hoop quilting.

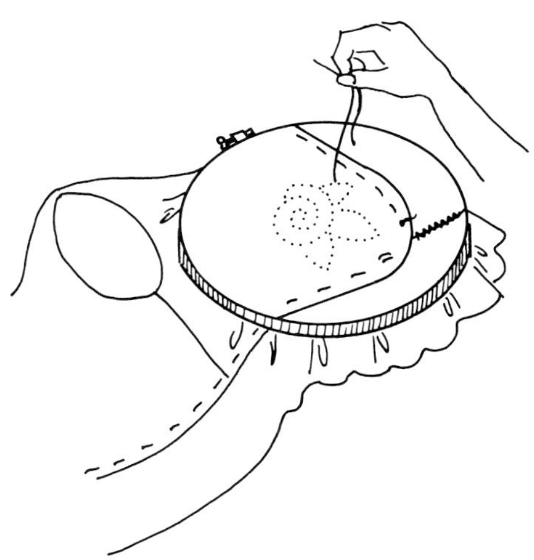

QUILTING AFTER PARTIAL ASSEMBLY. Assemble the garment to the point where major seams have been sewn. The garment can lay fairly flat. This will allow you to do most of your quilting in a hoop. Quilt to within ½" of any unfinished seams. Complete the garment assembly quilt-as-you-go style, blind-stitching the lining together. Connect any unfinished quilting lines across the seams.

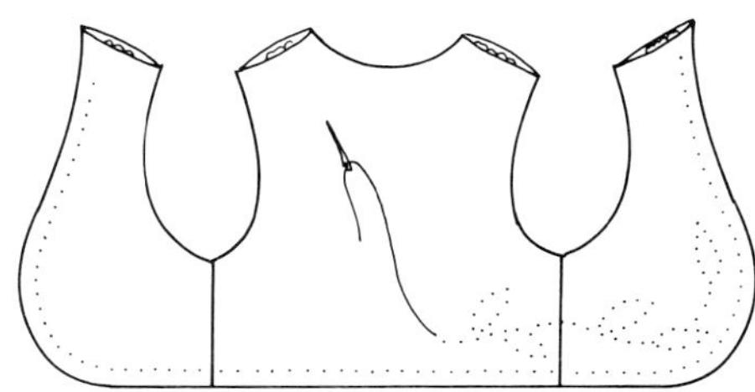

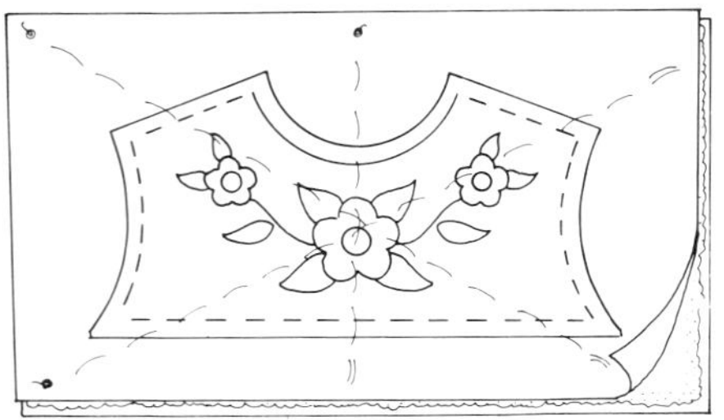

QUILTING ON SEPARATE PIECES. This method can be used for a vest that is to have all the edges bound or a garment with only one quilted section, such as the yoke of a dress. For this method, it's best to leave the garment section uncut so that you can work on a sizeable rectangular piece with lots of margin area. Start by basting the three layers together—top, filler, and lining—then quilt. In the case of a vest, quilt to within ½" of the side and shoulder seams. Quilt all the way up to the edges to be bound.

Cut out the quilted sections, then assemble the garment. Vest seams should be sewn quilt-as-you-go style. Dress yokes can also be done this way or sewn in the conventional manner.

Choosing the right thread

Your choice of thread will be determined by several factors. These include the type of fabric you're using, whether you will be quilting by hand or machine, and the "look" you hope to achieve. Keep in mind that a little bit of quilting on a special occasion silk vest will not get as much wear as a quilted wool skirt that you intend to use as a mainstay in your winter wardrobe. The wool skirt would need to be quilted with strong, durable thread, while the silk vest could be worked with a fancier, more delicate embroidery thread. Always make up a sample quilt sandwich and try out the thread you plan to use.

QUILTING THREAD. Can be used on all but the most delicate fabrics. Color choices are somewhat limited though, which may lead you to consider a different thread that may not be specifically labeled for quilting.

REGULAR SEWING THREAD. A good choice for almost any type of fabric. It works equally well for hand or machine quilting. For easier handling during hand quilting, run the length across a cake of beeswax.

BUTTONHOLE TWIST. Usually (and preferably) of silk. This is a thicker thread than silk sewing thread and is most commonly used for topstitching. Buttonhole twist gives a more noticeable quilting stitch with a nice sheen. This is a good choice for woolens and textured silks.

FINE PERLE COTTON. Another heavier, twisted thread, one that results in a more noticeable stitch. Use size #8, which is the finest weight available. A contrasting color of perle cotton can create a very interesting effect, much like Japanese sashiko quilting.

OTHER EMBROIDERY THREADS. Needlework shops carry a wide variety of threads, one of which might be just right for your garment. There are silks, rayons, linens, even metallics in varying textures. When selecting a thread, keep in mind that twisted threads such as perle cotton are stronger than soft, untwisted flosses. Some of the metallics and silks take practice at first. They tend to knot or kink up. They're especially beautiful on evening wear.

Hand quilting

Nothing can imitate or compare to hand quilting. In our opinion, delicate or flat finish solid color fabrics look best when hand, rather than machine, quilted.

If you've ever admired all-quilted bedspreads, or the elaborate feather motifs on older bed quilts, a vest or skirt is a good opportunity to try out these motifs without making a major time commitment. Even the most elaborate quilting design entails a relatively small amount of time and work compared to a full-sized quilt. Rose Bailey, who quilted our fancy white Baltimore Bride's Vest, worked an hour or so a day on the project and finished the vest in two weeks.

If you are a beginner, there are many books that can teach you how to quilt. Personal lessons, however, tend to be the most effective way to learn. The best way of all is to learn by helping out when a group of more experienced quilters gets together. Quilt shops, guilds, and adult education programs have competent teachers who can give you hands-on experience.

Most quilters strive to make their quilting stitches as small as possible. It's more important, though, to make sure your stitches are even. Don't expect to achieve the same tiny stitches on a medium weight wool flannel as you usually get on a cotton calico. On the other hand, a fine silk broadcloth and thin batting could allow you to magically increase your stitch-per-inch count.

Machine quilting

Unlike hand quilting, which creates a soft, broken line of stitches, machine quilting creates a crisper, more solid line. For many fabrics, this can be an attractive effect. If you are working with a napped fabric or a weave with a very pronounced texture, you may find that machine quilting is your best and only option. Hand quilted stitches can get so buried in a highly textured fabric, that they get lost from view. Machine quilting can stand up to napped and tweedy fabrics.

In most cases, regular sewing thread is the best choice for machine quilting. You may want to try finer machine embroidery thread or shiny silks and rayons. For bold stitching lines, try buttonhole twist. Metallic threads, which can fray during hand quilting, are often easier to machine quilt.

Sometimes people get unsightly puckers or "pooches" as they machine quilt. These are caused when the top layer of the fabric "creeps" during the stitching process. A little preparation can eliminate this problem. Before sewing, hand baste your "sandwich" carefully and thoroughly. Your basting lines should be placed every four to six inches.

In spite of its name, machine quilting does require that you spend some time with a hand needle. Sometimes the beginning and ending of your quilting lines will be sewn into a garment seam. If not, leave a 2″ tail of thread. Thread the tails into a needle, then bury them in the batting layer.

There are two ways to machine quilt. The first method works best for straight lines and gentle curves. Straight lines in parallel rows, chevrons, diamonds or "plaids" are best marked by laying out lines of ¼″ wide drafting tape. Stitch along one or both edges of the tape. Pieced designs can be stitched in the ditch or ¼″ from the seams.

Diane highly recommends the use of a walking foot or even-feed foot. You'll be amazed at how much this can help. You may also need to loosen the upper tension on your machine. Stitch at a slow, even speed, using your fingers on either side of the presser foot to keep the fabric taut. Leave a tail of thread at the beginning and end of each quilting line. Do not back stitch. Pull these loose threads to the lining side of the vest, then bury them in the filler layer. Always test out your stitching on a scrap sandwich of the same fabrics and batting.

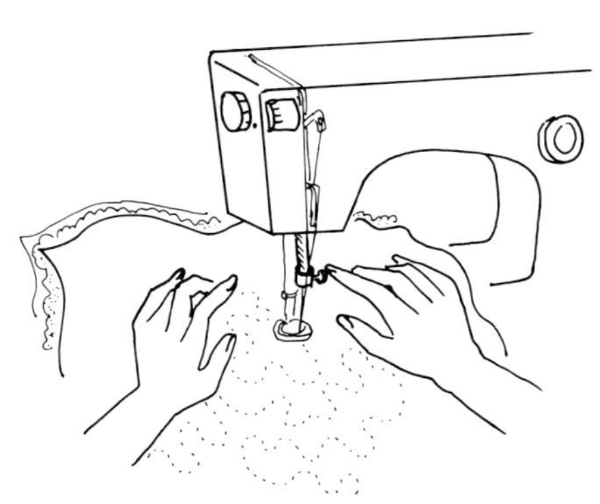

The second method is called free motion quilting. It allows you to quilt more elaborate designs such as feathers. Disengage or cover your machine's feed dogs and loosen the upper thread tension. Put on the darning foot and set the presser foot dial on the darning symbol.

To begin quilting, take one or two stitches in place, then start to move the fabric slowly while running the machine at a fast, even speed. The trick is to move the fabric *and* run the machine at a steady pace so that the stitches formed are consistent in length. You can move the fabric up, down or sideways, in meanders or curlicues. You can even sign your work in quilting. Free motion quilting takes more practice than the first method, so make a large test "sandwich" and spend some time experimenting.

For an in-depth look at machine quilting, we recommend *Heirloom Machine Quilting* by Harriett Hargrave.

Log Cabin Dress

Log Cabin Suit

Baltimore Bride's Vest (l and r) and Fan Vest (c)

Crazy Quilt Dress

Sawtooth Border Suit

Postage Stamp Dress

Pinwheel Panel Skirt

Dutchman's Puzzle Skirt

Flying Geese Suit

Leaves and Berries Vest and Quilted Skirt

Paisley Garden Vest

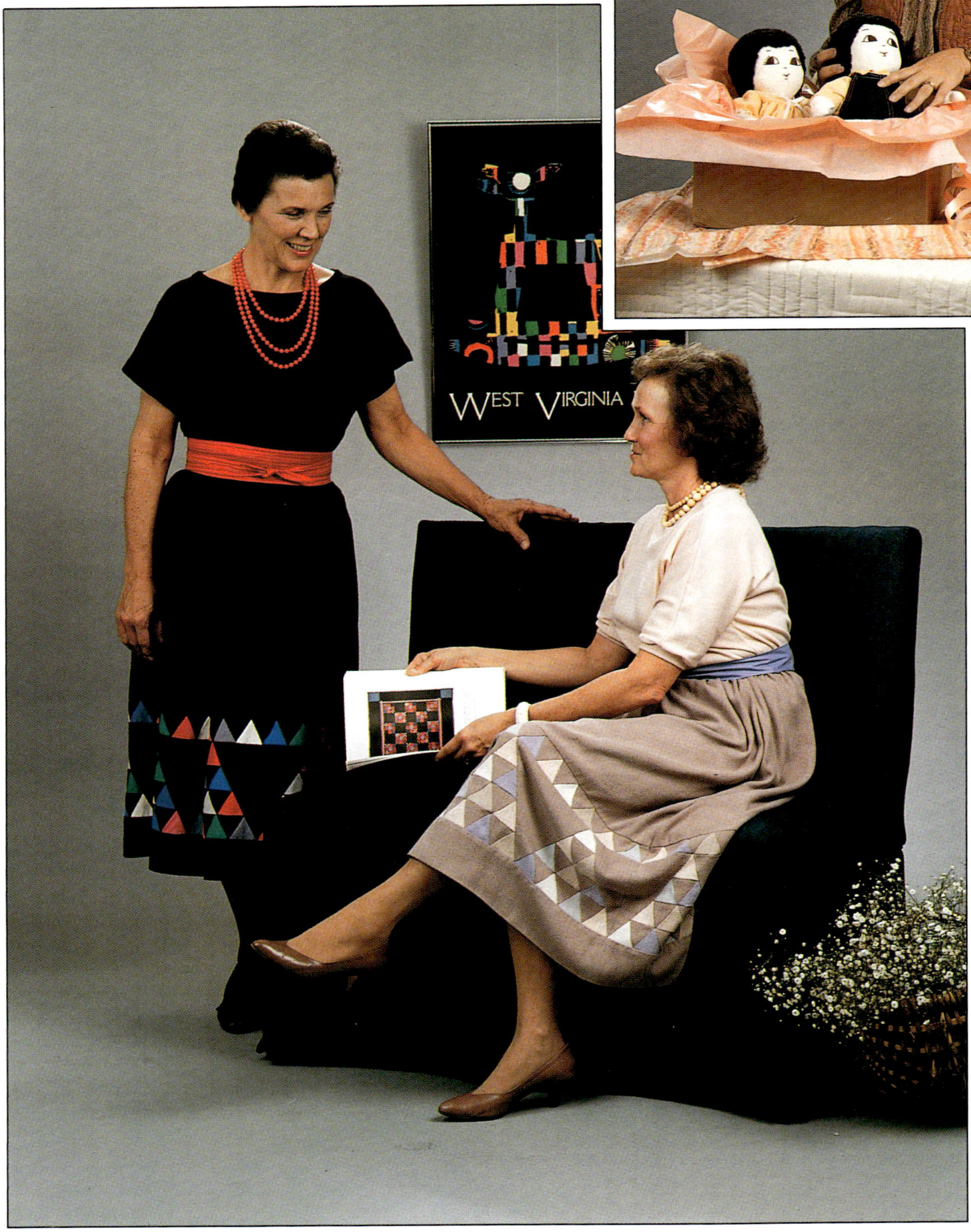

Floating Triangles Skirt

PART 2
MAKING THE GARMENTS

A FEW NOTES ON THE PATTERNS AND INSTRUCTIONS IN THIS BOOK

All patterns are drawn full size. When transferring patterns from the printed page, size conversions are not required.

Seam allowances are *not* included in these patterns. When tracing patterns for piecing or hand applique projects, always remember to add your own ¼" seam allowances.

Underlaps are not marked on the pattern pieces. If you're working on a machine applique project, be sure to add underlaps where they will be needed. To determine the location of underlaps, check the construction details for the specific garment.

All yardages in this book are based on a misses size 10. When figuring the amount of fabric you will need for a project, take into account your dress size and height, the fabric's width and nap, and the possibility of shrinkage. Also adjust for the desired fullness of any skirts or dresses.

8
LOG CABIN DRESS AND SUIT

To find a log cabin in Cabin Creek, West Virginia, we didn't have to go farther than the "hollers" around town. Tucked into the sides of the mountains, there were many homes constructed of brown/black logs, zebra-striped with white layers of plaster daubing. Some looked as though they could have been built in pre-Revolution days, back when the long, largely unexplored stretch of what's now West Virginia and Kentucky was called Fincastle County, Virginia.

We found a lot more log cabins, of course, at Cabin Creek Quilts' shops. The Log Cabin pattern is easily their best seller. Part of its appeal is its versatility. Each combination seems more interesting than the last. Even the names of the variations are intriguing. Courthouse Steps. . .Streak of Lightning. . .Barn Raising. . .Straight Furrow. And where else can a Pineapple have a chimney?

Within each variation, there's room for still more variation. You can distribute light and dark tones evenly and gradually, or you can arrange a stark light/dark contrast called Sunshine and Shadow. Even the number of colors you use is an important decision. In this busy pattern, restraint can create some eyecatching effects. We once saw an Amish Log Cabin constructed entirely of sober browns, greens and blacks, enlivened only with vivid pink chimneys.

Out in the hollers, one log is pretty much the same as the next. When building with fabrics, you have to select your "logs" with much more care. Because most log cabin arrangements hinge on some sort of light/dark color contrast, you'll want to start by dividing your fabrics into piles of lights and darks. As you do this, keep your mind open and creative. Diane has found that sometimes a fabric that she expected to use as a dark turns out to belong in her light pile or vice versa. Even after she's collected what seemed like a good variety of fabrics, all too often, the balance of tones is just slightly off. Then she's back to the sale bins and scrap bags, scrounging around for one more red with lots of blue in it.

As you plan the basic architecture of your Log Cabin blocks, it will help to step back often and examine the effect you're creating. Something that looks great up close can often be quite dreadful from a few paces away. Polaroid cameras are a big help here. As you try out different color and pattern arrangements, take a series of Polaroids. Later, you can set your photographs out side by side and decide which arrangement will be the most flattering to you and your garment.

If you do your creative work before you start sewing, your blocks will go quickly. You could very well build many Log Cabins in the course of one evening. Now that would be something to brag about, especially up in the hollers around Cabin Creek!

LOG CABIN DRESS

Construction notes:

Machine piecing. Beginner level.

We made our dress from Thai Silk's silk noil in a brilliant teal green. Silk noil is a four seasons fabric that sews and performs much like a good medium weight linen—but with far fewer wrinkles and better drapability. It's a perfect dress fabric for the office.

The log cabin blocks are cut from Concord's Country Cottons (100% cotton). We used light and dark shades of teal, terra cotta and gold. Scraps of teal silk noil from the dress body complete the blocks.

If you already have a set of log cabin templates and were considering using them for this project, think again. Log Cabin blocks must be quite small to work on clothing. The blocks we used for this dress are 2½" square. The center chimneys are only ¼" square. The finished width of each log is ⅜". Blocks of such a small size must be pieced carefully. The tiniest inaccuracy becomes quite noticeable. To avoid problems, Diane has developed a method using paper patterns as a base for sewing the blocks instead of the traditional muslin. The guidelines on the paper insure accurate piecing, and the paper foundation is discarded after the log cabins are completed.

What You Will Need

3½ yds. teal silk noil 36" wide

⅛ to ¼ yds. each of at least 8 cotton prints and solids in light and dark shades of teal, terra cotta and gold

⅜ yd. teal china silk for yoke lining

Teal thread, plus thread to blend with patchwork fabrics

Cotton cording for piping trim

Dress zipper
Basic Dress pattern
Patternmaking cloth
Rotary Cutter and Mat (optional)
Sheets of newsprint drawing paper
Template plastic

2DK

1DK

3LT

4LT

FULL SIZE PATTERN
LOG CABIN DRESS BLOCK

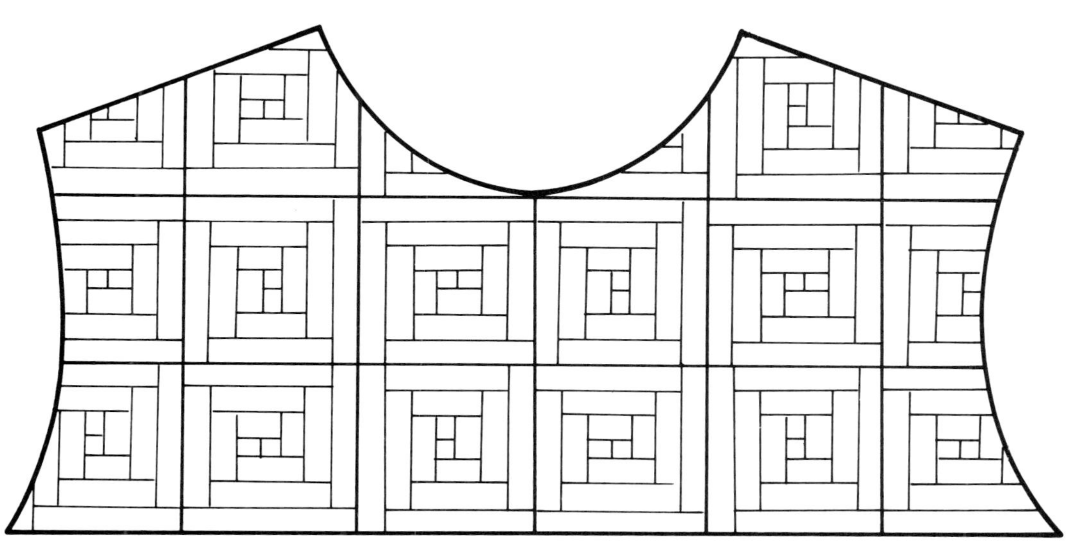

DIAGRAM: LOG CABIN DRESS YOKE

Directions

GET READY. Read through the complete instructions. Pre-wash all fabrics and cording.

ADAPT THE PATTERN. The yoke section of your Basic Dress Pattern should measure 5″ from the neckline to the bottom of the yoke. If you need to alter the yoke, make those adjustments now.

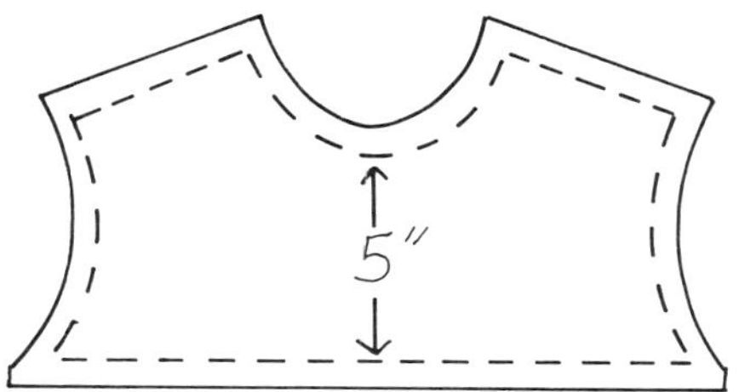

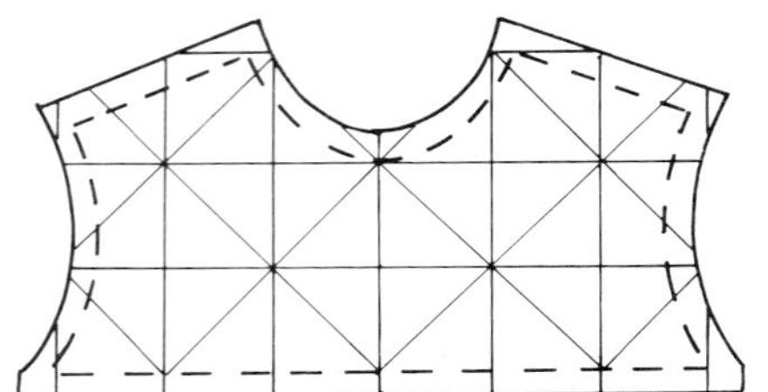

Draw the dress pattern onto patternmaking cloth, tracing the pattern of 2 ½″ blocks all over the yoke. Count how many blocks you will need to complete the yoke (about 20–24).

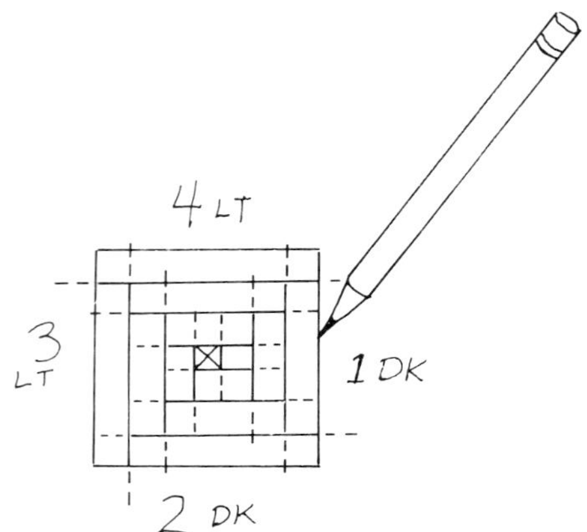

TRACE THE LOG CABIN BLOCKS. Use a *permanent* pen on sheets of blank newsprint. As you trace, extend all the seam lines as shown in the illustration here. Number the sides as to their sewing order. In addition, label each side as a light or a dark.

Make enough tracings for each block you need, including all information on each tracing. This will prevent confusion and sewing errors later.

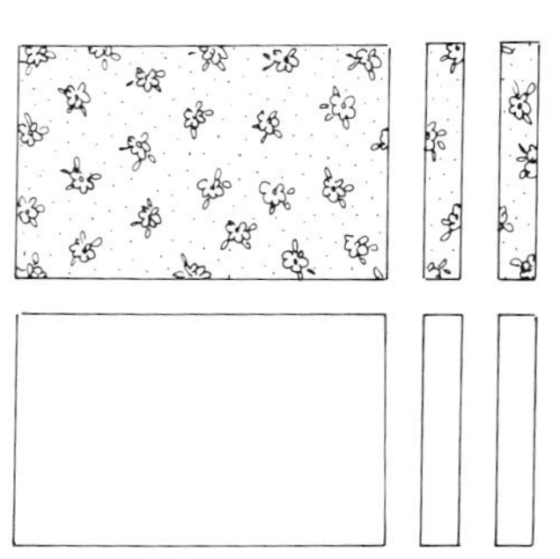

CUT THE FABRIC INTO STRIPS. Include the fabric that will form your center chimneys. Cut cottons or light- to medium-weight silks ⅞″ wide. Woolens such as flannel or gabardine should be cut 1″ wide. The length of these initial strips is not important because you'll be trimming each log to the correct length as you sew.

Separate your strips into a light pile and a dark pile. We sewed ours into blocks in a random order, but you may prefer to establish a pattern, sewing each fabric in the same position on every block.

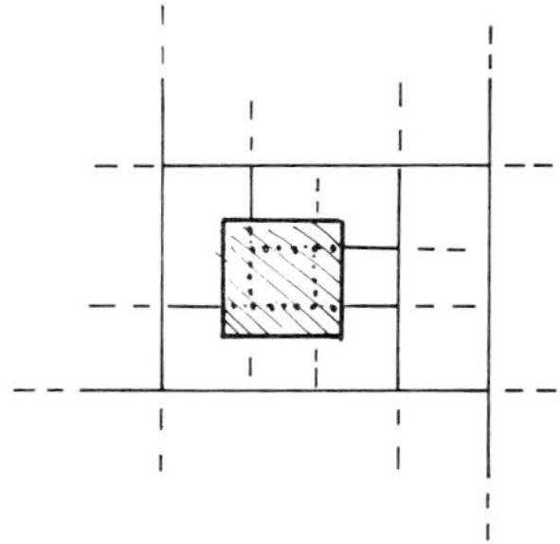

GET READY TO SEW. Thread your machine with a color that blends with all your yoke fabrics. Take a strip of the center chimney fabric and cut off a square. Position it on the center of the paper pattern.

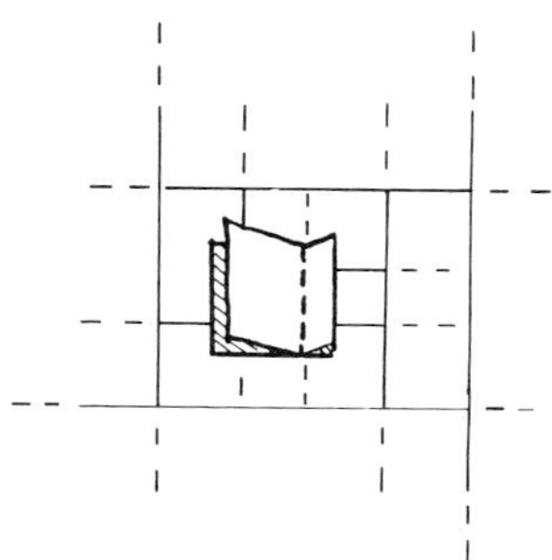

SEW THE FIRST LOG. Take the strip of fabric that will be your first log. Cut off a piece that is the same length as the chimney square. Place it face down over the chimney square so that the first seam to be sewn will be to your right. The seam lines that you extended on the paper pattern will show you exactly where to sew. Sew directly on this line.

Following that first seam, turn the paper pattern over and check to be sure your stitching landed exactly on your drawn seam lines. An incorrect seam will be obvious and should be fixed immediately.

Flip back the first fabric log and finger-press or iron into place. We prefer to iron.

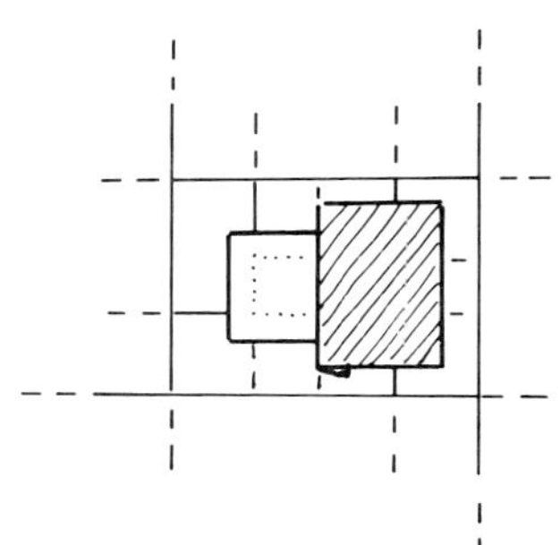

CONTINUE LAYING DOWN LOGS. After sewing and pressing each log, trim each log strip to the correct length. Use your paper pattern as a guide. Continue building each block, log by log, using these four steps: 1. Position 2. Stitch 3. Press 4. Trim to size.

Pay particular attention to the sewing order of each fabric strip and whether you're adding logs to a light side or dark side. We find that these blocks go faster assembly-line style. Sew the same log on a whole group of blocks—working on 4, 8, even 12 blocks. After that, start adding the next log to every block in a group.

When each block is finished, carefully tear away the paper backing. Any extra little shreds of paper will come off in the wash.

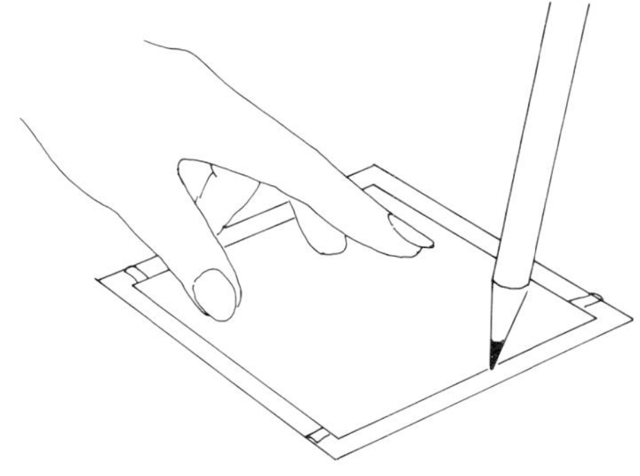

MARK THE COMPLETED BLOCKS. Cut a plastic template of the Log Cabin block. Use this to mark the outer seam lines on the wrong side of each block.

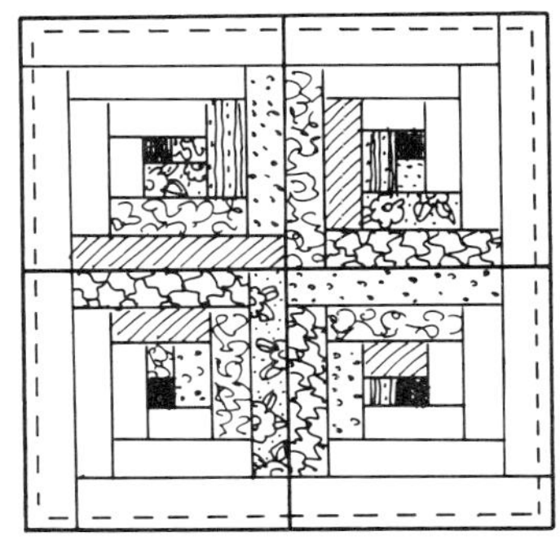

SEW THE BLOCKS TOGETHER. Join your blocks together so that each group of four forms a dark diamond. When your diamonds are completed, sew them all together into one piece of fabric. This assembled piece should measure slightly larger than the pattern for the dress front yoke.

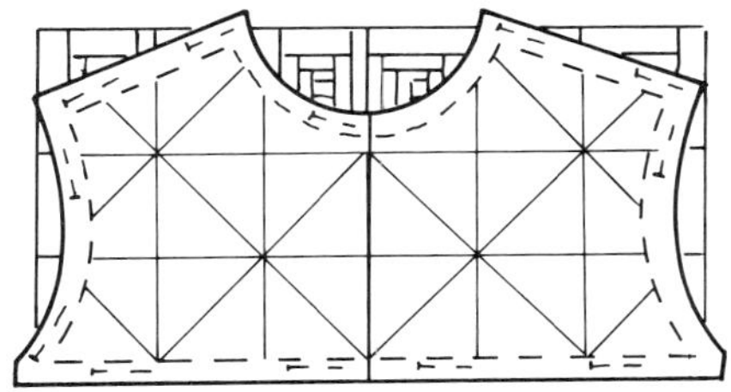

CUT OUT THE YOKE. Pin the yoke pattern to the pieced fabric, centering the design. Cut out the yoke. Staystitch the edges.

ASSEMBLE THE DRESS. For dress assembly, follow your commercial pattern instructions. Line the yoke, rather than using facings. To do this, cut another set of front and back yokes out of china silk or your dress body fabric. Add piping or cording at the neckline and bottom yoke seams if desired.

LOG CABIN SUIT

Construction notes:

Machine piecing. Tailored suit construction. Intermediate level.

We made our suit from a variety of light-weight to medium-weight woolens. Some were scrap trimmings from trouser hems. Others were salvaged from vintage mini skirts. To tie together these fabrics, we did have to purchase a few ⅛ or ¼ yard lengths of similar weight woolens. As you plan your yardage, allow extra of one patchwork fabric. This will be your jacket binding.

The main suit body fabric, which is also incorporated into the patchwork, is a brown, 100% wool tweed from G Street Fabrics in Rockville, MD. In planning the design, Diane chose the suit fabric first, then dipped into her scrap bag, searching for fabrics that could draw out the subtle colors in the tweed.

When working with lots of fabrics and two or more different block patterns, it's best to avoid any chance of a mix-up. To help, use our paper pattern method, which is described earlier in this chapter. This jacket takes lots of blocks, as many as 70 or 80 depending on your jacket size and its length. The actual sewing of the blocks is easy and goes quickly if you work assembly-line fashion. This means sewing the first light strip on a group of 8 or 12 blocks before stopping to press. After that first log is completed for every block, move on to the second log. Your work will appear to grow more slowly, but your consistency will be improved. The results are so spectacular, we feel it is definitely worth the effort.

What You Will Need

3¼ yds. (60″ wide) wool tweed (yardage covers jacket and gathered skirt)

1½ yds. muslin to make up jacket

⅛ to ¼ yds. of at least 11 light-to-medium weight woolens (challis, flannel, gabardine, menswear suiting)

Extra fabric for jacket binding

1¾ yds. lining material for jacket

Thread to match suit tweed and to blend with patchwork

Skirt zipper

Basic Jacket Pattern

Basic Skirt Pattern

1 yd. patternmaking cloth

1 or 2 large sheets of ⅛″ graph paper

Sheets of newsprint drawing paper

FULL SIZE PATTERNS LOG CABIN SUIT BLOCKS

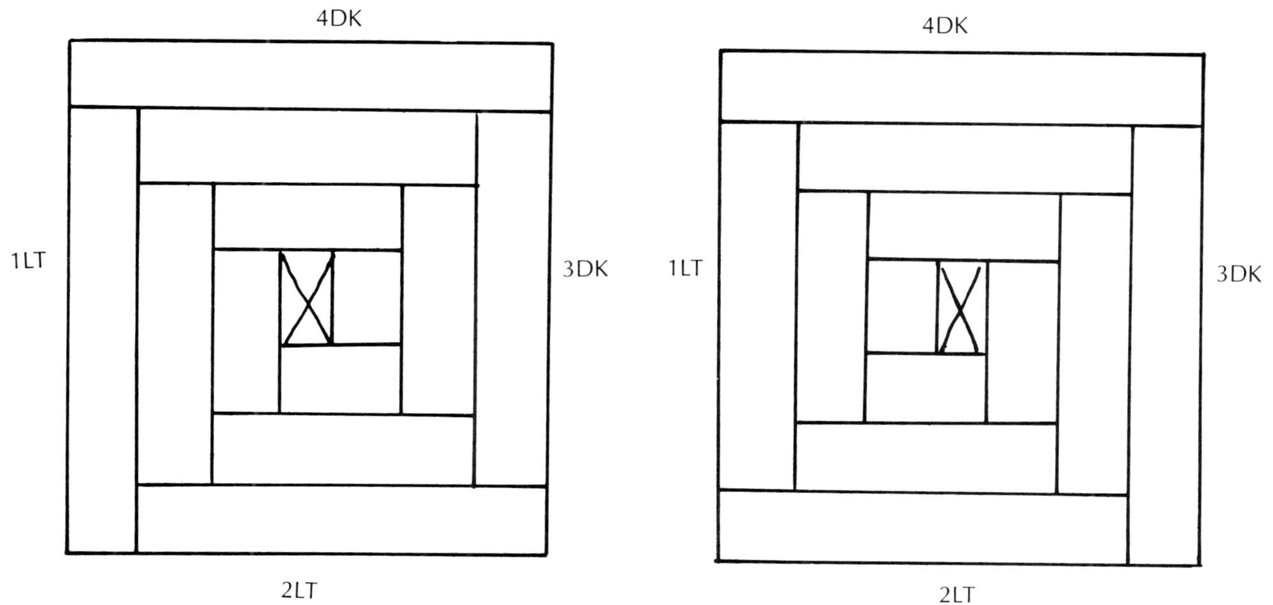

BLOCK #1 UPPER LEFT & LOWER RIGHT FRONTS

BLOCK #2 UPPER RIGHT & LOWER LEFT FRONTS

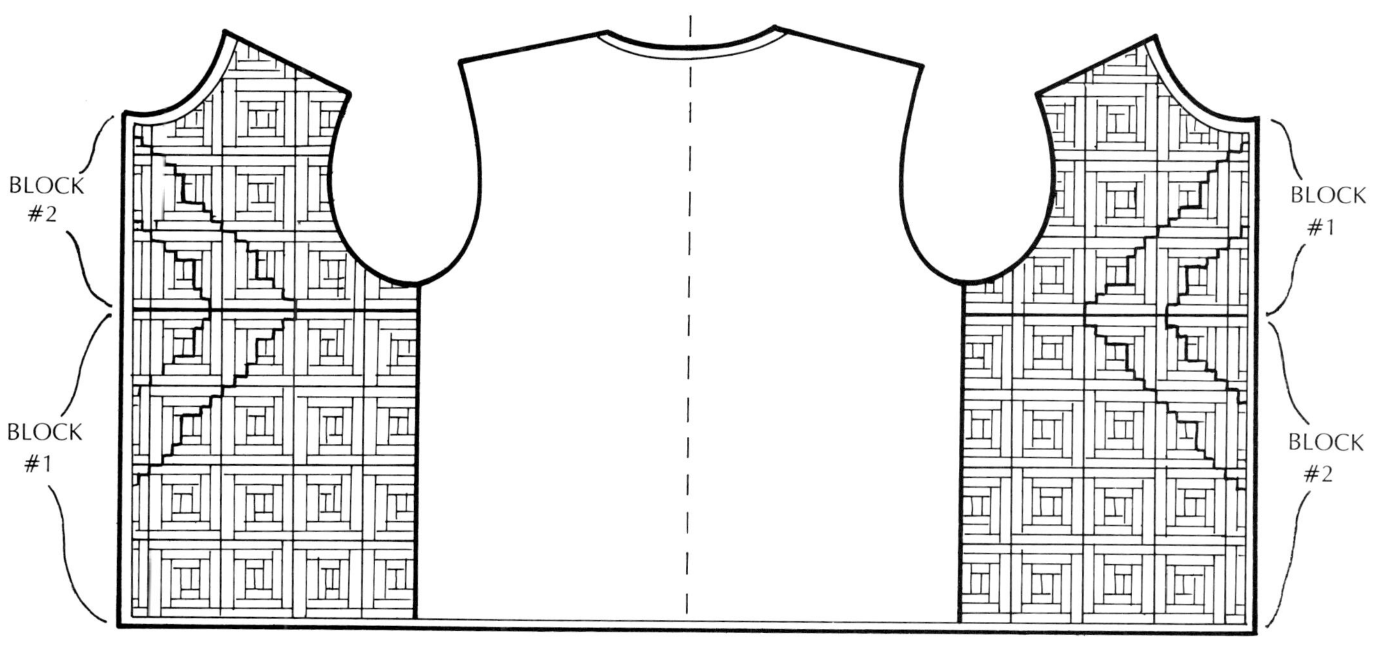

DIAGRAM: LOG CABIN SUIT JACKET

Directions

GET READY. Read through the complete instructions. Pre-shrink all woolens.

MAKE A MUSLIN OF THE BASIC JACKET. Your pattern must be adjusted now if you want to get a perfect fit. Determine the jacket

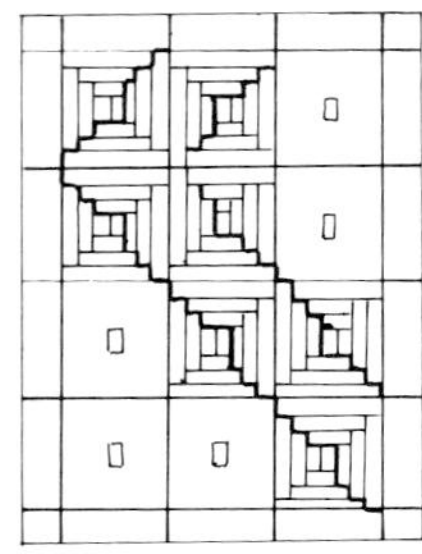

length now also. Draw any adjustments on the basic pattern and trace a final copy onto patternmaking cloth.

GRAPH OUT YOUR LOG CABIN BLOCKS. Trace a grid of 2½" x 2¾" rectangles onto a sheet of graph paper. Draw out half of the Barn Raising pattern. It is only necessary to actually draw the detail on the light/dark blocks which form the design. It's helpful to graph in the centers on the rest of these blocks. Shade the dark sections with a colored pencil.

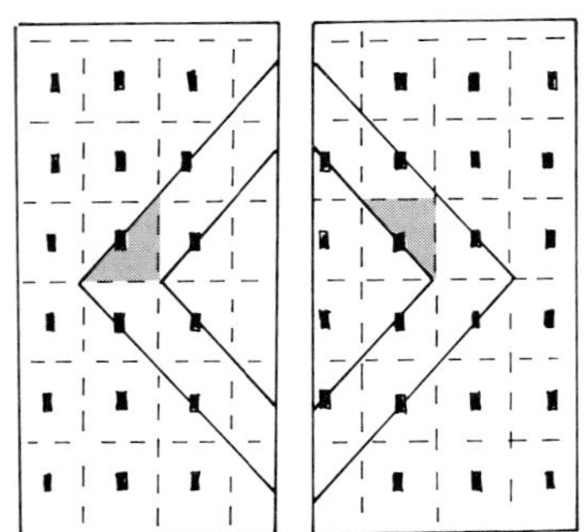

MAKE A MUSLIN "MOCKUP". Lay a piece of muslin on this graph and trace the design. Make a second muslin tracing. Turn one tracing upside down. You now have mirror image halves.

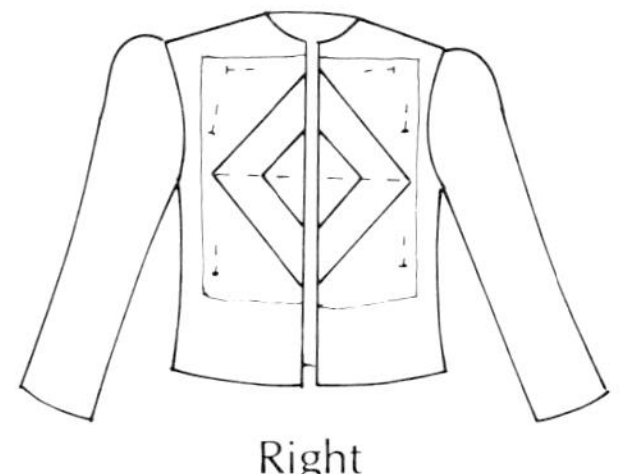

Right

Play with the placement of these muslin drawings, pinning them to the jacket muslin and trying them on until you get the arrangement and the fit just the way you like it.

A slim diamond shape, 2½ to 3 blocks wide on each front half, seems to look best on most people. Just be sure to line up the seams so that a row of logs is even with the center front where the binding will be added later. Also, try to leave an entire row of plain blocks (all light or all dark) below the bottom edge of your diamond. The design looks better if the visual center doesn't cut the jacket exactly in half horizontally.

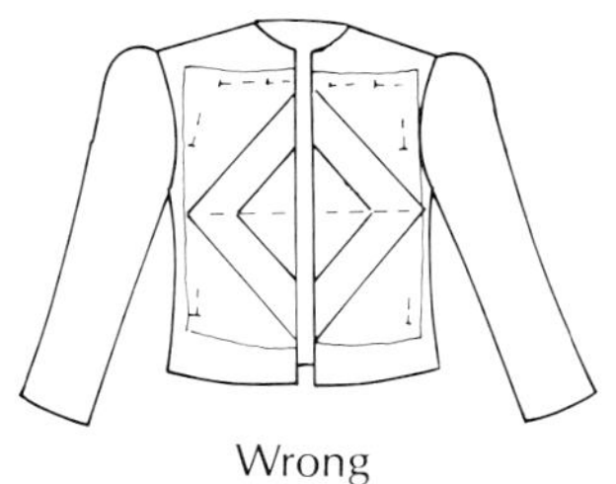

Wrong

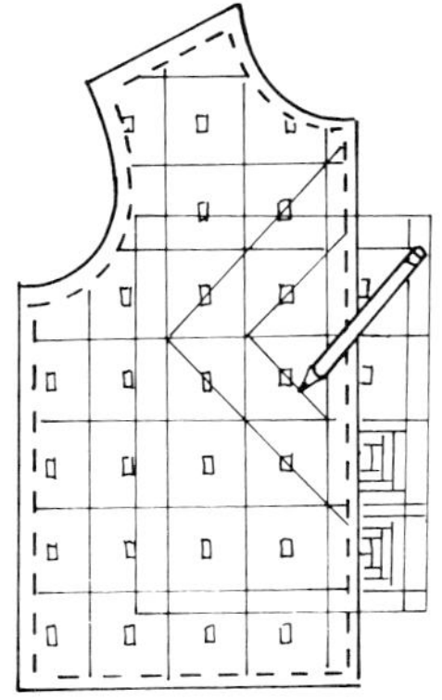

COMPLETE THE MASTER PATTERN. When you like your arrangement, take the jacket front you traced on patternmaking cloth and lay it on top of the graph of the log cabin blocks. Position the jacket front pattern to duplicate your muslin arrangement, then trace the blocks onto your pattern.

Now count the blocks to see how many need to be half light/half dark, and how many will be plain (all light or all dark). Don't forget to double the number. You will be making two front halves.

PREPARE THE PAPER PATTERNS. Trace the blocks onto newsprint with a permanent pen as described earlier in this chapter in the directions for the Log Cabin Dress. Be sure to label them either Block #1 or Block #2.

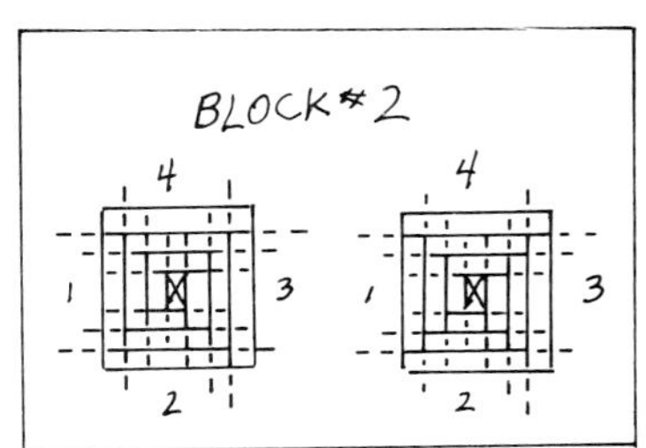

CUT FABRIC STRIPS. Wool should be cut 1″ instead of ⅞″ unless it is very thin (like challis). This allows for the "turn of the cloth", the extra bulk needed for folds. Separate your strips into a dark pile and a light pile.

SEW TOGETHER AND MARK EACH BLOCK. To sew the blocks together, review the assembly instructions in the directions for the Log Cabin Dress. As you finish each block and tear away the paper, keep the #1 blocks and the #2 blocks in separate piles, bags or baskets. Label each group.

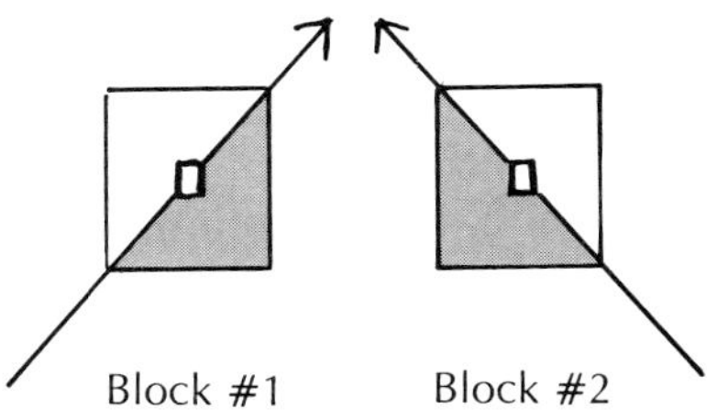

ASSEMBLE THE JACKET FRONTS. Lay out the blocks for one jacket front. If you have pieced them randomly, you may want to play with the positioning, rearranging a bit so that the same pink houndstooth check does not keep meeting itself at every block intersection.

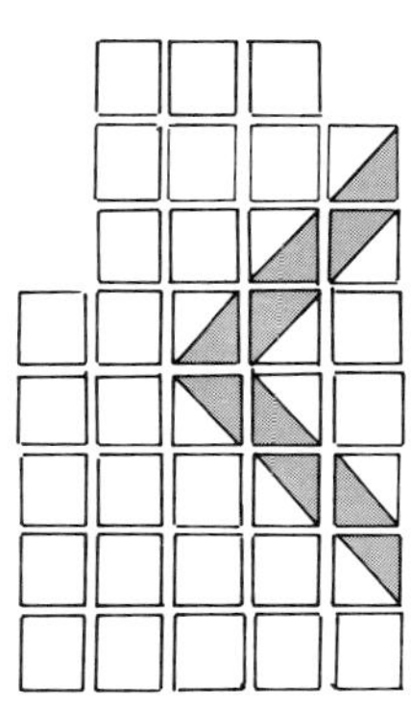

Sew the blocks into horizontal rows, then join the rows, matching all block seams. Repeat this procedure for the other half.

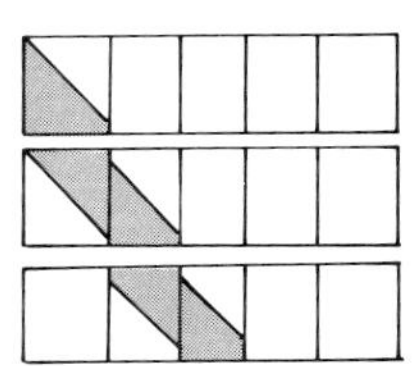

CUT OUT THE JACKET FRONTS. When the patchwork fabric is together, pin the master pattern to your patchwork. Cut out each jacket front. Mark the fronts. Staystitch the edges.

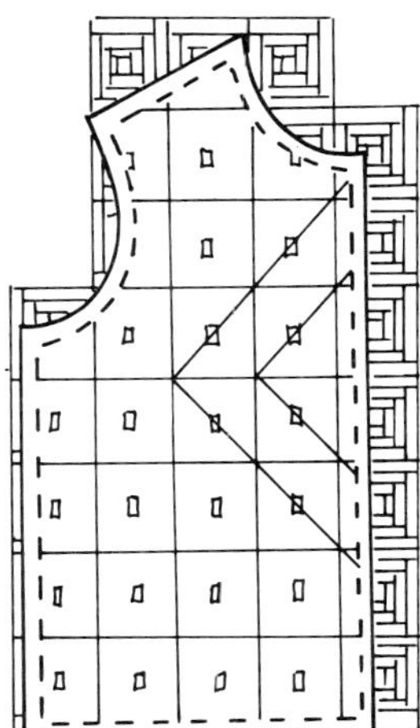

ASSEMBLE THE JACKET. Complete the jacket following the directions with your commercial pattern. The sleeves and back are unadorned. We show our version finished with ¼″ wide wool gabardine binding that covers the edge of the outer jacket and its lining. You could also use a matching Chanel-type braid or a knitted edge.

MAKE SKIRT. The skirt can be any style you want. The one we show in our photographs is a gathered skirt made from the Basic Skirt Pattern. Cut and construct the skirt according to your commercial pattern directions.

9
BALTIMORE BRIDE'S VEST

This bolero style vest is inspired by Baltimore Album Quilts of the 1840s. Like the individual blocks on an Album quilt, no two of which were ever alike, this vest is a show-off project. It gives you a great opportunity to create an heirloom while juggling your applique, quilting and embroidery skills. To add to the garment's versatility, we're showing this vest in two versions. The first uses the more traditional hand applique technique. The second calls for machine applique.

The heart motif, which gives our vest its name, has a special significance for Baltimore quilts, and particularly for bridal quilts. Baltimore quilts that have survived from the mid-19th-century tend to show surprising restraint in the use of heart shapes. In fact, hearts seem to have been reserved exclusively for bridal quilts. In that well-chaperoned era, hearts were not flaunted. Taken out of the bridal context, they were considered to be bad luck.

The rose-wreath structure of our nuptial heart is a classic Baltimore-style arrangement. You might consider substituting or adding bird, fruit or basket embellishments. But don't stop there. Embroider with silk ribbons. Trim with lace. Add fancy stitches, even elaborate beadwork. If you do, you'll be in good company. Many fine old Baltimore quilts contain these whimsical touches. In the flash of a needle, otherwise well-controlled Victorian ladies giddily crossed the line between matronly restraint and borderline gaudiness. Feel free to keep up the tradition.

After the vest was quilted and assembled, we washed it to remove the markings and all the dirt and smudges that seem to accumulate naturally on white sewing projects. The result was more than just a clean vest, we also got that nice, evenly "puckered up" look of a closely stitched antique quilt.

Hand Applique Version

Construction Notes:

Hand applique and quilting. Optional embroidery detailing. Intermediate level.

We made our vest and its lining from Concord's Country Cotton in white. The appliques are Concord's Country Florals. After the overall quilting was completed, we washed the vest one last time. This project is easily the most romantic and old fashioned-looking of all the garments in this collection. To keep the romance going, Diane suggests making the vest from white silk broadcloth with very pale pastel appliques.

What You Will Need

1¾ yds. (45" wide) fabric for body of vest (measurement includes lining yardage)

Applique fabrics (at least ⅛ yd. of each shade)

- 3-6 pinks
- 2 blues
- 2-3 greens
- 1 yellow

Thread to match all fabrics

Embroidery floss to match flowers and leaves

2¼ yds. of lace edging (optional)

Basic Vest Pattern

Tracing paper

Patternmaking cloth

Thin batting

Regular lead pencil

Water erasable pen

A rose, a book or catalogue about roses (for inspiration)

DIAGRAM: BALTIMORE BRIDE'S VEST

Directions

PREPARE YOUR PATTERN. Trace the Basic Vest Pattern onto tracing paper or patternmaking cloth. Trace the applique designs onto tracing paper. Lay the applique motifs *under* the vest pattern pieces and trace them in position onto the vest pattern. Trace each quilting motif separately onto tracing paper. Arrange them *under* the vest-plus-applique pattern so that they fill the blank areas of the vest exactly the way you want them. Except for the rose on the back, the applique pattern is symmetrical. Therefore, you can limit your tracing and arranging to only one side of the vest back, then fold the pattern in half and trace the mirror image onto the other side.

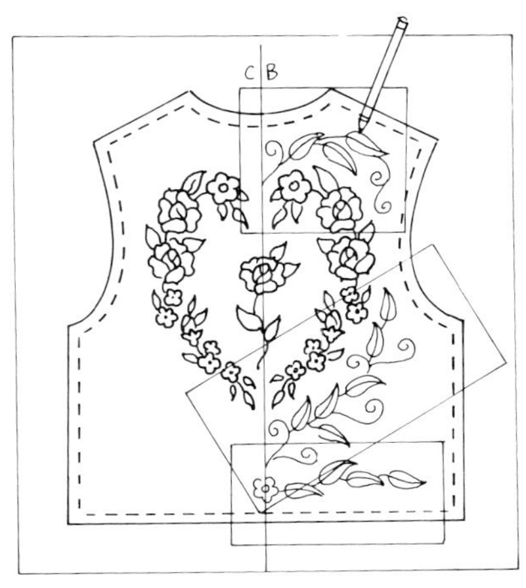

MARK THE VEST FABRIC. Tape the vest pattern to a light table or window. Lay the white fabric on top of the pattern. Trace the cutting lines onto the fabric with a regular lead pencil. Trace the applique designs with a water erasable pen. Don't mark the quilting design yet. For now, leave each vest section as a large rectangle of fabric. The fabric is easier to work with that way. After you've completed all the applique work, you can cut out the individual pieces.

DESIGN YOUR ROSES. This is the fun part, planning out your color placements and assembling different roses from different combinations of colors. If you've collected 3 to 6 shades of one color for your roses, go ahead and use them all. For inspiration, look at a real rose, or if they're not in season, study the photographs in gardening books or catalogues. One thing you'll notice is that colors can vary widely even within the same plant. Buds tend to be more vividly colored than fully-opened blossoms. As a general guideline, try to use your darkest shades in the center of each rose where the petals are more tightly packed.

Once you get going, start to vary each rose. Toss in a few surprises. One of the special characteristics of Baltimore Album quilts is the variety within each quilt. Repetition is anything but the norm. Try also to vary the placement of the fabrics used for the other flowers and leaves. Avoid making the left and right sides of the vest exactly the same. Your appliques will look more natural if the colors are not always in the same position.

APPLIQUE THE VEST. Review the chapter on hand applique and use methods you prefer.

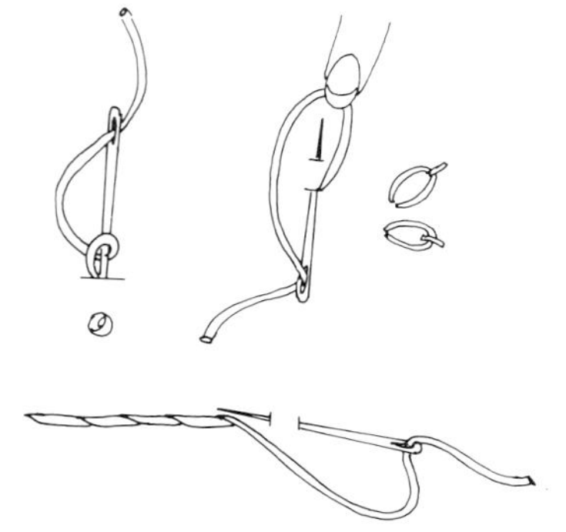

EMBROIDER THE VEST. First embroider the flower stems, using two strands of six-strand cotton floss. Then embroider the flower centers using four strands of floss to form French knots. This is all that's absolutely necessary to complete the design.

If you really enjoy embroidery, go ahead and embellish the flowers even more. Add French knots around flower centers, veins on leaves or radiating lines on flower petals.

Consider adding beads or tiny baby buttons for flower centers, or try using narrow ribbons instead of embroidery floss. Baltimore ladies of the 1850s embellished their Album quilt blocks with embroidery, ink drawings, feathers and ribbons.

REMOVE MARKINGS. When the applique and embroidery are completed, to remove the pen markings, soak the vest in two or three changes of plain, cool water. Allow the fabric to drip almost dry. While still barely damp, gently press out the wrinkles. Avoid pressing over the appliques or embroidery. If you must do so, put a thick towel on the ironing board. Place the applique face down on the towel, then gently press.

MARK THE QUILTING DESIGN. Lay the appliqued vest fabric on top of the vest pattern and lightly mark the quilting design with a water erasable pen.

ASSEMBLE THE VEST. Cut out the vest, lining and batting. Review the chapter titled "Assembling A Vest" and follow its directions. If you plan to add lace to the vest edge, do it now. Be careful not to iron over the pen-marked quilting designs when you press. Heat can permanently set marks from some brands of water erasable pen.

When the vest is assembled, baste all the layers together. Now you're ready to quilt. After you complete quilting, soak the vest well to remove all pen markings.

Simplification

If time or lack of skill is a concern, a basic flower design can be simplified considerably. A seemingly "short-cut" design may very well turn out looking quite as elaborate.

The easiest way to simplify this rose-wreath design is by eliminating or combining flower parts. A rose that calls for seven separate pieces of fabric can easily be redesigned to require only four or five pieces. The drawback is that you may lose some depth of color. The fewer pieces you use, the fewer opportunities for layering different shades of fabric. Also, by using fewer petals, your flowers may lose some of their definition and crispness. To avoid this, plan to spend time working with embroidery floss "drawing in" any otherwise lost detailing.

To simplify a rose, start by layering a piece of tracing paper over the rose pattern. Trace around the outer lines of the rose, then study the basic figure. Which parts are essential? What lines can be eliminated and still read as a rose shape? Experiment with colored markers or pencils to see how much variety and depth of color you can retain.

Before

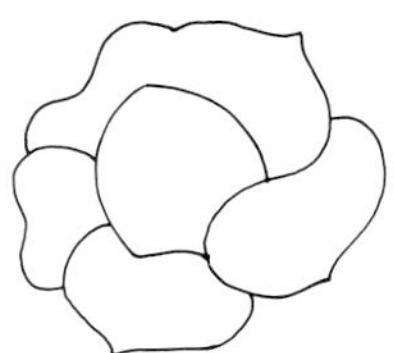

After: simplify center and combine petals

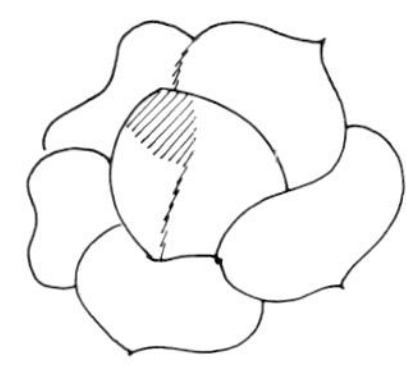

Embroidery stitches add details

The Pen Is Worth a Thousand Stitches

In the heyday of Baltimore style applique, good penmanship was as prized as tiny stitches. So if a quilter had it, she flaunted it. Autograph quilts were the most common use of ink on applique, but the use of ink didn't stop there. On the vest back, in the center, Diane has placed a rose. A Victorian lady might have chosen instead to letter in an inspirational Bible passage, a snippet of Shakespeare, or a tribute to a mourned relative. Over the course of 25 or 36 Album blocks, a quilt's inscriptions could range from colorfully sentimental love poetry to secessionist war whoops.

A Baltimore quilter might also sketch in a "vignette", a drawing of her home, a scenic wonder or a military monument. Military motifs were an important source of civic pride around the Port of Baltimore, especially after the 1840 election of President William Henry Harrison. He was the local celebrity by way of being a hero of the War of 1812, a conflict long dear to the hearts of Baltimore's citizenry. Log cabins, eagles, powder kegs and Old Ironsides quickly began appearing on Album blocks and proper bedsteads all on account of the memories stirred by a general turned politician. It brings one back to reality to consider what inspirational themes a Baltimore quilter might choose today to ink onto a quilt block or vest back.

Machine Applique Version

Construction Notes:

Machine applique and quilting. Intermediate level.

Everything old is new again. This vest shown here *couldn't* be worked as a hand applique project. To show the contrast between hand applique and machine applique, we purposely chose fabrics that would be difficult or even impossible to hand applique.

The vest body is constructed from J.B. Martin's Matinee® Velvet. Don't be fooled by the luxurious feel and deep coloring of this velvet. It has 100% cotton nap woven into a rayon back, it's washable and resists marring and crushing in spite of all the pressing, sewing and handling that goes with machine applique.

For the appliques, we used a variety of scrap bag satins, taffetas and moire faille. Against the dark background color of the rich velvet, these shiny, fancy fabrics contrast beautifully with the bright-on-pale coloration of the hand appliqued vest. This is a good example of how different a design can look when the fabric and color contrasts are changed.

As you stitch the appliques, you may be surprised to find how easy satins, taffetas and other luxury fabrics can be to work with. These fabrics also bring out the contrast between hand and machine work. The applique edges are more clearly defined, very crisp and bold. You can play up this feeling by using a contrasting, lighter or darker toned thread in your satin stitch.

What You Will Need

Vest fabric: Dark green velvet (40" wide, with nap). 1 yard for vest. For skirt, consult your pattern's yardage chart.

Lining fabric: 1 yd. matching dark green taffeta or use one of the applique fabrics.

Applique fabrics (at least ⅛ yard of each shade) or large scraps of moire, faille, satin or taffeta

Several shades each of pinks, blues and greens

Sewing thread to match the velvet plus colors to coordinate with the appliques

Basic Vest Pattern

Thin batting such as Fairfield's Cotton Classic

Large sheets of tracing paper

Stamping powder, talc, cornstarch

Scrap of felt fabric

Directions

PREPARE THE PATTERN. Follow directions given in the hand applique version for adapting the applique design to fit your vest size.

Draw separate right and left fronts and label each.

PERFORATE THE PATTERN. Perforate the applique designs on all vest pattern sections. Be sure to perforate from the *wrong* side.

APPLIQUE THE VEST. For instructions on press-basting and stitching, review "machine applique techniques" in Chapter 6.

ASSEMBLE THE VEST. Follow the directions in Chapter 4 choosing whichever method you prefer. Velvet tends to creep, so baste or use lots of pins before sewing. An even-feed or walking foot will help.

PREPARE THE VEST FOR QUILTING. Quilting lines tend to disappear easily on velvet and other napped fabrics. Therefore it is better to mark the vest after it has been assembled and all layers are basted together.

MARK AND QUILT THE VEST. Start by choosing the best quilting design for machine techniques. The elaborate design provided for the hand applique version of this vest is not appropriate for novice machine quilters. Straight lines or a simple crosshatching pattern are a much better choice. These lines can be easily drawn with a ruler. Use ¼″ drafting tape to mark the straight lines. When quilting, sew along one or both sides of the tape.

If you prefer to work a somewhat elaborate design, use the perforated pattern method. Draw your quilting design on the tracing paper vest pattern. Perforate the design from the wrong side. Working one section at a time (vest back, left front, right front), lay the pattern piece in position on the vest. Hold it down with weights. Go over the perforated quilting design with stamping powder. When the design is "pounced", remove the paper pattern. Go over the powdered design with a chalk pencil. After marking, quilt by machine or hand. Bury your thread ends in the batting.

Thread for Machine Applique

For the machine versions of this vest, we used silk thread. Silk seems to emphasize the sheen of moire and satin appliques.

As always, *work a test swatch*. It is especially important for this design because:

1. Silk thread is usually finer than regular sewing thread and therefore requires that your satin stitches be a bit closer together.

2. Velvet pile tends to "eat up" some of a zigzag width. Set your zigzag a little wider to compensate for the thick nap of your background fabric.

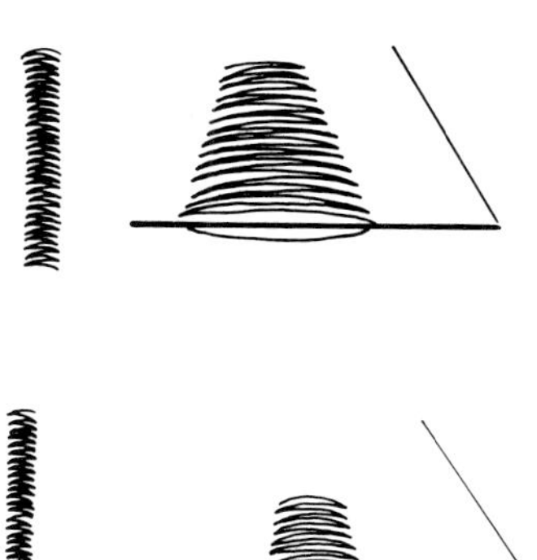

ADOLFO

10
CRAZY QUILT DRESS

This slim, softly gathered velvet dress is based on a late Victorian fad that was truly a craze. . .the Crazy Quilt. In a fit of delightful lunacy, shocking, impractical dress fabrics, traffic-stopping colors, even luxurious ribbons and trims were pieced together in seemingly haphazard triangles and trapezoids. But for all their brazenness, these new quilts were as sentimental as their Baltimore cousins. With a difference, of course. Baltimore Album Quilts tugged poetically at the heartstrings. Crazy Quilts behaved more like exuberant valentines.

There's no explaining the theory behind these happy designs, but their timing is quite logical. By 1880 new technologies had made fancy dress fabrics, machine-made laces and fancy embroideries less costly and more practical. Leftover scraps of watered silk, silk velvets, damask and taffeta, even brocades could be saved and traded for patchwork. Quilters could also purchase new fabric scraps by mail order. Magazines like *The Delineator* and *Godey's Lady's Book* advertised pre-cut, pre-assembled quilting kits complete with transfers or patterns for embroidery.

New technologies also explained the dazzling coloration of Crazy Quilts. The coming of William Henry Perkins's aniline dyes in 1857 made possible a dizzy array of brilliant, lasting colors. Aniline green came first, igniting a fad for green everything. Mauve came next, followed by true, non-fugitive browns, violets, reds and a better black. Of them all, the mauves and lavenders were the longest awaited and most sought after. The mania for these shades was so intense that the 1880s are still known as the Mauve Decade. Pieced together and balanced with black, then embroidered with golds and oranges, these quilts made stained glass windows look poor as church mice.

Once pieced, Crazy Quilts were simply tied together because most of the fabrics were too delicate or too heavy to be quilted. They didn't need to be quilted because, as parlor show pieces, they didn't get the same wear and tear as bed quilts. Crazy Quilts were used as lap rugs, piano shawls, table covers or throws for fainting couches. Modest uses for a pattern that is anything but shy!

Construction Notes:

Machine or hand piecing. Hand Embroidery. Lace and ribbon trim. Beginner level.

The dress body and sleeves of our Crazy Quilt Dress are made from J.B. Martin's Matinee® Velvet, a 65% cotton, 35% rayon blend. This luxuriously napped, light-absorbing velvet is the perfect foil for the shiny fabrics in the dress yoke. Unlike some high-nap velvets, Matinee Velvet is surprisingly easy to care for. Before cutting, we washed the velvet in cold water and tumbled it in the dryer at the permanent-press setting. The fabric must be removed the instant it is just dry. After tumbling, the fabric will look even prettier.

As with any high nap fabric, it must be carefully cut, with the nap. Press seams with care, between layers of terrycloth. If you have to rip and redo a seam, you'll find that the old seam line may show. So, baste and try on as you go.

For the yoke, choose any variety of fancy fabrics, ribbons and lace. Because you're combining fabrics of many textures and fiber contents, your finished dress must be dry cleaned.

What You Will Need

Velvet or other dress body fabrics (for yardage, see your pattern's "with nap" instructions)

Fabric scraps for the patchwork; medium-weight satin, moire faille and brocade

A piece of muslin, batiste or sturdy lining fabric, cut slightly larger than the front yoke pattern for use as a foundation for the patchwork yoke

Lining fabric for completed yoke (doubles as neck facing)

⅜ yd. heavy Venice-type lace (one that will lie flat around a curve)

Embroidery floss

Dress zipper

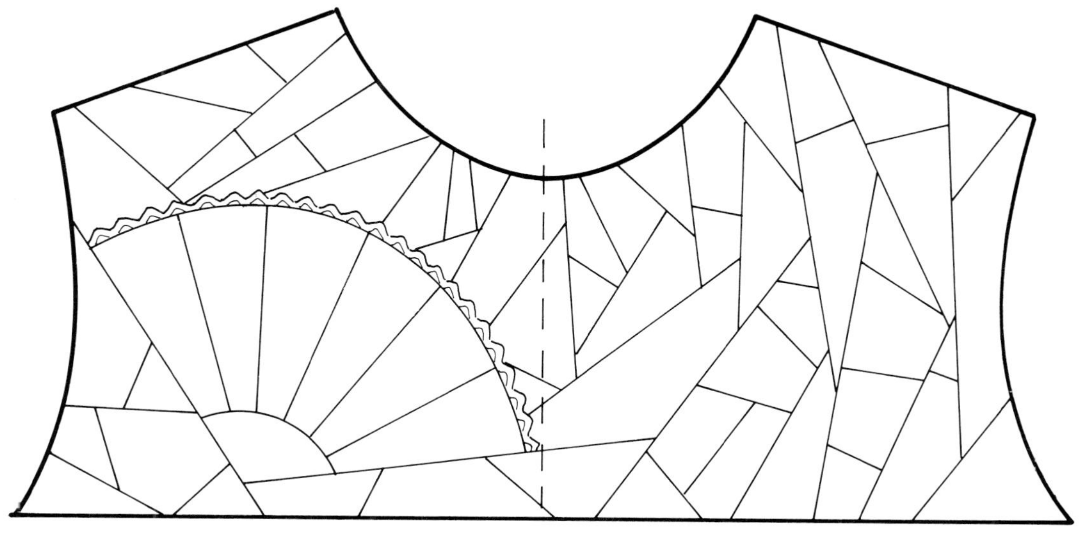

DIAGRAM: CRAZY QUILT DRESS YOKE

Directions

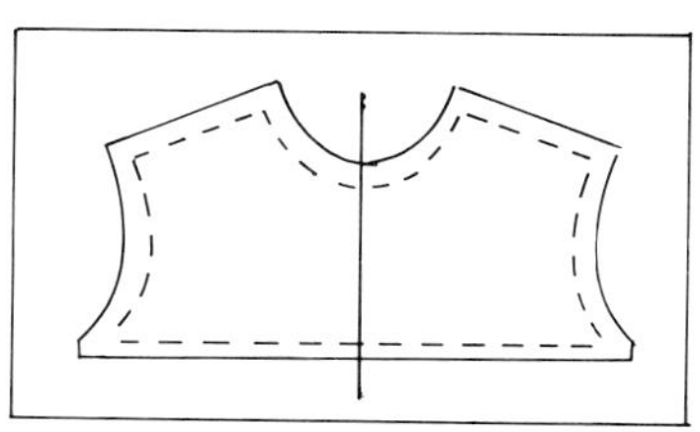

PREPARE YOKE FOUNDATION FABRIC. Using a pencil, trace the front dress yoke onto your foundation fabric. Include cutting and seam lines. Mark the center front, allowing the line to extend above and beyond the yoke at least 1″.

ASSEMBLE THE FAN. If you plan to include a fan on the yoke, this should be assembled first. Trace the fan blade and fan bottom onto template plastic. Cut out the templates. Mark and cut out six fan blades in six different fabrics, plus one fan bottom, adding ¼″ seam allowances on all sides. Sew the fan blades together, then press seam allowances to one side.

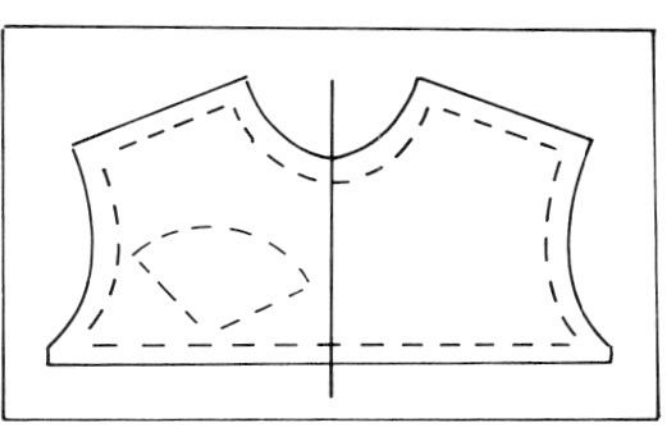

DETERMINE FAN POSITION. When deciding where you'd like to place the fan on the front yoke, remember to leave room for the unattached fan bottom and all remaining 1¼″ seam allowances. Trace the fan onto the base fabric. This doesn't have to be absolutely exact. Now, set aside the fan and its bottom piece until the patchwork approaches that portion of the yoke.

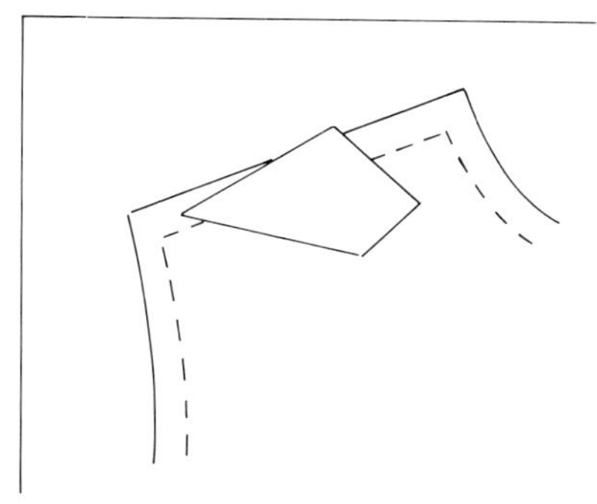

BEGIN CRAZY PATCHWORK. Select a scrap of fabric and cut a three or four sided piece about 2″ across. Pin it on the foundation fabric so that part extends beyond the cutting line of the shoulder.

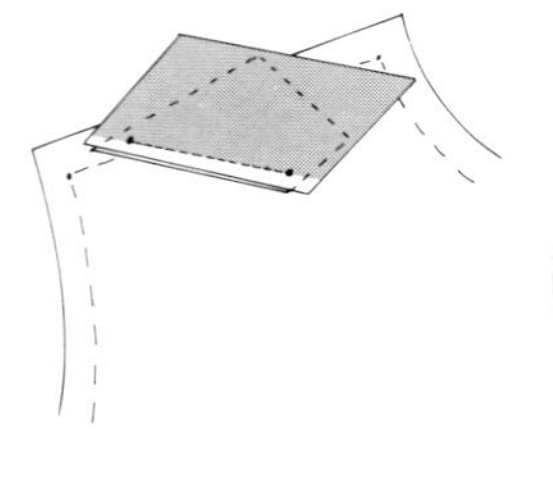

Lay a larger piece of fabric on top of that first shape, right sides together. One common edge should be aligned. Sew those two pieces of fabric together, ¼″ from the aligned edge.

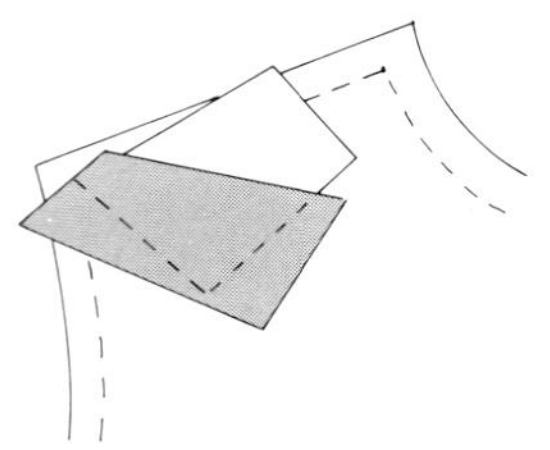

Flip back the second fabric, gently press the seam. Using a see-through ruler and a pencil, mark, then cut the second fabric into a patch shape.

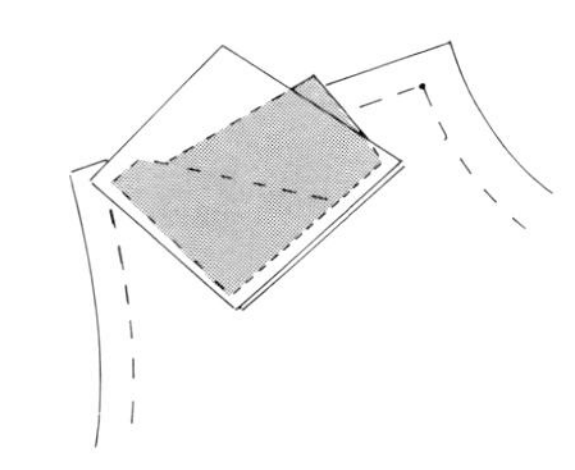

Place the third fabric, right side down, on top of the first two shapes. Align with an edge of one of the previous patches and sew another ¼″ seam.

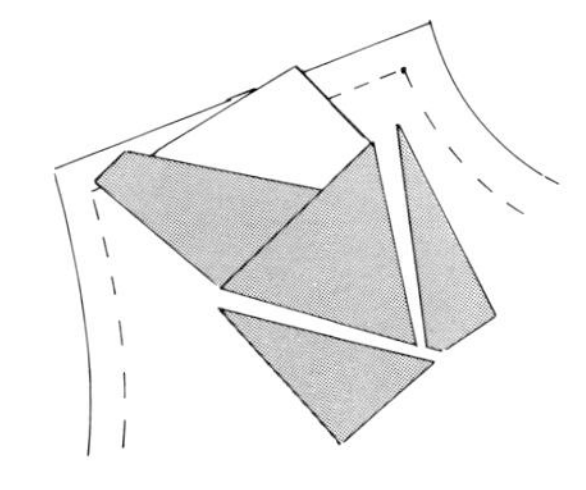

Flip the third piece back, press and trim into another Crazy patch. Continue down and across the yoke in this manner, extending the patches ½″ beyond all yoke cutting lines, until the patches overlap the placement line for the top curved edge of the fan.

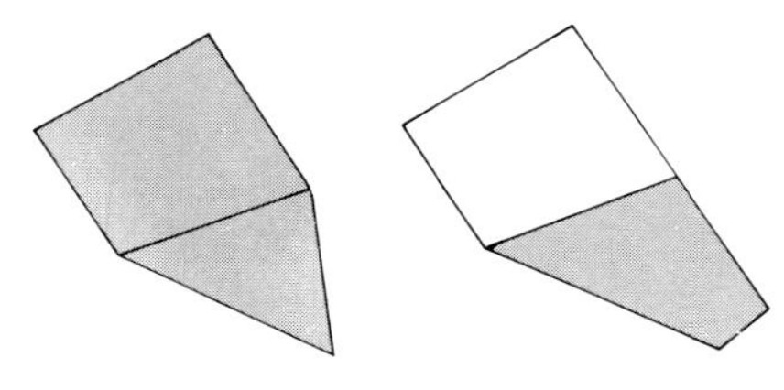

As you build your yoke, the size and shape of your patches will be entirely up to you. When you join patches, though, be careful to make angles that move outward like these.

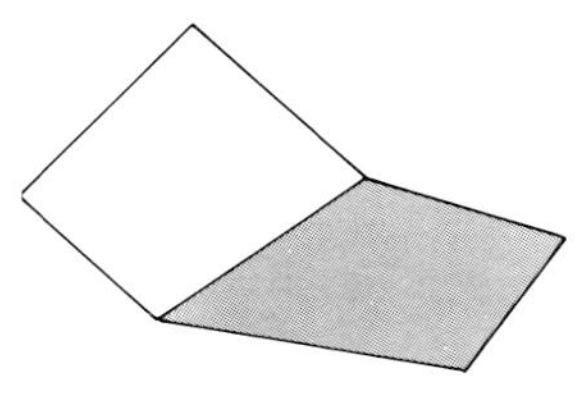

Avoid this kind of angle.

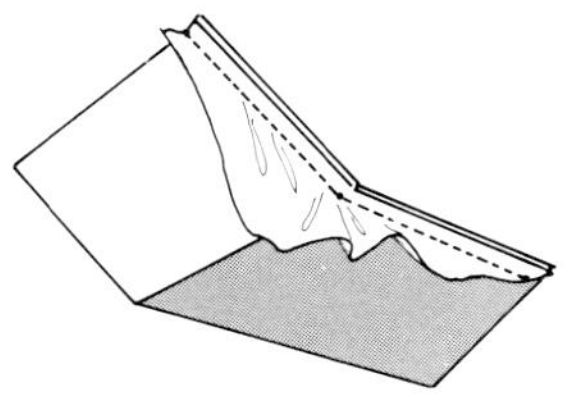

The patch above will look just fine until you try to add the next patch to it. See what happens.

Though Crazy Quilts may resemble crop land, you must always plow straight. No contour farming. Except for the fan, it's best to avoid making curves. The fan is the exception because its curve is attached by using applique techniques.

Think Small

A dress yoke is not a very large area, so try to keep your patches in scale. Crazy Quilt patches tend to take a life of their own and can grow uncontrollably. You may discover your patches growing larger as the edges you sew them to become longer. This can be avoided by strip piecing. Another way to limit the size of your patches is by using ribbons in addition to fabric strips.

How to Strip Piece a Crazy Quilt patch:

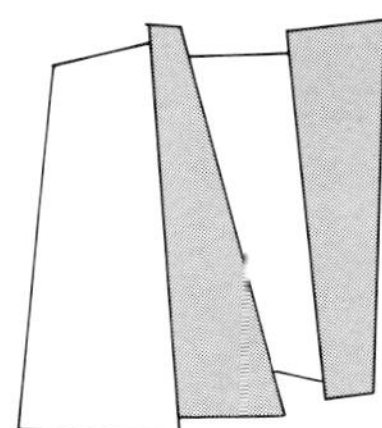

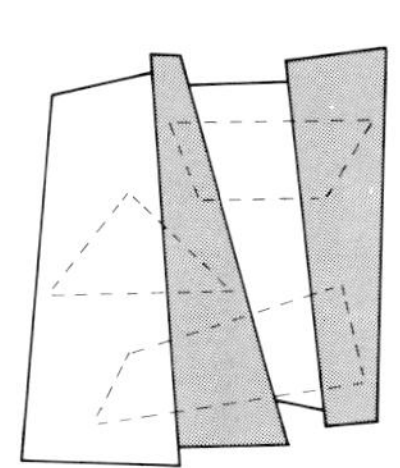

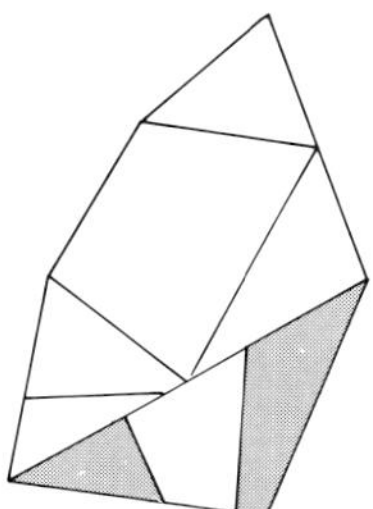

SEW FAN TO YOKE. The fan can be sewn to the yoke either by hand or by machine. The machine method is useful for a fan including heavy velvets. The hand method looks neat and delicate and is a good choice for light-to-medium weight non-raveling fabrics.

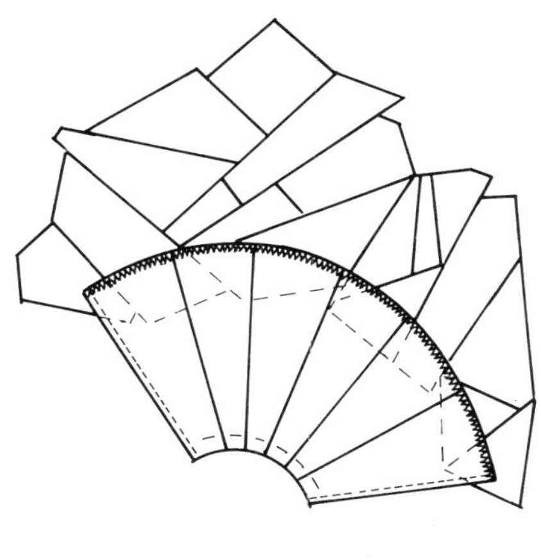

Machine Method

Trim away the seam allowance on the outer curved edge of both fan and fan bottom pieces. Pin the fan blades in place, making sure the entire top curve overlaps the Crazy patchwork. Straight stitch within the seam allowance along both sides of the fan blades. Zigzag along the top curved edge.

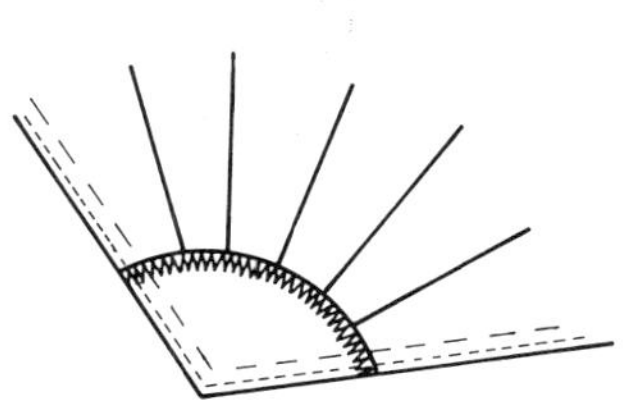

Pin the fan bottom piece in place on top of the fan blades. Straight stitch within the seam allowance along the two straight sides. Closely zigzag along the curved edge using thread that matches the fan bottom.

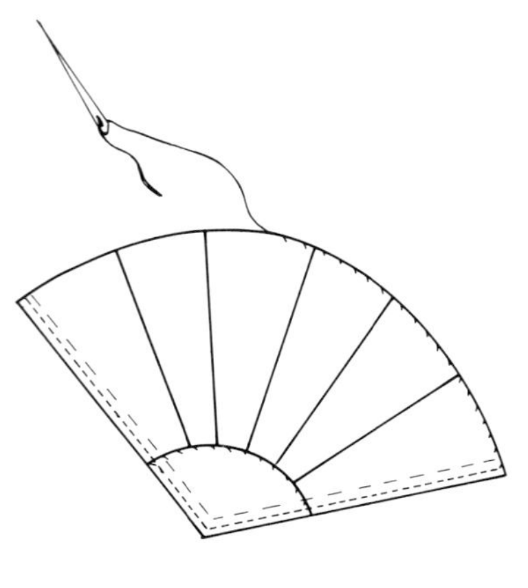

Hand Method

Pin fan blades in place. Turn under the top curved edge and hand applique it to the yoke. Pin fan bottom in place on top of the fan blades. Hand applique the curved edge to the fan. Straight stitch within the seam allowance along the two straight sides.

SEW LACE ONTO FAN. Pin the lace along the curved edge, covering the line of zigzagging or overlapping the hand applique edge. Sew in place with a narrow, widely-spaced zigzag. The curved edge of the fan bottom may also be trimmed with lace if you like.

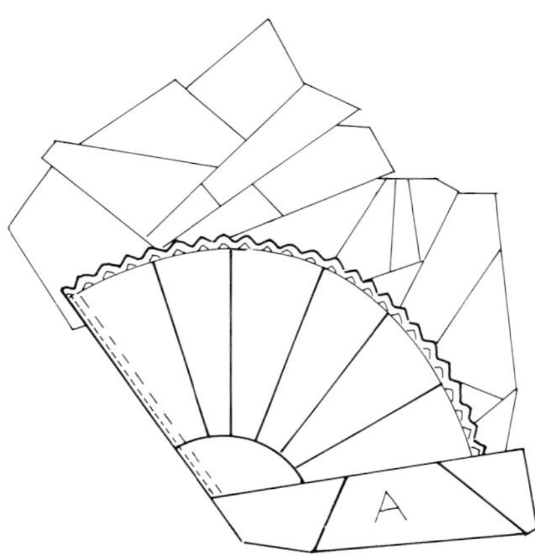

EXTEND PATCHWORK BEYOND FAN EDGES. The two straight sides of the fan are now ready to be finished off with Crazy patchwork. To do this, think of the fan as a completed crazy patch. Since the edges are so long, it will be necessary to use strip piecing. (See A&B)

Construct a length of strip piecing long enough to cover one edge of the fan and the necessary seam allowances. Starting with the horizontal side of the fan (A), sew your strip-pieced patch the length of this edge. Flip open the new seam and press gently. Using the see-through ruler, trim the bottom of the long patch even with the vertical edge of the fan.

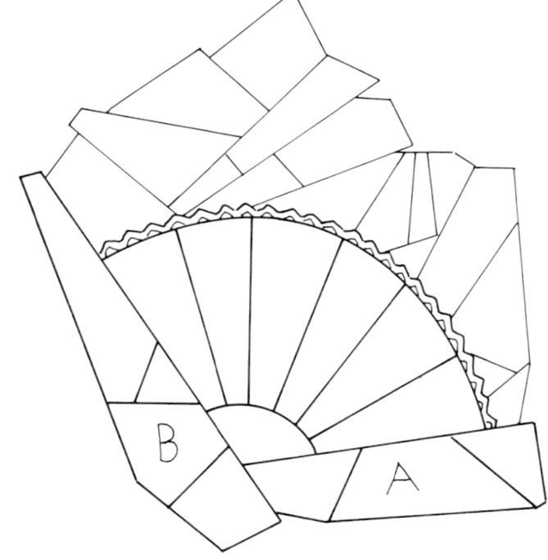

Sew another section of strip pieced fabric along the vertical side of the fan.(B) Flip open. Press gently, then trim even with the rest of the Crazy patchwork. Continue sewing patches until the entire yoke is covered.

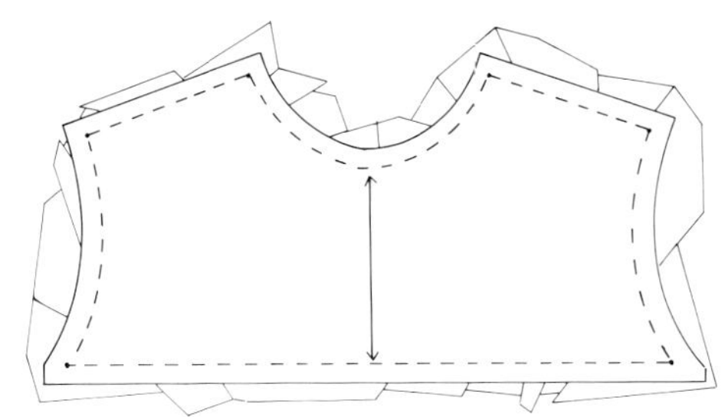

MARK YOKE. When the patchwork is completed, lay the paper pattern for the front yoke on top of the patchwork. Match up center front lines. Trace the cutting lines. Baste along these lines. Mark in the sewing lines with chalk.

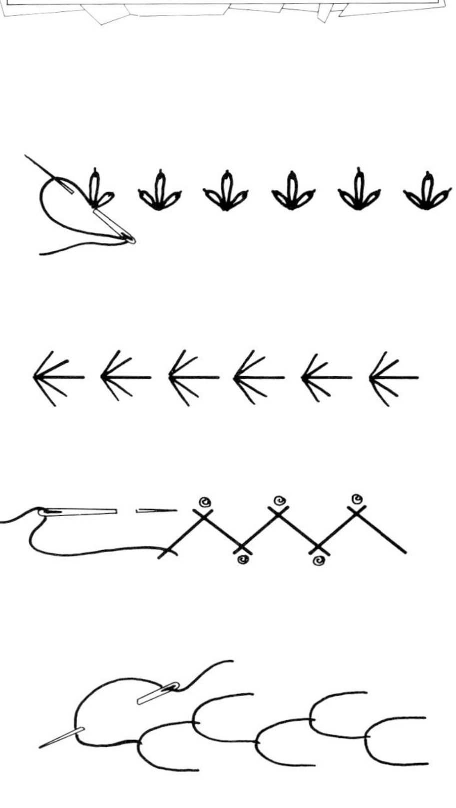

EMBROIDER THE PATCHWORK. The yoke is now ready to be embellished with embroidery stitches. For inspiration, Diane suggests that you take a look at *Crazy Quilt Stitches* by Dorothy Bond and *The Crazy Quilt Handbook* by Judith Montano. These are just two of many excellent sources listed in the Appendix.

Another good source of inspiration is fine heirloom quilts pictured in quilt books and magazines. Study the photographs with a magnifying glass, paying particular attention to how embroidery stitches were used. Observe the way some are placed over, others next to the seams connecting each patch. Notice also how colors are used on old quilts, and how, occasionally, several colors are included in a single row of stitches.

EMBROIDERY THREAD. Regular 6-strand embroidery floss comes in the most colors; however, it may not be shiny enough on fancy satins and brocades. Perle cotton has a bit more sheen. Size #8, the thinnest kind that comes wound in balls (rather than skeins), is a good weight for this type of embroidery. Sizes #5 and #3 are probably too heavy. Silk buttonhole twist is beautiful, but it is becoming difficult to find. For the dress shown here, Diane used Marlitt rayon embroidery floss. The shiny rayon has just the right look. She separated the four-strand floss and used two strands. Rayon floss is a bit more difficult to use than cotton floss, but the beautiful shiny colors are worth the trouble. Cut your threads into strands no longer than 15″. Every so often, as you embroider, allow the strand to hang loose and untwist itself. To make the thread more manageable dampen it lightly with a wet paper towel as you work.

If you use silk fabrics for your patchwork, consider using silk embroidery floss. It is more difficult to work with, but the results are quite beautiful. Most antique Crazy Quilts were embroidered in silk.

When embroidering, stop your rows just inside the ⅝″ seam allowance. Later, after the garment is constructed, these allowances will be trimmed. If you sew too far out into the seam allowance, your threads could be clipped and later pull loose.

CONSTRUCT THE DRESS. Follow your pattern instructions, treating the Crazy patchwork yoke like a regular piece of fabric. Instead of using facings, line the yoke.

11
FAN VEST

Our Fan Vest is a variation and simplification of the Crazy Quilt theme. In the Crazy Quilt Dress, a fan figure is built into the patchwork yoke. Surrounded by crazy patchwork and elaborate embroidery, a carefully pieced fan might be expected to get lost in the crowd of bright jewel tones and jagged angles. Instead, a well-placed fan gives the eye a focal point; it can lend order to a disorderly quilt pattern.

In this vest, the Crazy patchwork fan is removed from its more familiar home, a busy Victorian setting, and placed on a lighter, more open, plain background. Despite this dramatic uprooting, the fan pattern retains its eyecatching appeal, a quality that explains the fan's persistent popularity.

In the 1920s and 30s, cotton scrap quilts, in all their possible variations, reached a peak in popularity. Patchwork from those decades is characterized by the use of cotton candy pastels in lively prints. Pieced into multibladed fans, these prints created equally cheerful memory quilts in which one could detect bits of old pinafores, summer dresses, even Granddad's old underwear. Many of these all-cotton heirlooms remain in excellent condition today in spite of the fact that the quilts, and the garments that preceded them, were well worn and much laundered.

In addition to being a good use for random, unmatched fabric scraps, fans earned their popularity because they are so easy to piece, either by hand or machine. They're also a good use for slippery silks or difficult-to-handle brocades, fabrics that might not work in more complicated piecing designs. Even extremely delicate or fragile fabrics can be pieced in the fan pattern if they are fused to light-weight interfacing before cutting.

When worked in delicate silks, the fan pattern takes on a whole new personality. As the fan motif moves away from the Crazy Quilt setting, and then again away from the sunny-day pastels of the '20s and '30s, the Oriental influence of this design becomes apparent. Soft, delicately colored silks and silk batting can make this vest reminiscent of an antique silk kimono. In keeping with the Oriental mood, Diane designed a butterfly pattern for the vest's quilting motif. In the vest shown here, the butterflies are in flight, scattered randomly across the vest. If you prefer more quilting—and a firmer-bodied vest—the background can be filled in with simple cross-hatch quilting lines.

Construction notes:

Hand or machine piecing. Hand Quilting. Intermediate level.

The vest shown here is 100% silk. Silk body. Silk lining. Even the filler is a soft silk batting.

For the shell and lining, we used a mauve Thai silk. This lustrous silk has irregular slubs running horizontally across the surface. Before cutting, we pre-washed it and it came out beautiful. The fabric was amazingly easy to sew.

For the fan blades, we used a variety of silks in shades of cream, mauve, pale gray and blue. If you're making a blouse or dress to wear with this vest, try to work some of this fabric into the fan patchwork.

The fan blades can be trimmed with lace, ribbon or fancy embroidery stitches. For inspiration, see the instructions for the Crazy Quilt Dress (Chapter 10). If you use lace, be sure that what you choose will bend around a curve, yet still lie flat. For a rich feeling that complements luxurious Thai silk, look for a heavy cotton Venice-type lace.

Silk batting gives this vest a softness and drape that must be seen and felt to be appreciated.

What you will need

1⅞ yds. Thai silk (36″ wide) in mauve (measurement covers vest shell and self lining)

Several large scraps or ⅛ to ¼ yd. lengths of silk solids and prints

2¼ yds. ½″ wide one-sided ecru lace

2 yds. ½″ wide ecru daisy lace

Thread to match vest fabrics and lace

Basic Vest Pattern (shorter, bolero-length version)

1 yd. patternmaking cloth

2 packages silk batting

Artist's tracing paper

Compass

Template plastic

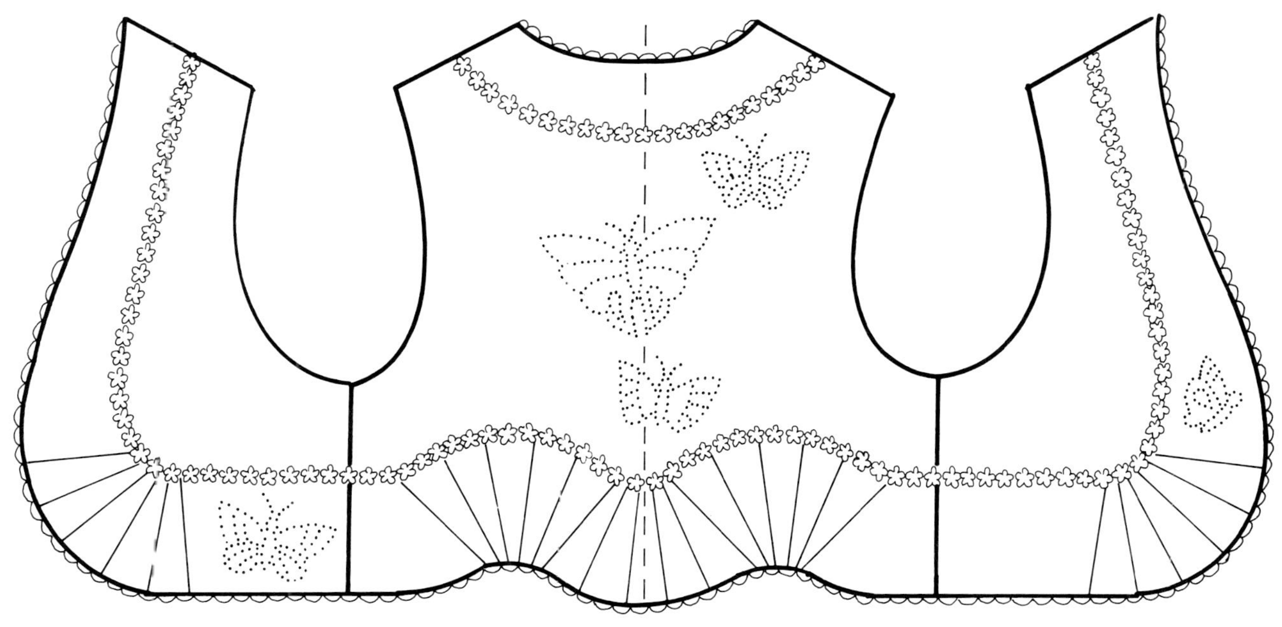

DIAGRAM: FAN VEST

Directions

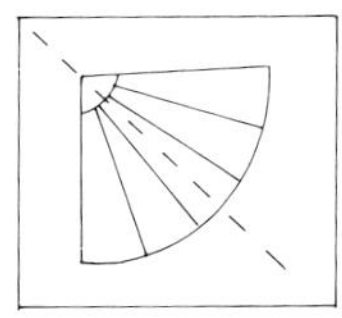

GET READY. Review chapters 4 and 7 on Assembling a Vest and Quilting.

Review Instructions for Crazy Quilt Dress.

Read through the complete instructions.

Pre-wash all fabrics and notions.

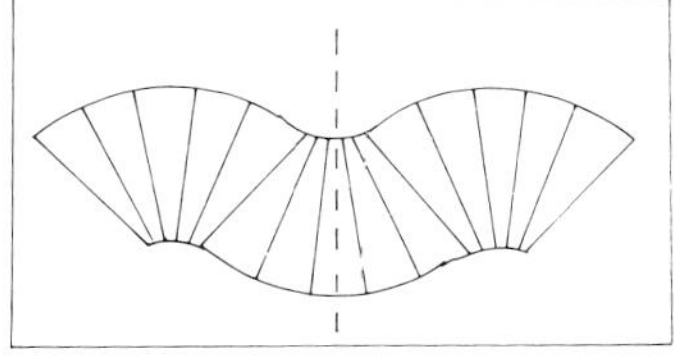

ADAPT THE PATTERN. Trace the fan onto a sheet of artist's tracing paper. This is the fan for the vest front. To make the design for the vest back, take another sheet of paper and trace the fan again. Add another fan, facing the opposite direction, to either side.

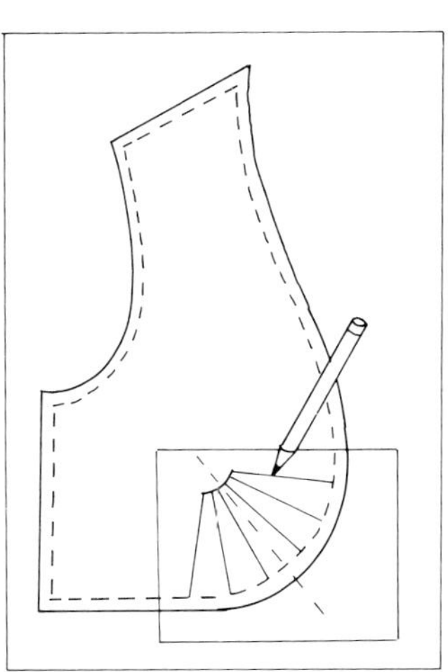

Trace the vest pattern onto patternmaking cloth. Position the fan design along the curved seam of the vest front. Adjust the curve a bit if necessary.

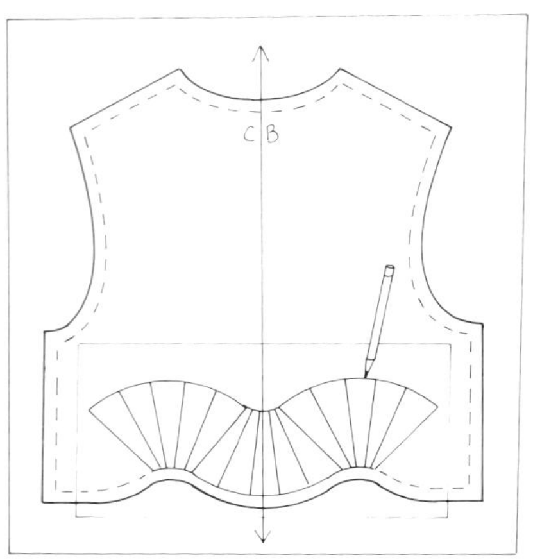

Trace the three fans onto the vest back. Adjust the curves, if necessary, so they flow smoothly.

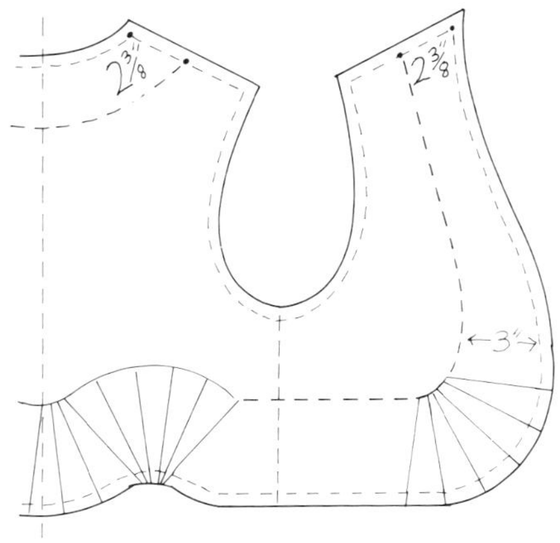

Draw a line for the daisy lace that connects all the fans. This line is more flattering if it starts out closer to the vest edge up at the neckline, then gradually widens out to meet the fans. Follow the illustrations as drawn, and mark the dots down, then connect with a continuous line.

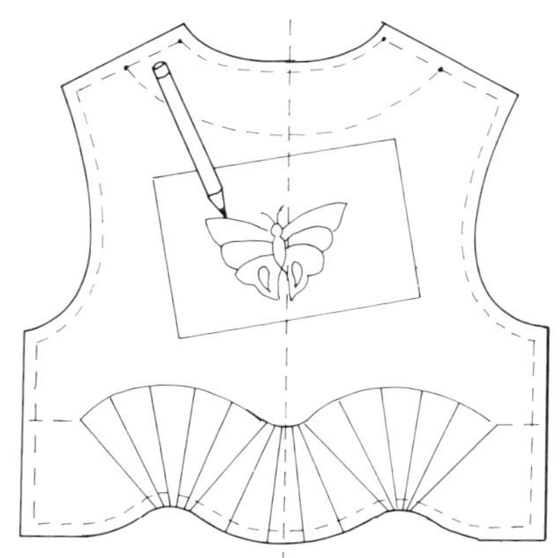

MARK THE QUILTING DESIGN ON THE PATTERN. Trace the butterfly figures onto a sheet of artist's tracing paper. Scatter these figures randomly over the vest back pattern. Add one butterfly to each half of the vest front.

Draw in parallel quilting lines in the margin between the daisy lace and the edge of the vest.

If you prefer to have even more quilting, fill in the rest of the vest with crosshatching or rows of double lines.

Your master pattern is now completed.

CUT OUT THE VEST AND LINING. Lightly mark the quilting design and the position of the fans on three vest sections. Set the vest sections aside.

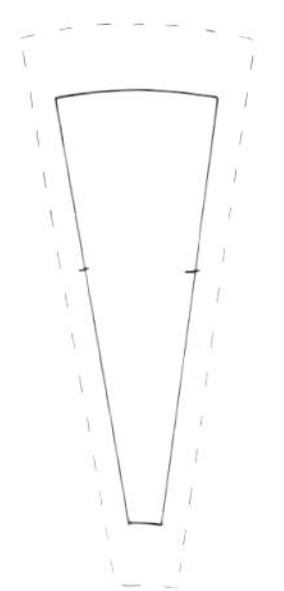

MAKE THE PIECED FANS. Trace one fan blade and the pattern for an entire fan onto template plastic. Be sure to include the line for matching the fan blades.

Mark and cut out the fan blades, marking the guidelines with a dot. Add 1/4″ seam allowances to the sides of each blade, and add a bit more than 1/4″ to the top and bottom edges, which will later be appliqued.

Piece fans, using the full-fan template to check for accuracy as you work. Sew three fans together to form the back.

APPLIQUE THE FANS. Pin each fan into position on each vest section. Applique. Trim away the vest fabric behind each fan, unless the fans are pieced from very delicate fabrics.

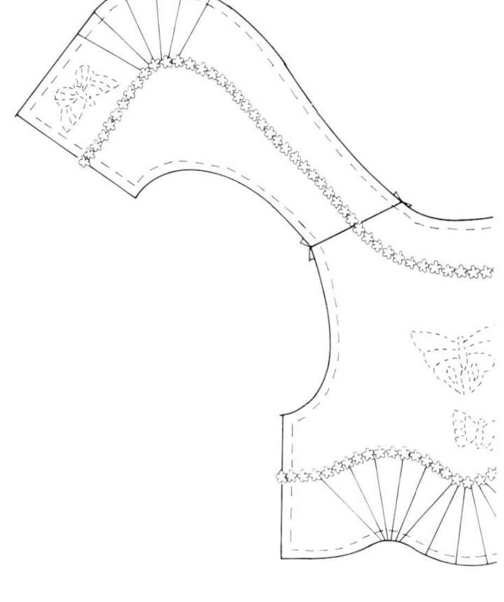

SEW THE VEST TOGETHER AT THE SHOULDERS. Trim and press open the vest shoulder seams. Apply the daisy lace by hand or with a zigzag stitch. The center of the daisies should be positioned directly over the edge of the appliqued fans.

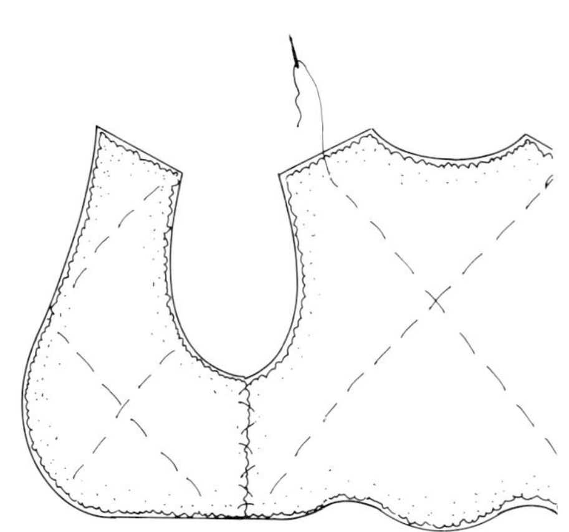

ASSEMBLE THE VEST. Lay the vest shell flat, wrong side up. Spread out the silk batting and cut to fit each vest section. Baste the batting to the wrong side of the vest.

Baste the one-sided lace along the neck and hem seam lines, right sides together. The lace should face *away* from the edge of the vest.

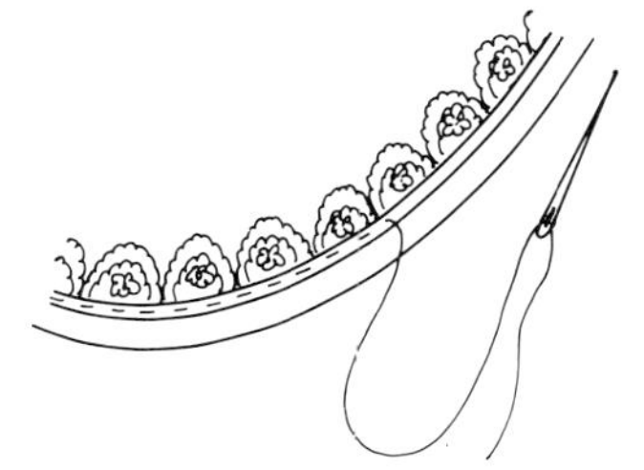

COMPLETE VEST ASSEMBLY. Follow the directions for sewing in Chapter 4 and turning the vest through an open side seam.

After the vest has been turned, remove the basting stitches that hold the batting in place. Re-baste through all three layers. Quilt, using matching silk or cotton thread.

12
POSTAGE STAMP DRESS

We call this dress a "postage stamp dress" because the bright squares that fill the yoke and parade around the hem remind us of postage stamps from places with exotic names and balmy climates. In truth, though, the Postage Stamp pattern is really just one variation of the Mosaic Square or Checkerboard pattern.

The Nine Patch, the Sixteen Patch, Irish Chain patterns and their colorful jewel box variations are all based on the idea of simple repeated squares. Squares can also be used to paint pictures and perform feats that are most often left to applique. For the Bicentennial, the Cabin Creek Quilters created a patchwork portrait of West Virginia's New River Gorge. In this quilt, thousands of tiny blue, green and brown squares come together to create a velveteen photograph of a soaring bridge spanning a dramatic, unspoiled waterway.

In our dress, with so many colors coming together in perfect parallels and crisp corners, the design looks complex, and perhaps a bit tedious to execute. It's not. Strip piecing makes fast work of putting this dress together. And because you're working in assembly line fashion, your strips of blocks are guaranteed to be uniform throughout.

Of course postal workers do need to take a few precautions to insure accuracy. With so many small elements coming together, ill-matched or uneven seams can quickly throw your work off. So make sure your sewing machine foot, or the throat plate, is accurately marked for ¼" seams. If not, get a new attachment, or mark a guideline on your throat plate. This simple precaution will assure that all your postage stamps will be first class.

Construction notes:

Strip piecing. Intermediate level in cottons, silk noil, wool flannel. Advanced level in silk shantung, challis, or napped fabrics.

While the patchwork design for this dress is quite simple, the difficulty level for the entire project is determined by the choice of fabrics. We used 100% silk shantung from Thai Silks in Los Altos, California.

Shantung is not a fabric for beginners because it is hard to cut accurately with scissors. We used a rotary cutter to cut out the dress pieces and the patchwork strips, plus a generous amount of silk pins and a new, fine needle in the sewing machine. If silk shantung is not for you, try pima cotton or silk noil. Though your dress will not drape as fluidly, the sewing will be dramatically easier.

As you plan this dress, decide whether or not you will be wearing it with a belt and with what kind of heels. Heel height and belt affect the length of the dress and the position of the border motif.

What You will Need

Silk Shantung (54″ wide)

- 2¼ yd. bright navy
- ¼ yd. each of berry, rust, gray-green, teal, dark turquoise, light blue and lavender

Sewing thread to match dress body

Dress zipper

Basic Dress Pattern

4 yards patternmaking cloth

Rotary cutter and mat

Silk pins

Size 70/10 sewing machine needles

Sewing machine foot (or throat plate) with 1/4″ markings

1 large sheet of graph paper

Artist's tracing paper

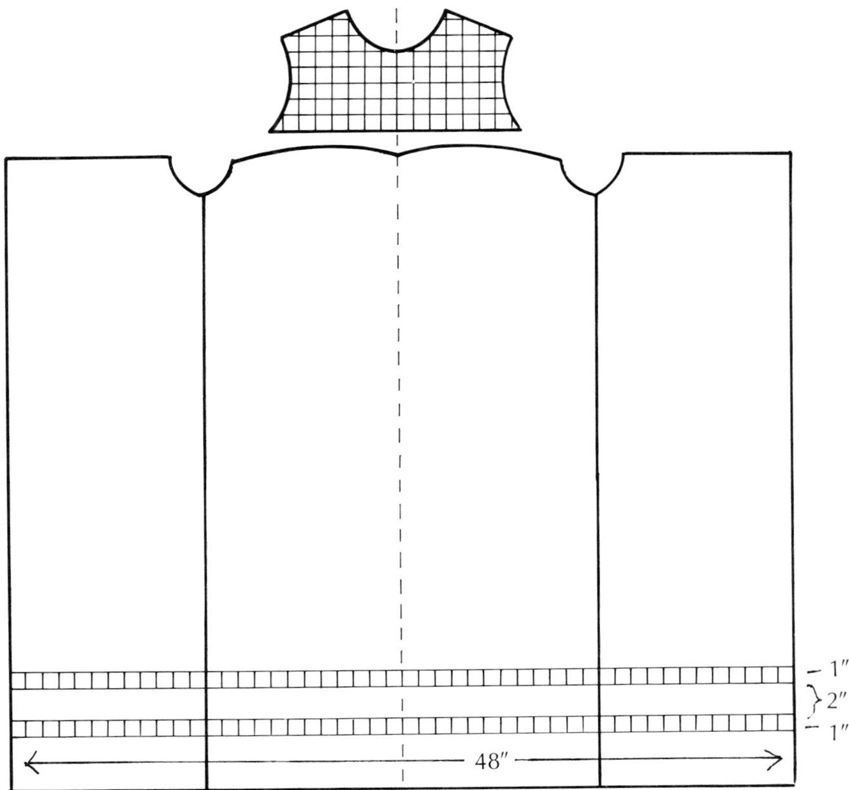

DIAGRAM: POSTAGE STAMP DRESS

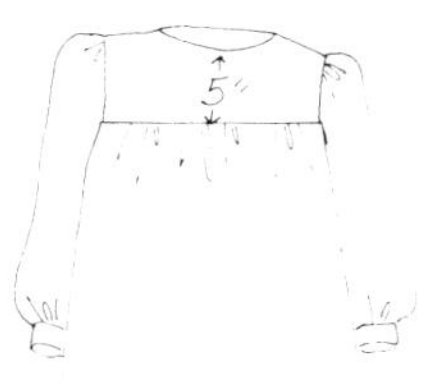

Directions

GET READY. Read instructions. Pre-wash all fabrics.

ADAPT THE BASIC DRESS PATTERN. The front dress yoke should measure 5" from neckline seam to bottom yoke seam. The dress body should have a 48" circumference at the hem. Draw a copy of the dress pattern (with changes) on patternmaking cloth, then set aside.

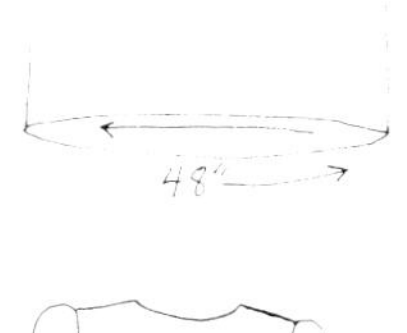

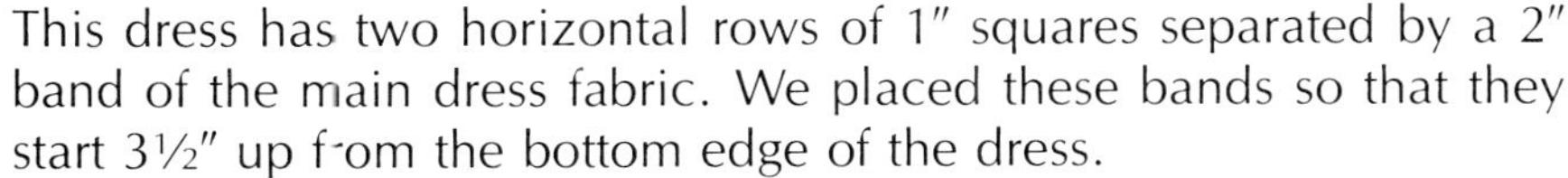

This dress has two horizontal rows of 1" squares separated by a 2" band of the main dress fabric. We placed these bands so that they start 3½" up from the bottom edge of the dress.

If you are not sure where these bands should be placed, make a muslin of the basic dress. Take a long strip of muslin and draw a facsimile of the three border bands. Pin this to the dress muslin and try it on. Play with the position of the bands until you are satisfied with the proportions.

Now draw the three bands on the dress front and back pattern pieces in the correct position, and your master pattern is complete.

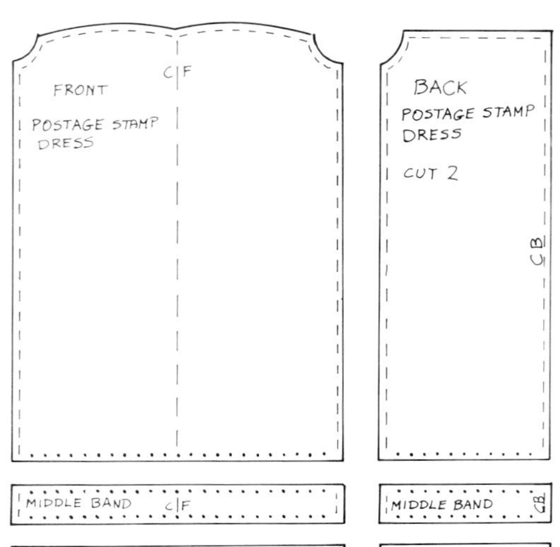

PREPARE THE WORKING PATTERN. Retrace the plain upper sections of the dress front and back as well as the 2″ wide bands and the bottom hem band. Add seam allowances to each pattern piece. Add the hem to the bottom band. These are the pattern pieces you will use to cut and mark your fabric.

CUT DRESS FABRIC. Cut out all dress pieces including sleeves, back yokes, and a set of front and back yokes that will form the lining. Mark, then set aside.

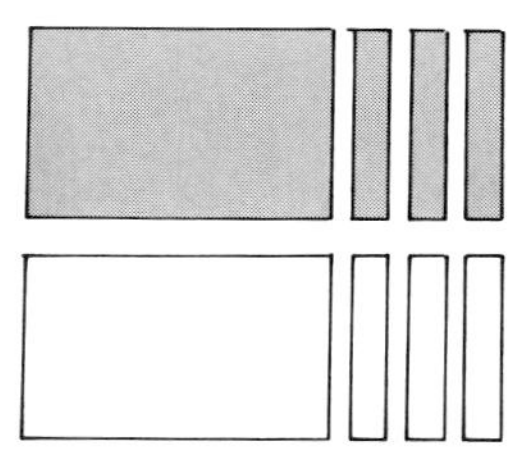

CUT STRIPS. Using a rotary cutter, cut 1½″ wide strips of all the fabrics. ¼ yard fabrics will give you strips about 9″ long. This is a good working length.

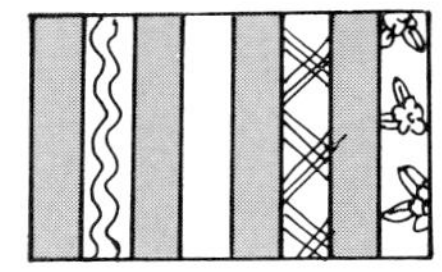

SEW THE STRIPS TOGETHER. Arrange the strips into several groups of eight to eleven, being sure that every other strip is navy. Sew them together, taking ¼″ seam allowances. Each sewn strip will end up 1″ wide. Make at least four or five different groupings.

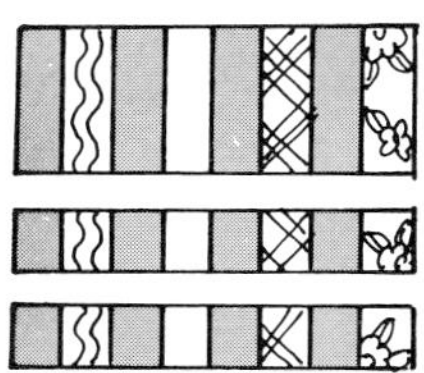

CUT THE PIECED STRIPS APART. Cut across the stitching, forming 1½″ wide strips of rectangles that alternate navy with other colors.

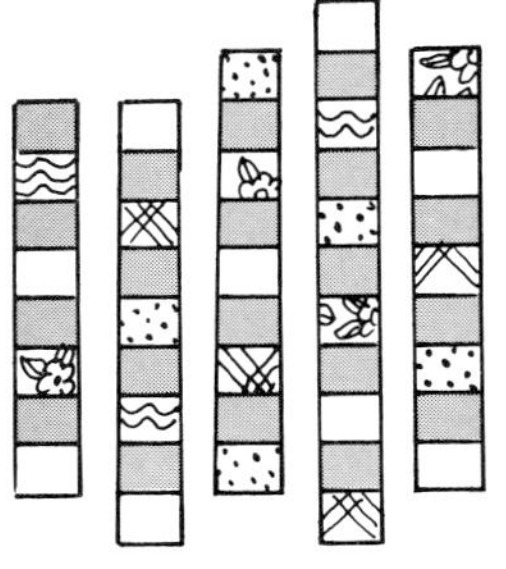

REARRANGE THE PIECED STRIPS. Aim for a random distribution of colors. For even more variety, turn some strips upside down. Be sure the navy rectangles are staggered to form a checkerboard effect.

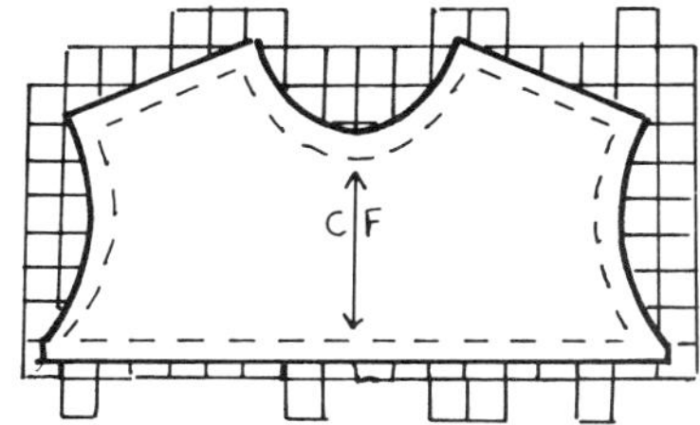

SEW YOUR CHECKERBOARD TOGETHER. Sew the pieced strips together, taking 1/4" seams. You will end up with 1" squares. Sew enough pieced strips to create a piece of patchwork fabric slightly larger than the front yoke pattern.

CUT OUT THE YOKE. Pin the yoke pattern in place on the postage stamp fabric. Mark and cut it out. Stay-stitch around the yoke.

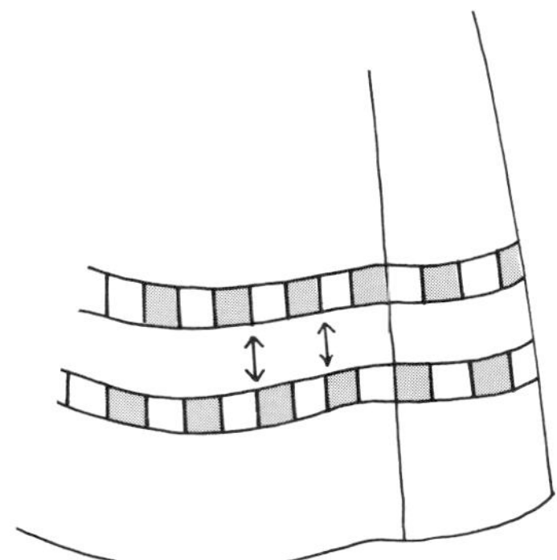

MAKE PATCHWORK BANDS. Sew the leftover pieced strips together end to end, making two patchwork bands for each dress section. Keep in mind that the alternating pattern of navy squares must continue uninterrupted even when the dress is sewn together at the side and back seams.

PIN DRESS BANDS TOGETHER. Check the illustration. Notice that the bands of patchwork squares line up with each other across the plain 2" band. While the colors alternate throughout, a navy square must face a colored square every time.

SEW ALL FOUR BANDS TOGETHER.

ASSEMBLE THE DRESS. Join the completed new border to the rest of the dress body, both in front and back. Assemble the dress, applying a self lining at the yoke. For a neat, finished look on the inside, at the hem area. cover the patchwork borders with China silk or any fine, thin lining fabric. Blindstitch in place.

13
SAWTOOTH BORDER SUIT

This suit was inspired by a last minute detail—the decorative borders on bed quilts. In many quilts, borders are often an afterthought, nothing more than a simple strip of bias binding to hem off the edges. Some quilts, however, use borders as a major part of their design. In medallion quilts, the borders can be as interesting and intricate as the central motif. Often the patchwork or applique medallion at the center is enclosed and framed by multiple layers of complex borders.

It may sound like the tail wagging the dog, but some patterns that have come to look tired and over used when seen on quilt tops can look surprisingly fresh and new when they're used as borders. To prove that, we've created a suit that's all border. With no interior patchwork to distract from our decorative frame, the sawtooth piecing here looks crisp and modern. It's a dramatic foil for a classic gray flannel suit. The jagged red border is tempered by the Chanel-style tailoring and the texture of the fine wool flannel. This suit would be equally striking in black wool with bright cobalt blue borders. High contrast colors tend to create the most dramatic effect.

When planning a border for a garment, take some time to decide how to position your motifs. In a pointed design like the one shown here, the points should be placed to face inward. This helps contain your design and establishes a sharp "fence" around the garment, directing the eye toward the center of your work. This inward-directed optical effect can also help make the figure inside look smaller and trimmer. Carefully planned, a patchwork border really does what any good frame should do: it flatters the beautiful work of art that's on the inside.

Construction notes:

Hand or machine piecing. Tailored suit construction. Intermediate level.

The precise piecing of a sawtooth border requires a fabric that pieces well and stands up to the handling that comes with turning sharp, perfectly square corners. That's why, for our Sawtooth Border Suit, we chose G Street Fabric's washable wool flannel (75% wool, 25% polyester) in grey and turkey red. This flannel cuts, pieces and presses beautifully.

What You Will Need

2¾ yds. (54″ wide) grey wool flannel for jacket and skirt

¾ yd. (54″ wide) red wool flannel

2 yds. jacket lining material in a shade to match border

Thread to match

Skirt zipper

Basic Jacket Pattern (with center back placed on fold or center back seam)

Basic Skirt Pattern (60″ width at bottom edge)

Graph paper

Artist's tracing paper

Template plastic

3½ yds. patternmaking cloth

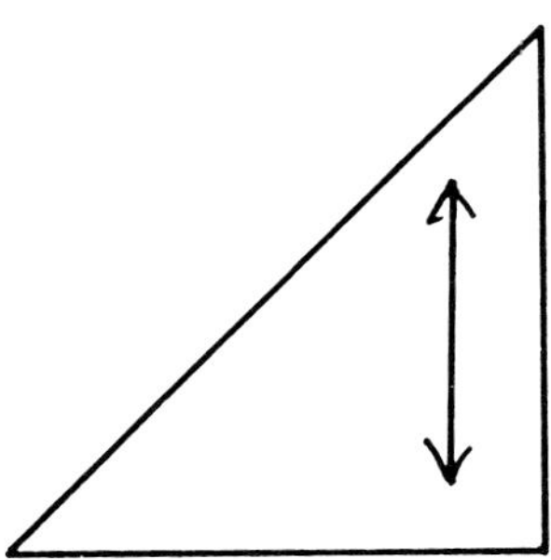

FULL SIZE PATTERN SAWTOOTH BORDER

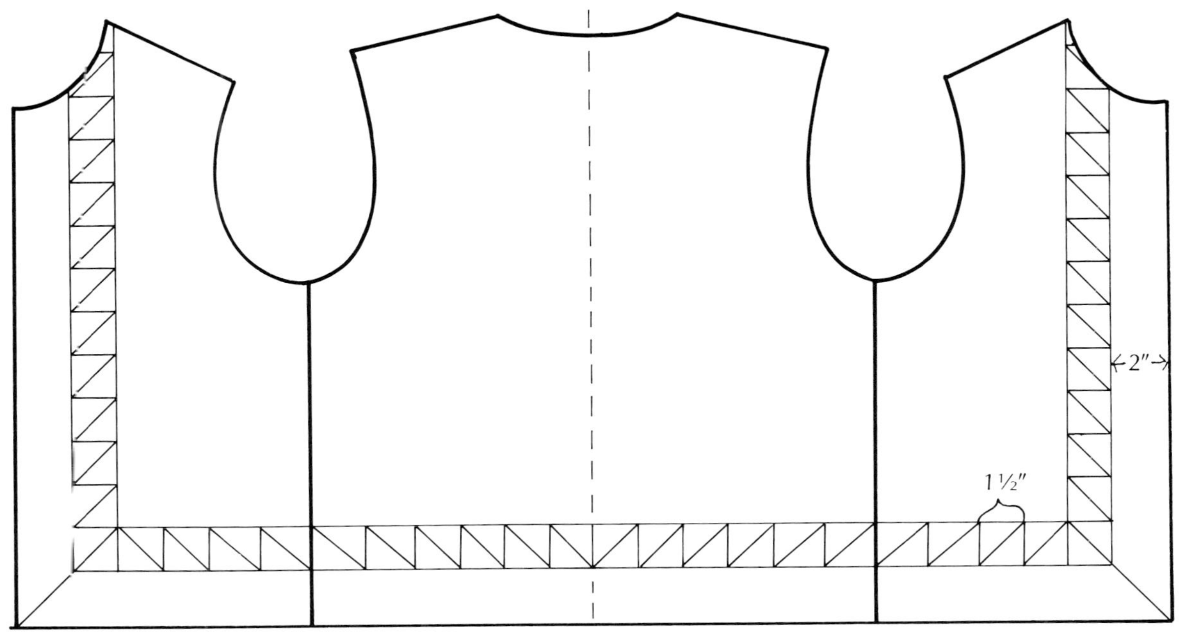

DIAGRAMS: SAWTOOTH BORDER SUIT

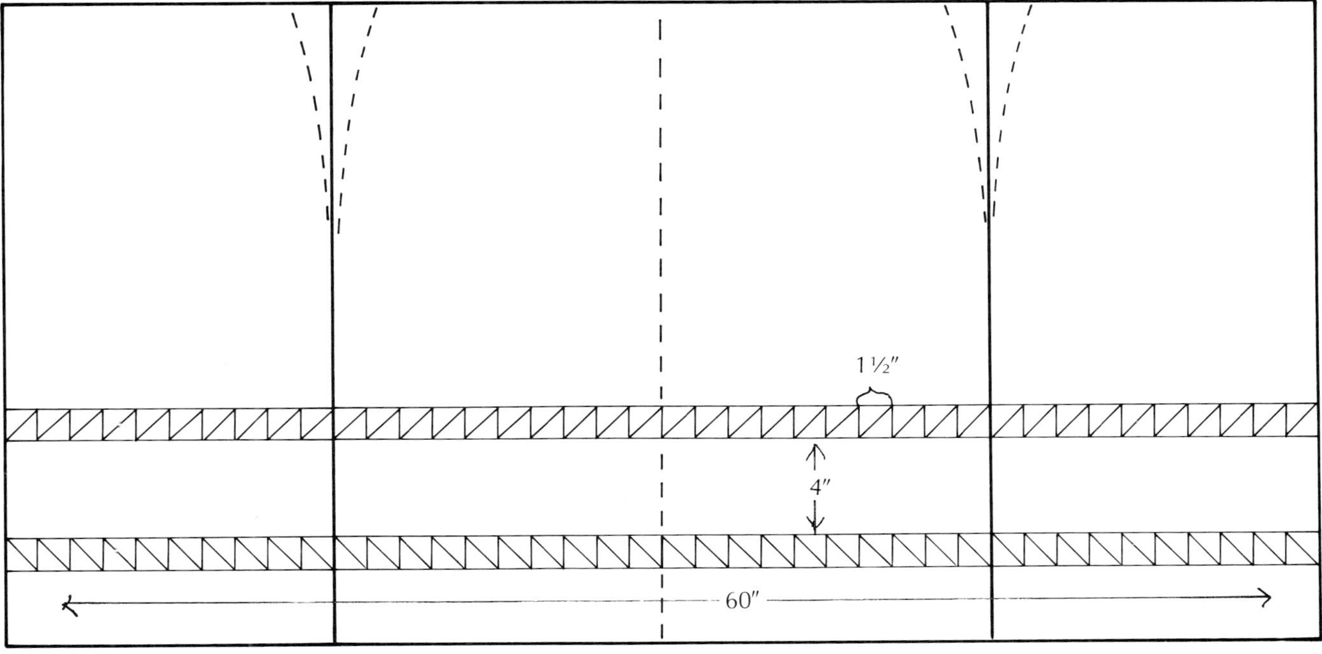

Directions

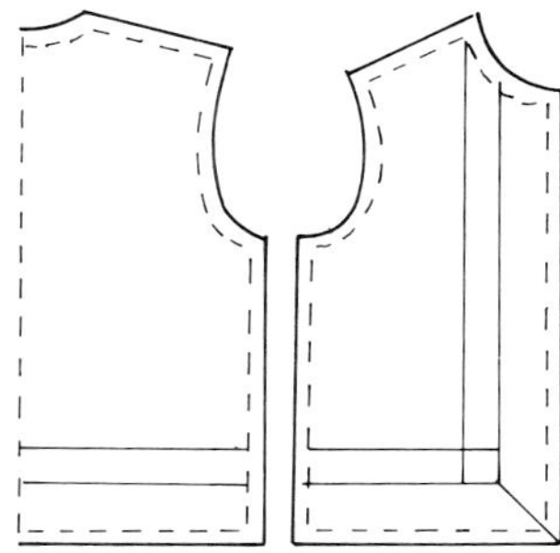

GET READY. Read instructions. Pre-treat all fabrics.

ADAPT THE JACKET PATTERN. Trace the jacket front and back onto patternmaking cloth. Draw the 2" wide red border on the jacket sections, including the seam line which miters the borders on the front. Draw a 1½" wide border beyond the plain red borders. This is the space for the Sawtooth blocks.

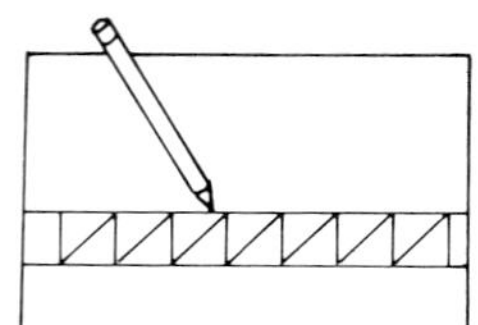

Graph a repeating section of the 1½" square Sawtooth blocks on a piece of graph paper. This will be used to make the plastic templates and to trace the patchwork design onto each pattern piece.

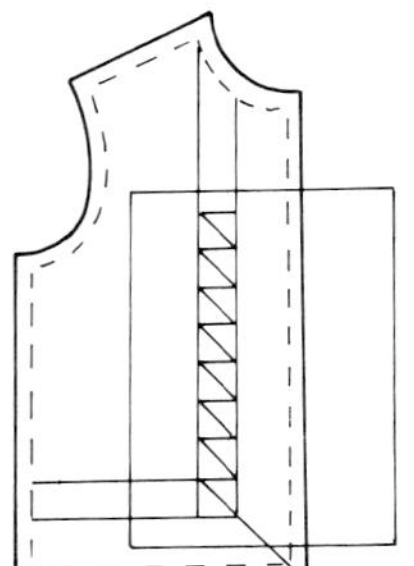

JACKET FRONT. As you work, refer to the diagram. Start with the square formed by the intersecting horizontal and vertical borders. Lay the jacket front pattern on top of the patchwork graph. Position the vertical border on top of the patchwork graph and trace the blocks. Be sure the triangles face in the correct position.

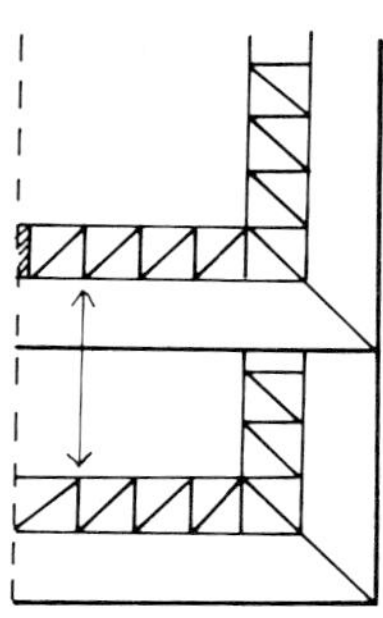

Place the horizontal border over the patchwork graph. If the blocks don't end evenly at the side seam, you will need to adjust it.

If the block nearest to the side seam falls just a little bit short, widen the last block into a rectangle.

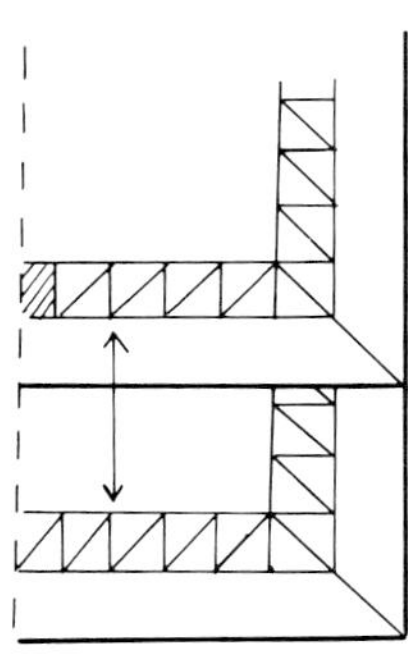

If there is a large space between the side seam and the nearest block, go back to the second-last block. Divide the space in half between that block and the side seam. You will be making two slightly narrower blocks.

The slightly rectangular shape of these adjusted blocks will not be noticeable when the jacket is finally put together. It is more important that the blocks all join smoothly and correctly at the side and back seams. Remember that you must make a separate set of templates for these adjusted blocks.

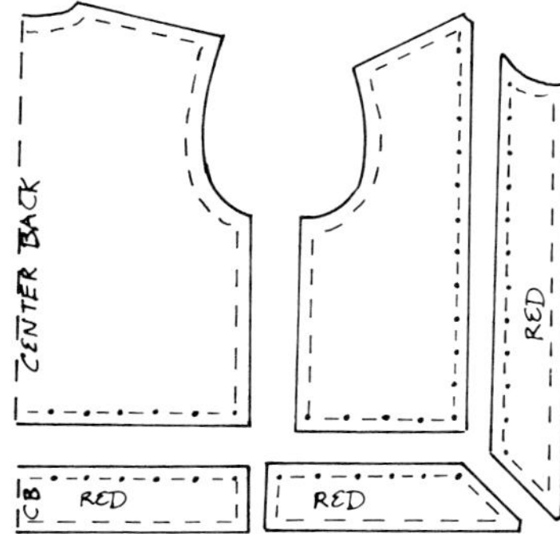

JACKET BACK. Start at the center back and graph the blocks toward the side seam. Adjust the blocks in the same way as described for the jacket front. You have now completed the Jacket Master Pattern.

MARK THE WORKING PATTERN. Retrace each separate part of the jacket front and back patterns, leaving space between them. Add seam allowances, then mark dots to match up with Sawtooth blocks. These are the pattern pieces you will use to cut and mark your fabric.

ADAPT THE SKIRT PATTERN. Your basic skirt pattern should measure 60″ (finished width) at the hem. Trace the front and back skirt sections on patternmaking cloth. Make a muslin version of the skirt.

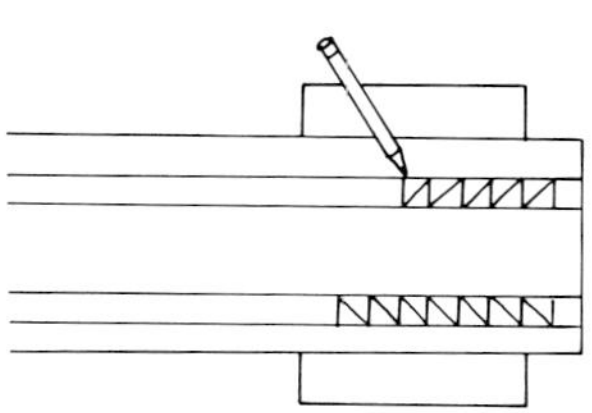

DETERMINE THE BORDER PLACEMENT. Take a strip of leftover muslin and draw a facsimile of the wide red band with the Sawtooth borders on either side. Pin this strip to your muslin skirt. Try it on and reposition the bands until you like the look. We placed our bands to start 3½″ from the hem edge.

When you have determined the correct placement for the bands, draw them on the skirt pattern. You have now completed the Master Pattern for the skirt.

MAKE THE WORKING PATTERN. Retrace everything onto patternmaking cloth except the Sawtooth borders, leaving some space between each piece. Add seam allowances, dots to match Sawtooth blocks, and hems deep enough to turn up, then blindstitch to the lowest Sawtooth border. These are the pattern pieces you will use to cut out and mark your fabric.

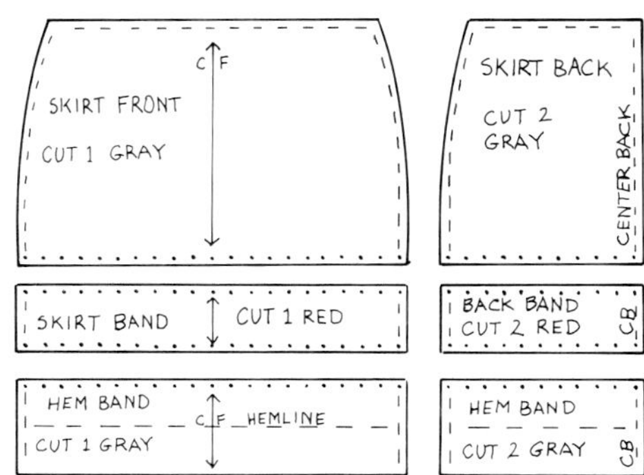

CUT OUT ALL JACKET AND SKIRT PIECES. First, lay out and cut all the garment sections. Then make a plastic template of the triangle for the Sawtooth borders. You should be able to cut most of the triangles from the odd-shaped scraps left from the garment sections, but watch the grain lines carefully.

PIECE THE SAWTOOTH BORDERS. Sew together pairs of red and gray triangles to form blocks.

Put the blocks together, following your pattern as to the number of blocks in each garment section. Don't forget that any blocks that were adjusted for the side seams must be cut, marked and sewn separately.

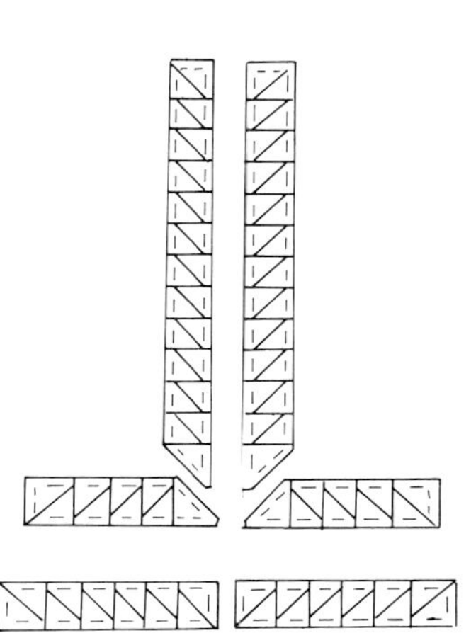

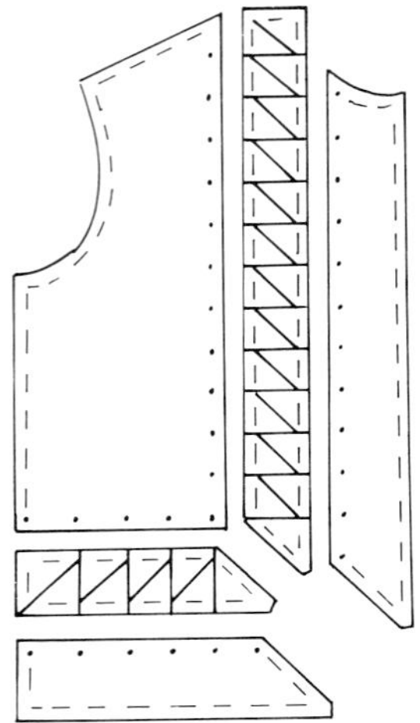

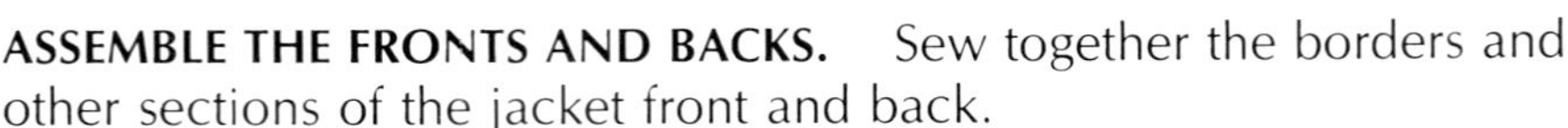

ASSEMBLE THE FRONTS AND BACKS. Sew together the borders and other sections of the jacket front and back.

Note: To turn the corner on a Sawtooth border, start at the corner and work your way out in either direction. You may find it easier to put the corner sawtooth block together at the time when the red outer borders are mitered.

As you assemble the jacket, don't worry if a patchwork block gets partly cut off at the neckline. The curve of the neckline seam will make this look all right.

ASSEMBLE THE JACKET. Finish sewing the jacket together. Insert lining. Topstitch around the edges of the jacket.

ASSEMBLE THE SKIRT. Sew the Sawtooth borders to each edge of the wide red band, lining up the Sawtooth borders so that all block seams are directly across from each other. Sew the bottom hem band to the Sawtooth borders.

Sew the remaining skirt sections together. Pin in the zipper and gather or pleat the skirt onto the waistband, lining the skirt if you wish.

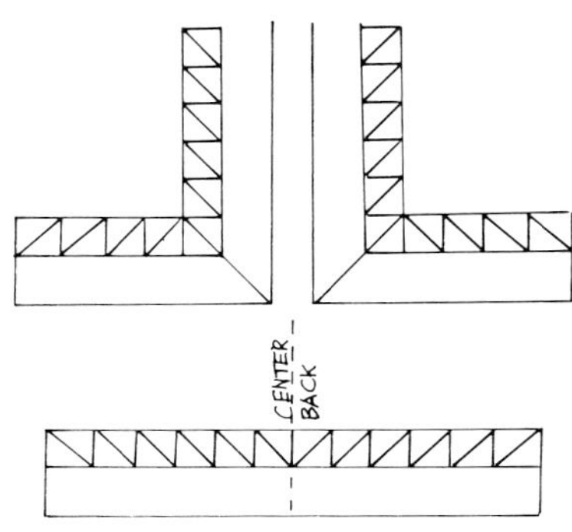

MIRROR IMAGES. Take a close look at the photographs of this suit. The jacket fronts are mirror images of each other, as are both halves of the jacket back. These mirror images are created by flipping the pattern over. The Sawtooth borders on each side of the red skirt band also mirror each other. Be sure the outer points of your triangles all point in the same direction as they go around the skirt.

COSMOPOLITAN

14
TWO PATCHWORK PANEL SKIRTS

In the Sawtooth Border Suit, we showed how borders can be used to finish and flatter a tailored garment. In that suit, the skirt has a wide Sawtooth border that runs parallel to the hemline. This is the classic way to use border panels in skirts and dresses.

In the next two garments, we turn that border panel 90° to create a vertical border. Now, with this panel in a front and center position, your patchwork is displayed to fullest advantage. Also, this vertical line, when gathered into a waistband, has a slimming effect, a flattering detail that makes even the fullest skirt look neater and trimmer.

The first panel skirt features a Pinwheel pattern. One of the easiest patchwork designs to draft and sew, this is a very good choice for those who have never made patchwork clothing.

The next skirt is the Dutchman's Puzzle Skirt, another pattern that uses triangles. In this pattern, the figures are smaller and arranged in a more complex manner. If the colors and prints are carefully planned, it can take on an intriguing oriental sophistication.

For both skirts, we recommend that you buy extra yardage of at least one of your fabrics to make a matching blouse.

PINWHEEL SKIRT

Construction Notes:

Hand or machine piecing. Beginner level in cotton, silk noil, or wool; advanced level in napped fabrics.

Because we had used this pattern a lot, most often in cottons or wool flannels, we decided to make it up in something new for this book.

We used Facile® in a deep violet-blue. The pinwheels, also cut from Facile®, are in five shades of pinks, peaches and reds. The blocks are arranged randomly. A strip of Facile® folded into the seams of the skirt panel forms self piping.

Featherweight corduroy, cotton velveteen or any other soft, napped fabric could be used to create a similar look and feel. These fabrics call for very careful cutting and piecing because the nap must run in the correct direction on every triangle within each block. Follow our system of notching the triangles and your blocks will come out perfectly.

If this is your first try at patchwork, we recommend that you choose a plain, closely-woven fabric such as cotton broadcloth, cotton chambray, silk noil or lightweight wool flannel. These fabrics will free you from the worry of nap directions. Lightweight wovens do still require a bit of care. You must take care when handling the triangles so that the long bias edges are not stretched.

What You Will Need

Facile® (45″ wide)

- 1¾ yds. Dark Blue including allowances for nap
- ⅛ yd. each of 4-6 shades of pink and red

Thread to match

Skirt zipper

Basic Skirt Pattern, any width at bottom, 29 ¾″ in length

1 sheet graph paper

Template plastic

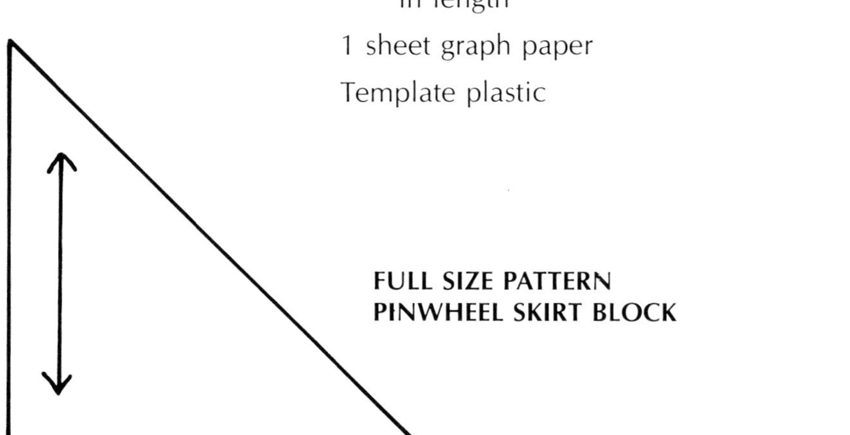

FULL SIZE PATTERN
PINWHEEL SKIRT BLOCK

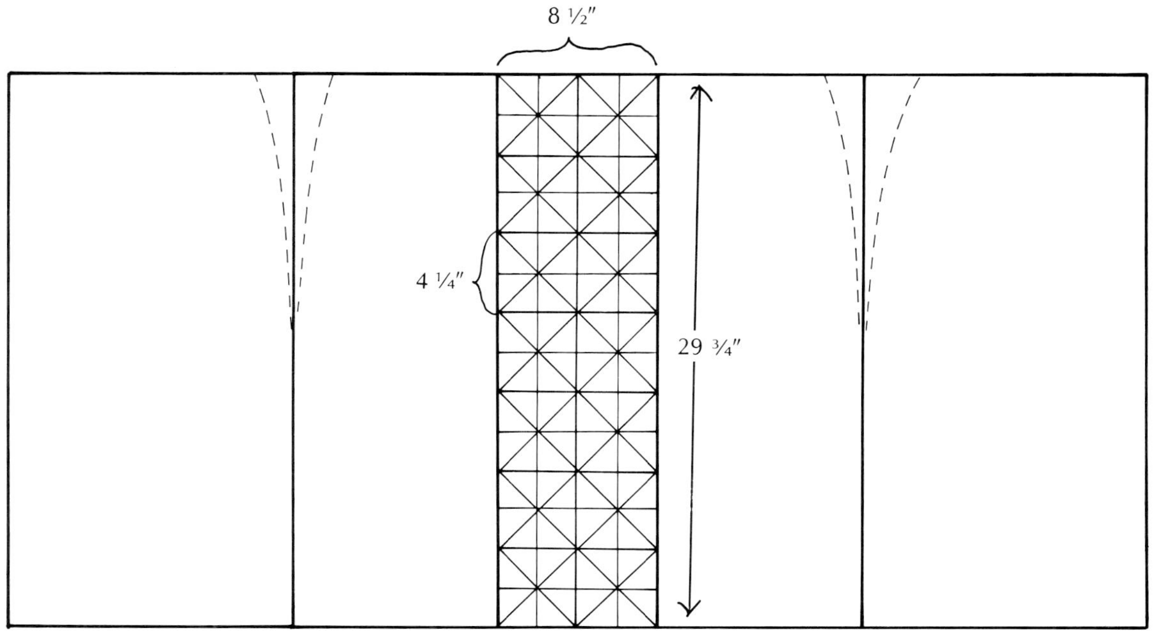

DIAGRAM: PINWHEEL SKIRT

Directions

GET READY. Read through all instructions. Pre-treat all fabrics.

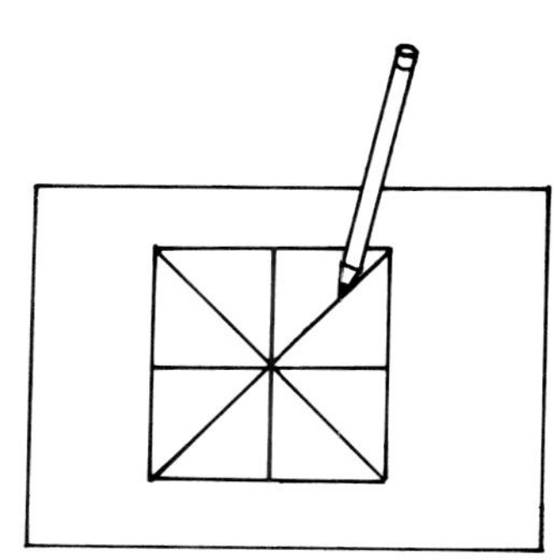

ADAPT THE PATTERNS. Draw the Pinwheel block on a sheet of graph paper. The finished block is 4¼″ square.

Trace the Bas c Skirt pattern onto patternmaking cloth. Line up the Pinwheel block with the top along the waistline seam and one side along the skirt's center front. Trace this onto the skirt.

Trace a panel of 14 blocks down the skirt, which means 7 side-by-side pairs of blocks. The skirt panel should measure 8½ x 29¾″. This completes the master pattern.

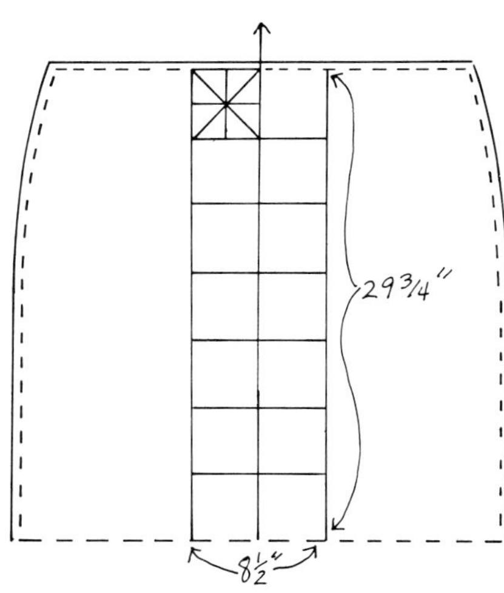

MAKE THE WORKING PATTERNS. Re-trace one of the side front sections onto patternmaking cloth. Add seam allowance, hem and dots to mark position of patchwork block seams. Use this pattern, plus the skirt back and waistband from the Master Pattern to cut out the skirt.

CUT OUT THE SKIRT. If you are working with Facile® or any other napped fabric, be sure to follow the nap, laying all your sections in the same direction. Mark each section, then set aside.

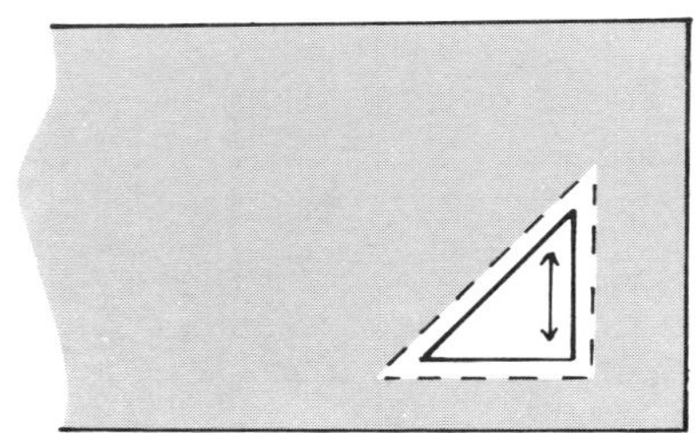

MAKE THE PINWHEEL BLOCKS.

For fabrics without nap. Make a template of the triangle from template plastic. Mark and cut out the pinwheel triangles, adding a ¼″ seam allowance. Be sure both short sides of the triangle are on the straight grain.

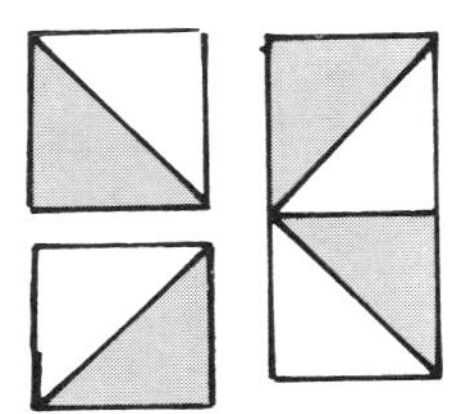

Following the piecing diagram here, sew the pinwheel blocks together, pressing the seams toward the darker fabric. Join all blocks to form the entire skirt panel.

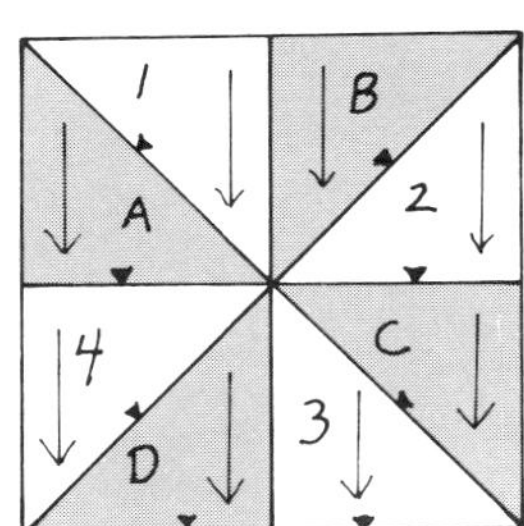

For fabrics with nap. When cutting and assembling napped patchwork, it's easy to get confused and turn a piece the wrong way. So work slowly and carefully. We recommend cutting and sewing just one block at a time.

To start, trace an *entire* pinwheel block onto template plastic. Letter the background triangles (in this case, the darker color), and number the foreground triangles (the lighter tone). This system will not only help you position your nap correctly, it assures that your templates are never flipped. Mark an arrow for the nap direction, then mark a notch to indicate which side is the bottom edge. Now cut apart the plastic template into individual triangles.

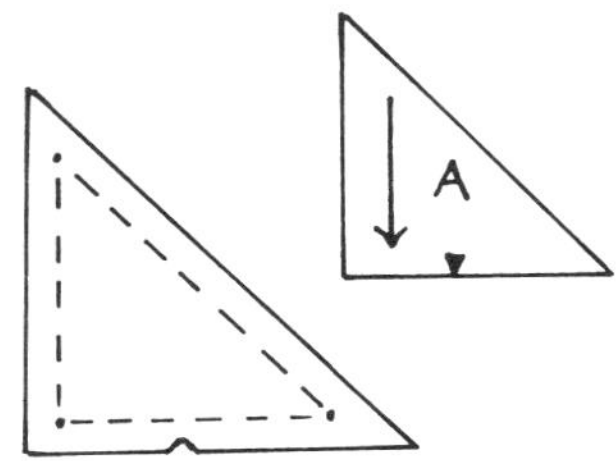

Using these specifically marked templates, mark and cut out the pieces for one block, adding ¼″ seam allowances. At the bottom edge of each triangle, make a notch in the seam allowance.

ASSEMBLE THE BLOCKS. Sew each block together, either by machine or by hand. Pad your ironing board with a towel and use a scrap of fabric as a pressing cloth. Press all seam allowances to one side, unless you are working with heavier fabrics such as velveteen or wool. In that case, press the seam allowance open. To get Facile® blocks to lie flat in the center, clip into the final seam allowance ½″ from the center, then press open. (Facile® does not ravel.)

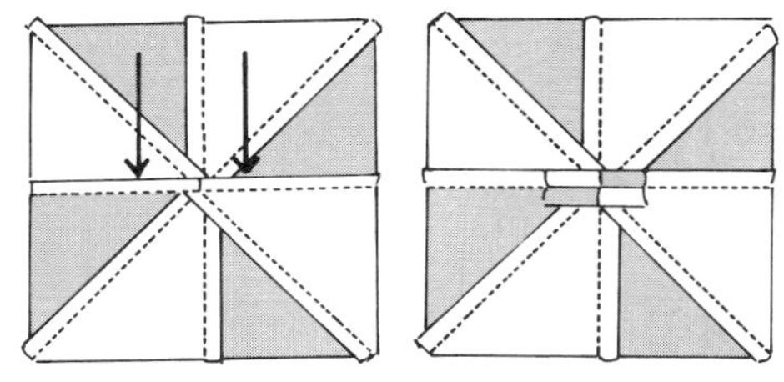

When all 14 blocks are assembled, sew them together to form the skirt panel.

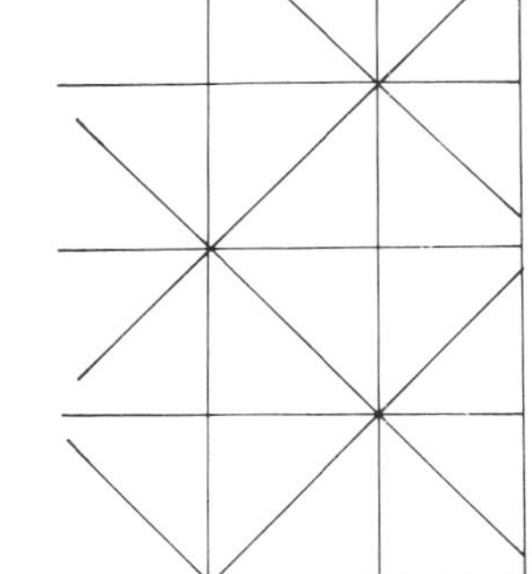

MAKE THE PANEL "PIPING". Cut two strips of fabric measuring 1″ x 31″. For fabrics such as cotton broadcloth, you may wish to sew a piece of soft cord into each strip. For Facile®, or any heavier fabric, simply fold the strip in half lengthwise. Baste these folded strips of "piping" along the side seams on either side of the patchwork panel.

HEM FRONT PANEL AND ASSEMBLE SKIRT. Because of the patchwork panel, this skirt has a faced hem at the center front. That means that there will be a seam on the hemline at the center panel. The side front sections have their own hem allowance. This part of the front hem is simply folded under.

To hem-face the front panel, cut a facing strip 3 inches by 9 inches. Sew this strip to the bottom edge of the patchwork panel. This becomes the hem for that section of the skirt. The seam line marks the hem line.

Do not hem the Facile® skirt. It will look too lumpy at the bottom of the patchwork panel. Just carefully cut off the skirt at the correct length, or sew two rows of topstitching along the hemline, then trim the Facile® right below the stitching.

Now you're ready to assemble the skirt sections. Sew each side front section to the center panel. Sew the skirt backs to the assembled skirt front. Put in the back zipper.

Gather or pleat the skirt. To gather Facile®, run a zigzag stitch over a piece of string or perle cotton, and pull string.

ATTACH WAISTBAND, FINISH HEM. For regular woven fabrics, attach the waistband as you would on any gathered skirt. Top stitch the waistband in place. Finally, turn up the hem and slip stitch in place.

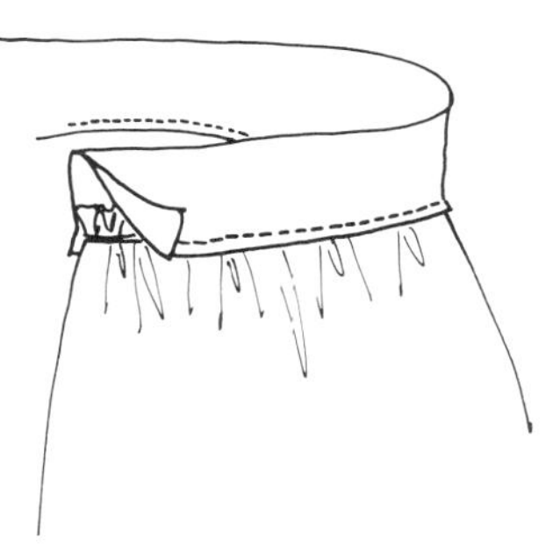

To attach a Facile® waistband with the least amount of bulk, eliminate the waistband seam allowances. Press fusible interfacing onto the wrong side of the outer half of the waistband. Topstitch the waistband in place.

DUTCHMAN'S PUZZLE SKIRT

Construction notes:

Machine or hand piecing. Beginner level.

We made this skirt from Stylecrest's "Antonio" and "Pimalene", 100% pima cottons that are available in prints and coordinating solids. This smooth, soft, closely woven fabric is perfect for piecing. Soft and drapable, these "dress" cottons can be used much the way you might use silk broadcloth or lightweight wool challis. The darker prints have a seasonless quality, which means that with dark tights and a sweater, a summer skirt can become a winter outfit.

What You Will Need

Stylecrest "Antonio" pima cotton print (36" wide)
1¾ yds. peach/black print

Stylecrest "Pimalene" pima cotton solid (36" wide)

½ yd. black

¼ yd. peach

Thread to match

Skirt zipper

Basic Skirt Pattern, any width, 30" in length

2½ yds. patternmaking cloth

Template plastic

FULL SIZE PATTERN
DUTCHMAN'S PUZZLE BLOCK

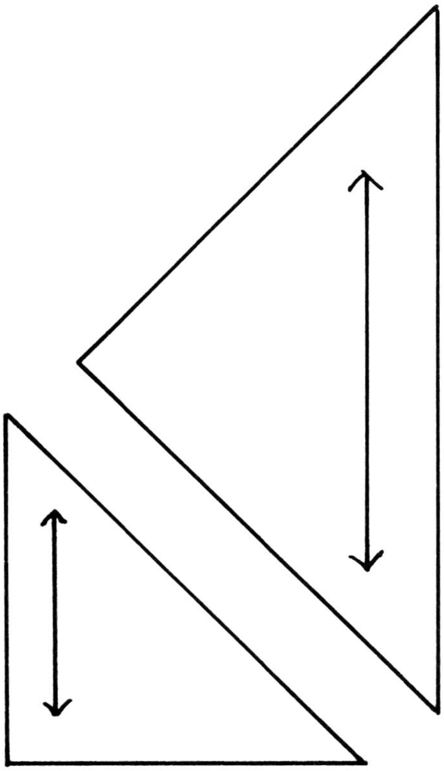

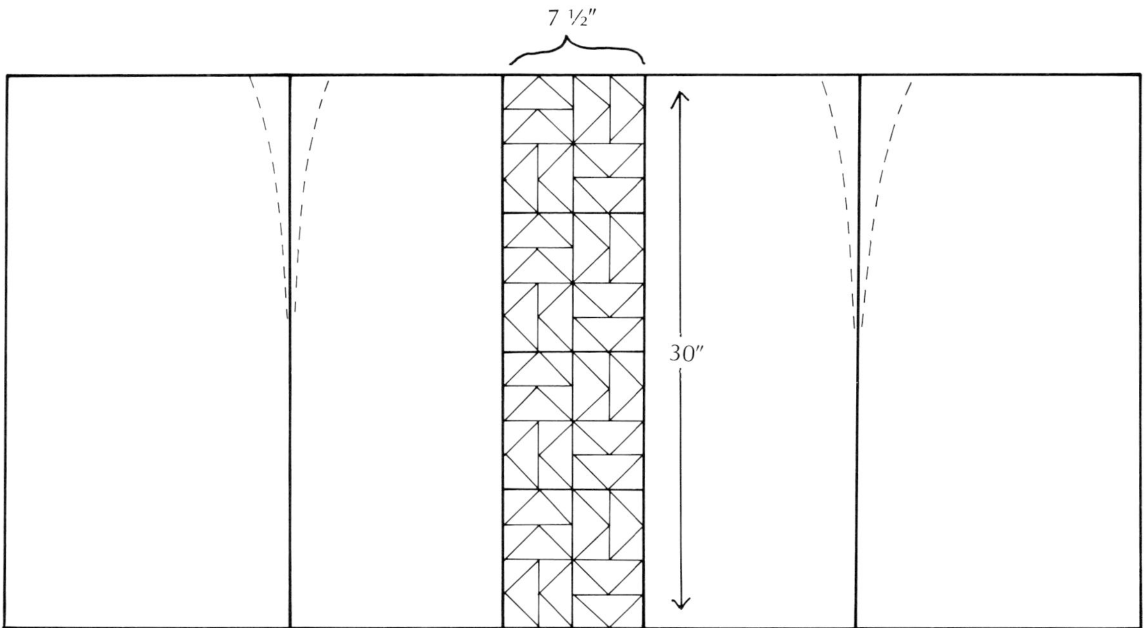

DIAGRAM: DUTCHMAN'S PUZZLE SKIRT

Directions

GET READY. Read through the complete instructions. Pre-wash all fabrics.

PREPARE THE MASTER PATTERN. Draw the Dutchman's Puzzle block, full size, onto graph paper.

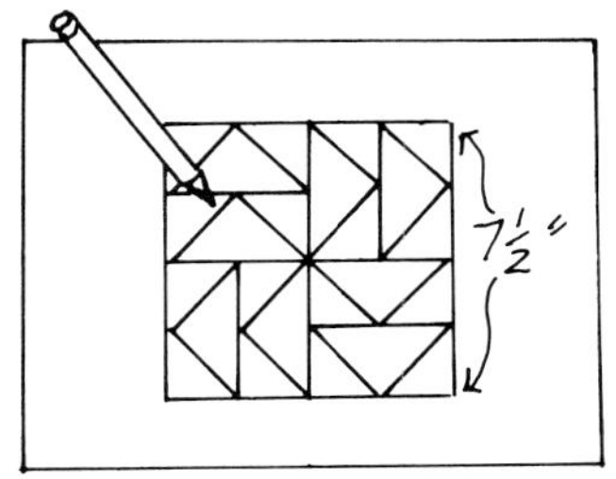

Trace the skirt onto patternmaking cloth. Lay the skirt front pattern over the graphed block. Line the top of the block up along the waistline seam, centering the block over the center front. Trace this block onto the skirt pattern.

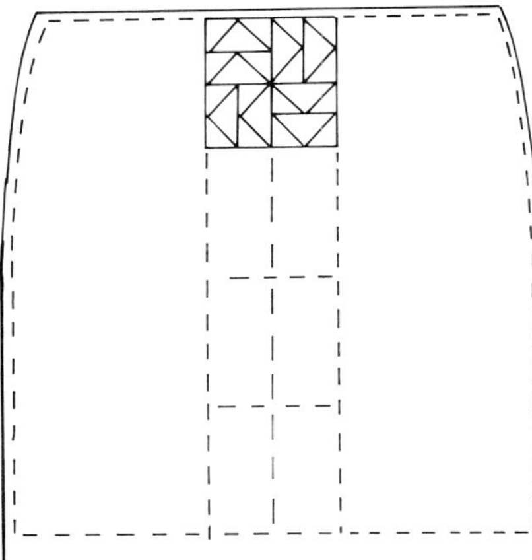

Trace three more blocks, each directly below the other. You now have a four-block panel down the center front of the skirt. This panel should measure 7½" x 30". Trace the waistband pattern. You have now completed the master pattern.

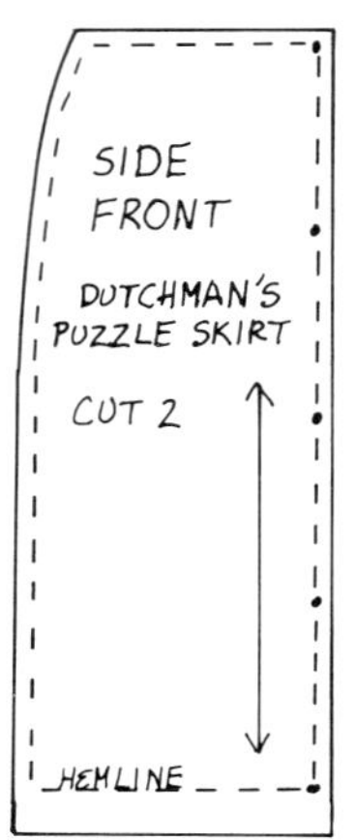

MAKE A WORKING PATTERN. Lay another piece of patternmaking cloth on top of the master pattern skirt front. Trace one of the side front sections. Use dots or notches to mark where the side seam lines up with each block intersection. Add the seam allowance and hem. This is the pattern you will use to cut out the skirt fronts. Use the master pattern skirt back to cut out each back section.

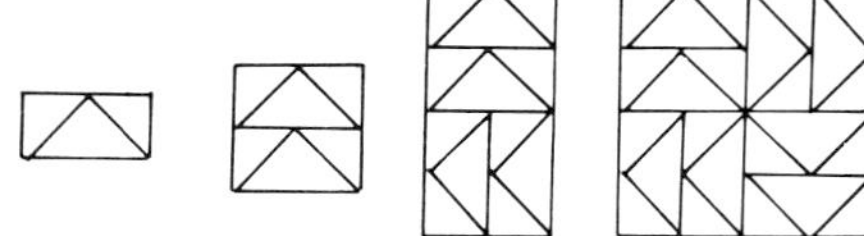

MAKE THE PATCHWORK BLOCKS. Make plastic templates of the triangles that create the Dutchman's Puzzle pattern.

Mark and cut out all fabric patches, adding a ¼″ seam allowance.

Following the four-step piecing diagram shown here, assemble the triangles into individual blocks. Press as you go, checking against the markings on the master pattern to make sure your blocks are perfectly square. They should measure 7½″ along each seam. When all four blocks are assembled, sew them together into one long panel.

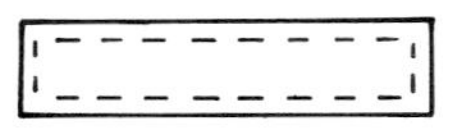

ATTACH HEM TO PANEL. Cut a piece of main skirt fabric 2½ x 8″. Sew this along the bottom edge of the bottom block, taking a ¼″ seam. This will be turned up as part of the hem when the skirt is assembled.

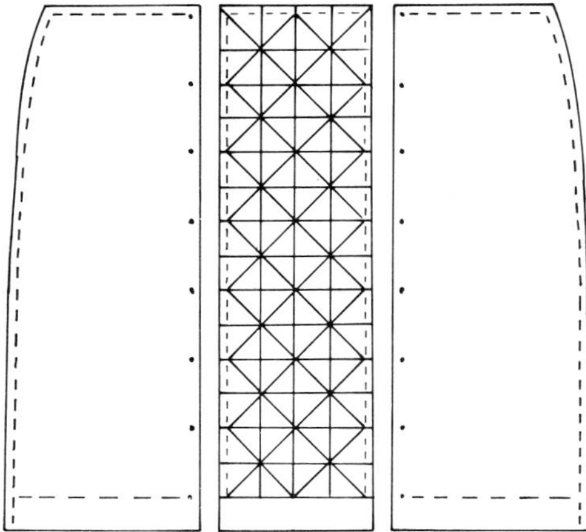

ASSEMBLE THE SKIRT. Sew the side fronts to the center panel. Sew skirt front to back sections. Put in zipper. Gather or pleat skirt onto waistband. Hem skirt.

WHEAT
Chex

15
FLYING GEESE SUIT

As we were working on this suit, methodically piecing together all the long rows of Flying Geese blocks, we started wondering how Cabin Creek Quilts makes its own Flying Geese quilts. At the Co-op's shop, Judy Parcell and Bonnie Masters told us that for a pattern like this, they need a quilter who's a real perfectionist. More likely than not, that means a quilter of the West Virginia persuasion.

Before a quilter can become a member of the Co-op, what does Cabin Creek look for in the quilter's work? Neatness of course. Neat stitches. Careful pressing. White fabric that stays pristine despite hundreds of hours of handling. Beyond these basic requirements, they look for the details that show an insistence on perfection. They want quilters who take pride in little things like mitered corners, and neatly turned and blindstitched bindings. As to quilting, Cabin Creek insists that stitching lines be carefully marked, then accurately followed. And stitches must not only be small, they must be uniform in size. In piecing, they look for neatness, consistency and the ability to create sharp, even points and corners. Some piecing patterns show off these skills more than others. The Flying Geese pattern is one of them.

Sewing small triangles in a row is a simple enough task. Putting *rows* of rows together is a bit more tricky. Any little inaccuracy becomes apparent. Flying Geese blocks must be cut, marked and pieced very precisely. Then the rows must be carefully assembled to insure that they all line up exactly even with each other horizontally. When Flying Geese blocks run up a jacket front, the jacket opening emphasizes this effect. The slightest error can be quite glaring.

When choosing fabrics for this suit, go for the easy piecers: fine pima cotton, plain weave silk noil or closely woven wool flannel. Avoid anything that's slippery, stretchy or unforgiving when you may need to rip and restitch.

If your skills and patience are up to it, don't be scared off by our warnings. The finished suit manages to be both businesslike and very dramatic. It's well worth the effort.

Construction notes:

Hand or machine piecing. Tailored suit construction. Advanced Level.

100% wool is a good choice for this design. Tiny triangles require lots of handling to come together in matching long, straight rows. Wool flannel can take it. Excess fabric can be eased into a seam without being noticeable. With a bit of steaming, a slightly stretched-out bias edge will settle back into place.

Good wool can also undergo ripping and resewing without becoming ragged. For our Flying Geese Suit, we chose a fine black Anglo® wool flannel and a slightly lighter weight black-on-white wool plaid. Both fabrics are available through G Street Fabrics.

For a warm-weather suit, try a fine pima cotton or a plain-weave silk noil in pale shades.

What You Will Need

2 yds. muslin

Anglo® wool flannel in black (60″ wide)

- 1½ yds. for jacket
- Additional yardage for coordinating skirt (see your pattern directions)

¼ yd. black and white plaid wool (54″ wide)

Black China silk

- 2 yds. for jacket lining
- See pattern for skirt lining yardage

Black thread

Skirt zipper

Basic Jacket Pattern

Skirt pattern of your choice

2 yds. patternmaking cloth

Graph paper

Template plastic

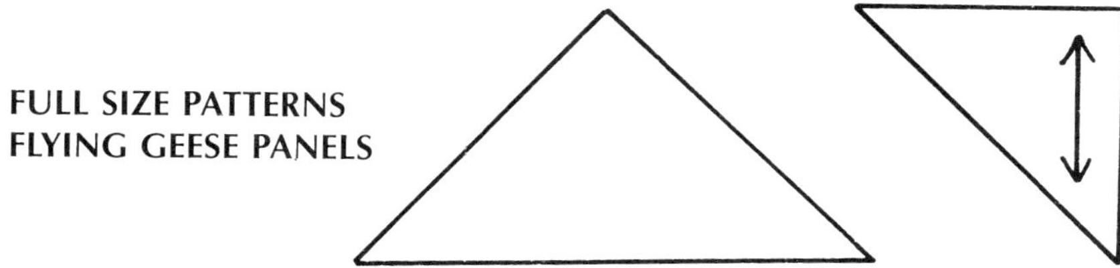

FULL SIZE PATTERNS
FLYING GEESE PANELS

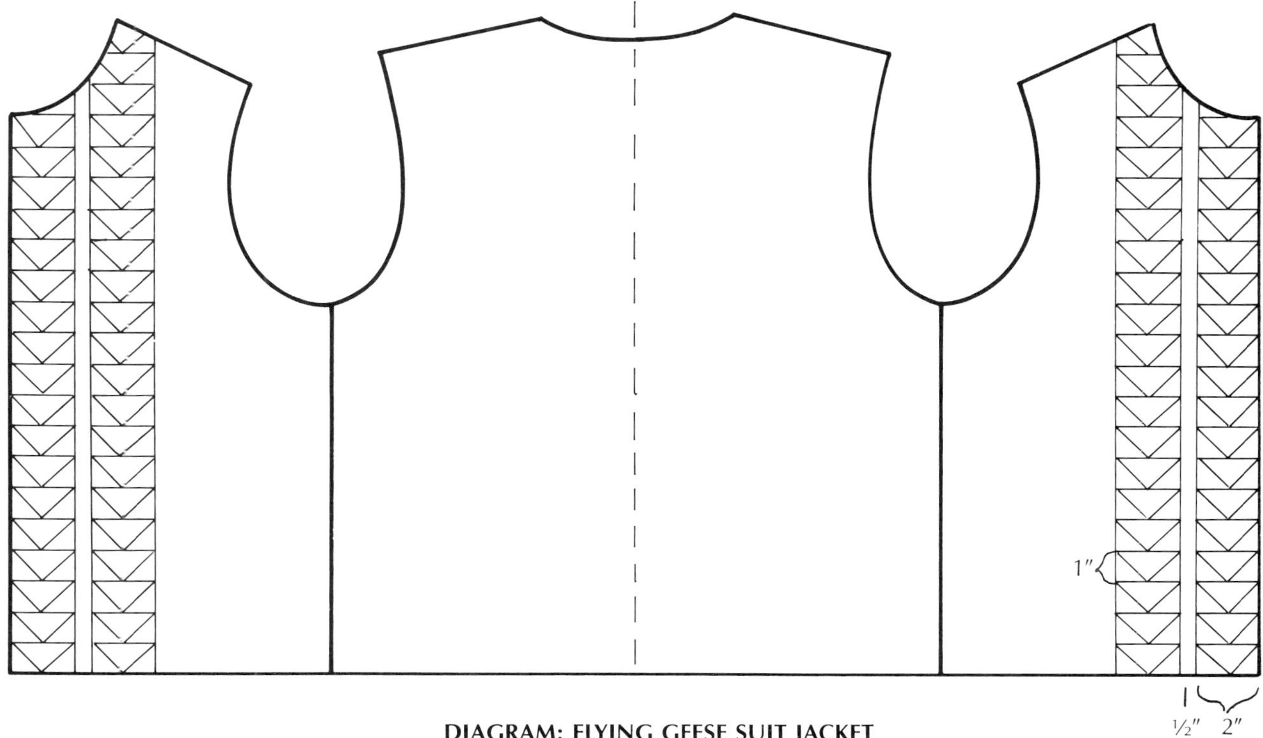

DIAGRAM: FLYING GEESE SUIT JACKET

Directions

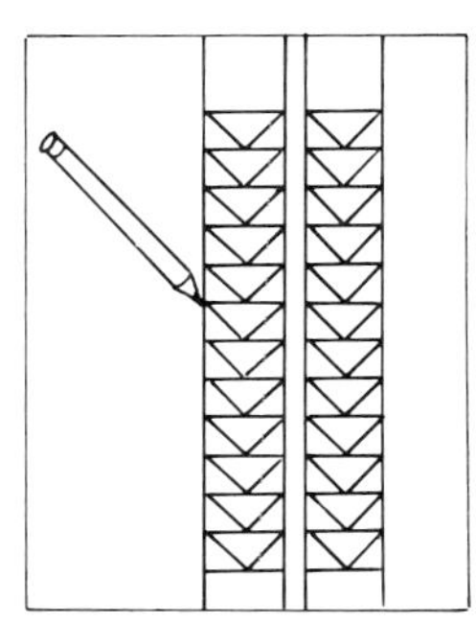

GET READY. Pre-treat all fabrics. Read through instructions.

PREPARE THE JACKET PATTERN. Make a muslin version of the jacket. Determine the jacket's finished length. Trace the jacket pattern, including the front and neck facing, onto patternmaking cloth.

Draw a section of the Flying Geese panels onto graph paper. Each block measures 1″ x 2″. The two rows are separated by a ½″ wide strip.

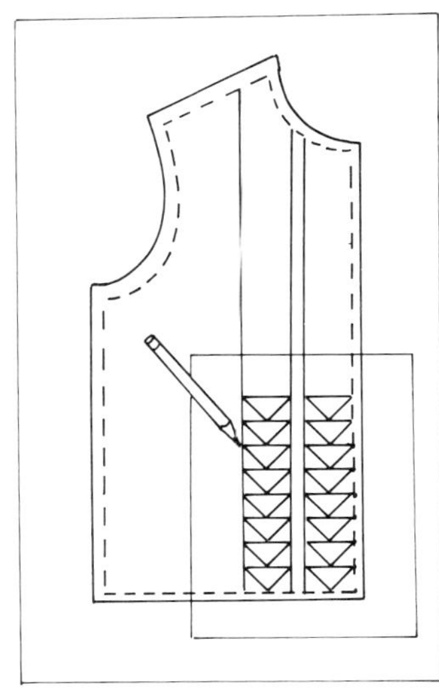

Align the edge of the Flying Geese panel with the jacket pattern's front seam line. The bottom block should line up with the jacket hem. Trace the Flying Geese panel onto the pattern. Your master pattern is now completed.

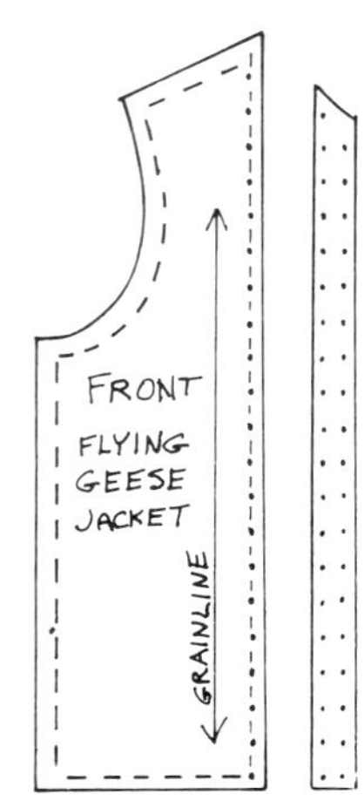

MAKE THE WORKING PATTERN. Retrace the unadorned side section of the jacket front and the ½″ wide strip. Add seam allowances and dots to show where these pieces meet the seams of each Flying Geese block.

CUT OUT THE JACKET, SKIRT AND LININGS. Use the master pattern to cut out the back jacket lining. Mark all pieces and set aside.

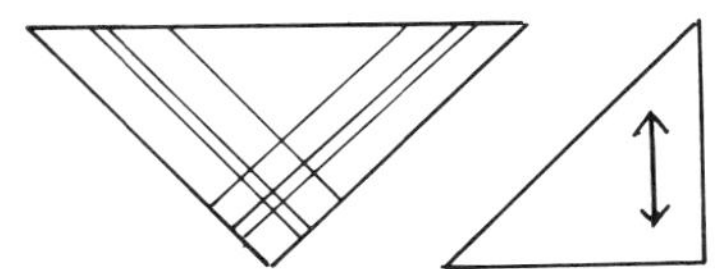

CUT OUT THE FLYING GEESE BLOCKS. Trace the two triangles onto template plastic, then cut them out. Use them to mark the wrong side of the fabrics. If your contrast fabric is a plaid, draw the position of the plaid weave on the "goose" triangle so that you can mark and sew every block exactly the same. Cut the triangles out, adding a ¼″ seam allowance.

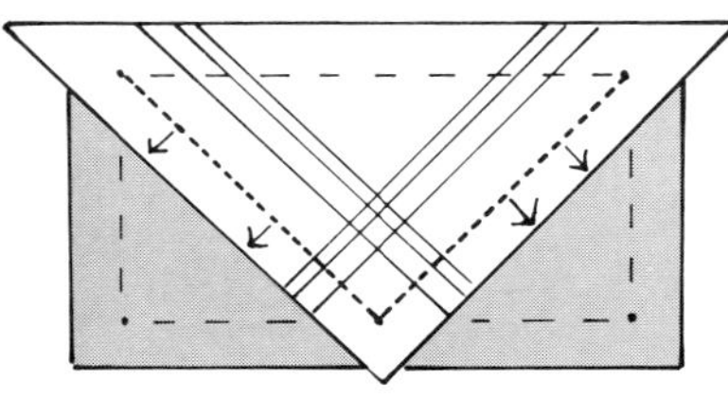

PIECE THE TRIANGLES INTO BLOCKS. This can be done by hand or machine. We chose to hand piece, since our two fabrics were of slightly differing weights and weaves. Sew from the bottom point of the "goose" triangle out toward each corner. Take care in handling the pieces. Avoid stretching the long bias edge of the goose triangle.

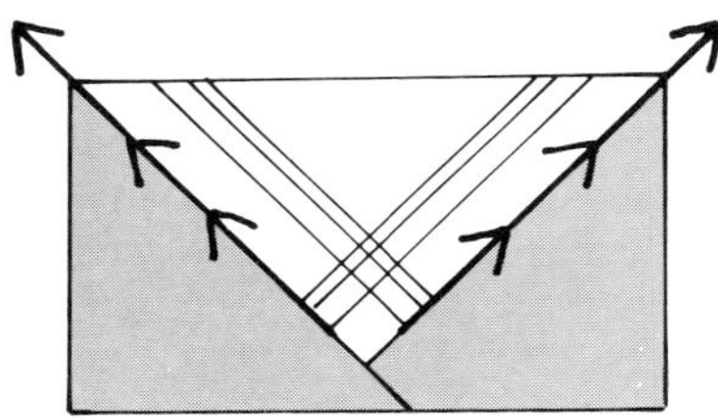

Press the seams away from the goose triangles.

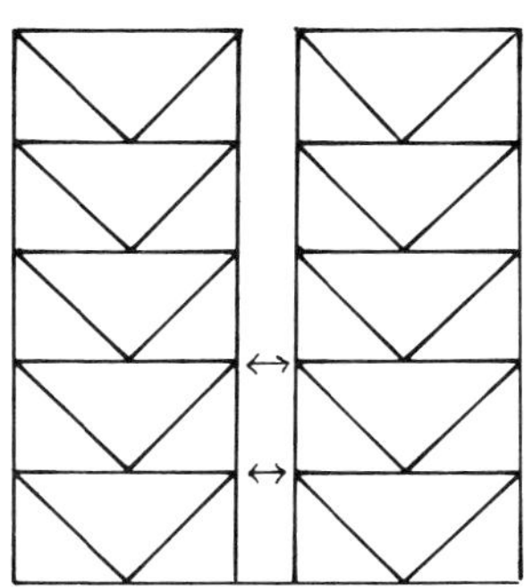

PIECE THE BLOCKS INTO ROWS. Sew the blocks together, measuring frequently to be sure they are accurate. Remember that the blocks must be uniform in order to line up with each other across the ½″ separating strips. The blocks must also meet evenly at the center front opening.

JOIN THE ROWS TO THE LONG ½″ STRIPS. It helps to hand baste before you sew. Match the dots on the ½″ band to the block seams. Be sure that the blocks line up across the strip. Trim the seam allowances and press them away from the blocks.

ASSEMBLE THE JACKET FRONTS. Sew the jacket fronts to the Flying Geese panels, matching the dots on the jacket to the block seams.

ASSEMBLE THE JACKET. Follow the directions with your commercial pattern. If the Flying Geese don't match up quite right across the front opening, you can correct this by easing in the too-long panel.

MAKE THE SKIRT. Use the commercial pattern of your choice.

ALLOW FOR TURN-OF-THE-CLOTH.

Most wools have a bit of thickness to them. So if you stitch the facings and flying geese panels together right at the points of the triangles, the points will look cut off when the facing is turned back and pressed. To avoid this, stitch just a tiny bit beyond the points, out into the seam allowance. The points will look just right.

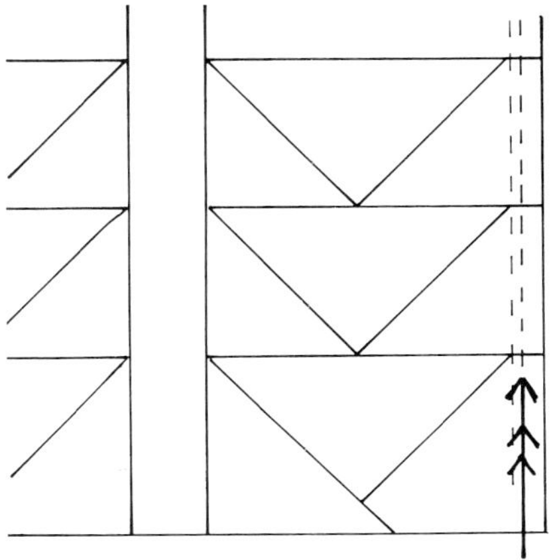

16
LEAVES AND BERRIES VEST AND SKIRT

"Honey, where were you during the Bicentennial? I coulda done great things with this pattern!" That's what a customer at Cabin Creek's Downtown Charleston shop said when Diane pulled from a garment bag her Leaves and Berries Vest, followed by its matching skirt and dress. That day, we were matching Cabin Creek's red and green home furnishings to the colors in Diane's appliqued and quilted vest. "I'da lengthened the skirt, laced up the front of the vest, and tucked up a calico apron. I would have looked just like Betty Zane at the Battle of Fort Henry."

That customer deserved an A+ in both American History and the History of Fashion. In Early American times, quilted clothing offered much more than just a practical way to keep warm. Throughout the 18th century, on both sides of the Atlantic, quilted petticoats were both the height of fashion and the basic uniform of everyday dress. To our ear, "petticoat" sounds like undergarment. Back then, however, a petticoat was exactly what the word said: a petite coat, worn for warmth and fashion. The only thing "under" about this garment was the manner in which women layered and draped their gowns at the time. Current fashion called for the "open robe" dress, a two-piece garment consisting of a lightweight overdress and an exposed underskirt. The outer skirt was split open from waistline to hem, revealing an elaborately quilted petticoat. Often, the overskirt was tucked up and puffed with panniers, a wire, bone, or basketry frame that emphasized and displayed the underskirt to fuller advantage.

Layering of skirts also allowed for some cheerful variety. After all, in this era any woman who owned more than one dress knew to count her blessings. So by interchanging one overdress with different petticoats or vice versa, many dresses could be created from only three or four separate pieces. In its shorter, more contemporary version, a quilted skirt can be just as practical and stylish.

The matching appliqued and quilted vest is also designed for the same qualities. With only a little planning, this vest can be the basis for many coordinated outfits. It's designed to be worn with both the quilted skirt and the simple paisley dress shown in our photographs.

For the sake of variety this Leaves and Berries Vest doesn't even have to be an applique project. The entire applique-plus-quilting design could be worked in quilting stitches.

The vest in our photographs is worked with machine applique. Hand applique looks just as nice. With this technique, the stems should be embroidered with a stem or chain stitch using double strands of six-strand floss or perle cotton.

LEAVES AND BERRIES VEST

Construction Notes:

Machine applique and hand quilting. Adaptable for hand applique. Beginner to intermediate.

Our vest and its matching lining are made from Stylecrest's off-white pima cotton broadcloth. For the appliques, we used scraps of deep red and fir green prints and solids. The berries are cut from the same rayon challis used for the vest's coordinating quilted skirt. Chances are, some of your applique fabrics will come from your scrap bag. For a nicer, more coordinated outfit, plan on purchasing at least one of your fabrics in enough quantity to make a matching skirt (quilted or plain) and/or a matching dress.

The fabrics in this vest are vividly colored, so be sure to wash all your material at least once. The completed vest looks even better after washing, so you'll never need to dry clean it.

What You Will Need

1⅞ yds. (36″ wide) solid color cotton (measurement covers vest and self lining)

Scraps of solid and print cotton in deep reds and fir greens

Thread: off white, fir green, deep red

Basic Vest Pattern (bolero length if vest is to be worn with Basic Dress)

See-through ruler

Wonder Under® or fusible webbing (such as Stitch Witchery®)

Large and small sheets of tracing paper

Stamping powder and piece of felt

DIAGRAM: LEAVES AND BERRIES VEST

Directions

GET READY. Review chapters on applique techniques and perforated patterns. Read through all instructions. Pre-wash fabrics.

PREPARE THE PATTERN. Trace the vest front and back onto the large sheet of tracing paper. Set aside.

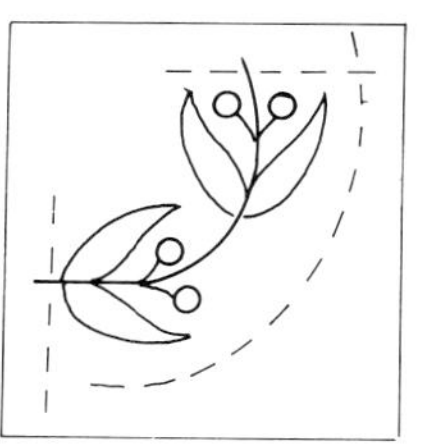

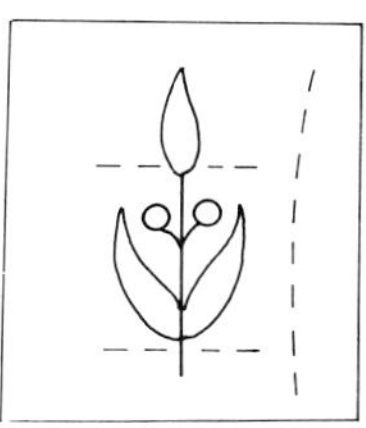

Trace the Leaves and Berries applique motifs onto small sheets of tracing paper. Draw each unit (front curve, end unit, basic unit) on a separate sheet of paper.

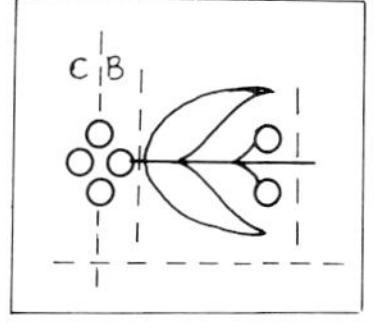

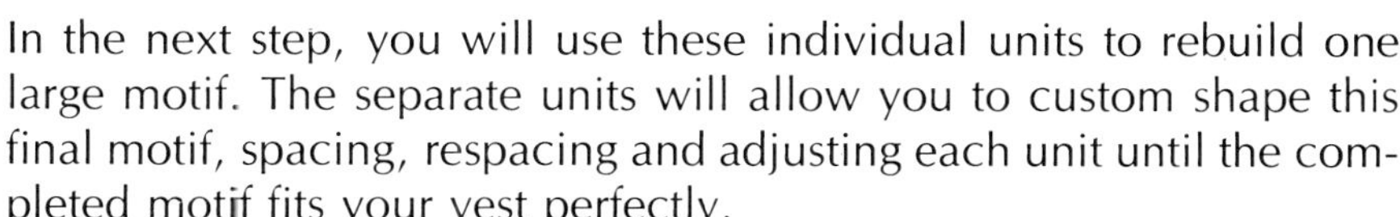

In the next step, you will use these individual units to rebuild one large motif. The separate units will allow you to custom shape this final motif, spacing, respacing and adjusting each unit until the completed motif fits your vest perfectly.

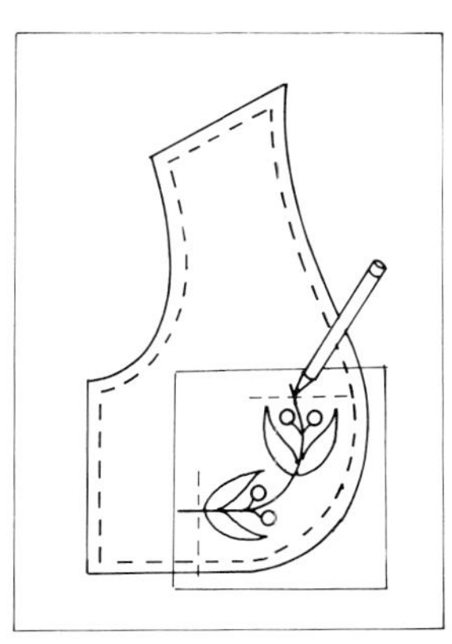

Lay the applique units *under* the tracing paper vest pattern. Position the front curved unit first so it fits onto the curve of your vest front.

Add on each remaining unit, one by one, adjusting each until you have them spaced as you want the final piece to look.

How to Custom Fit the Applique Design to Your Individual Pattern

If the applique design is too short: If the applique design needs to be lengthened, add another basic unit of leaves in the front, just above the curve. You can also try spacing the individual units farther apart.

If the applique design is too long: Reduce the spacing between each set of leaves by overlapping each of the units ⅛" to ¼".

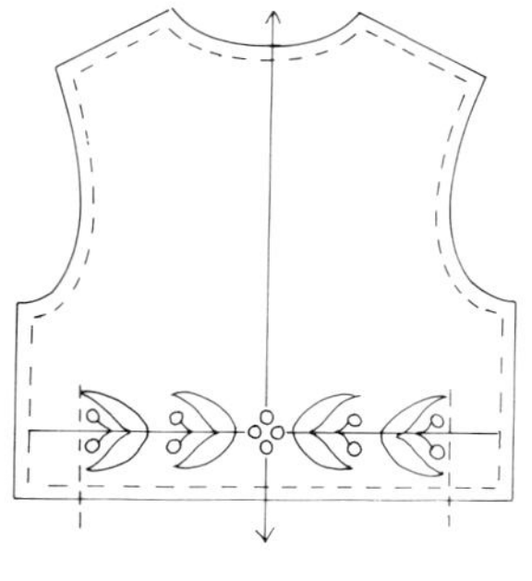

If the design doesn't fit from the center back to side seams: If the design is too short and doesn't reach the side seams, adjust the motif in one of the following ways:

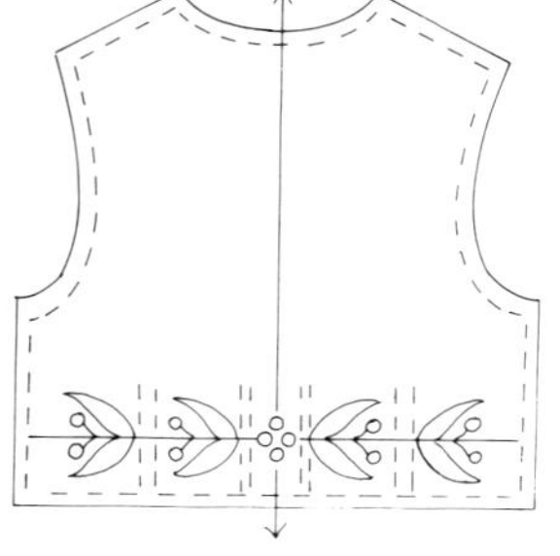

For a small gap, space all the leaves a bit farther apart.

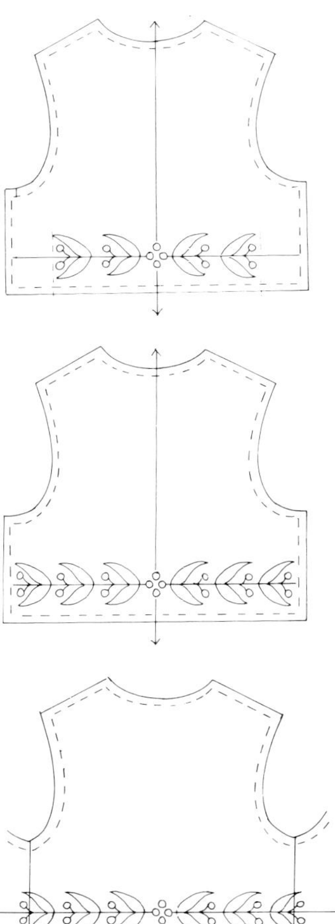

For a larger gap, add another leaf unit. If this makes your motif too long, space all the leave units a bit closer together.

If a leaf unit runs across a side-seam: No need to readjust. Instead, applique all the other leaves and berries first. Then sew the vest together at the side seams. Finally, applique the side seams' leaf units.

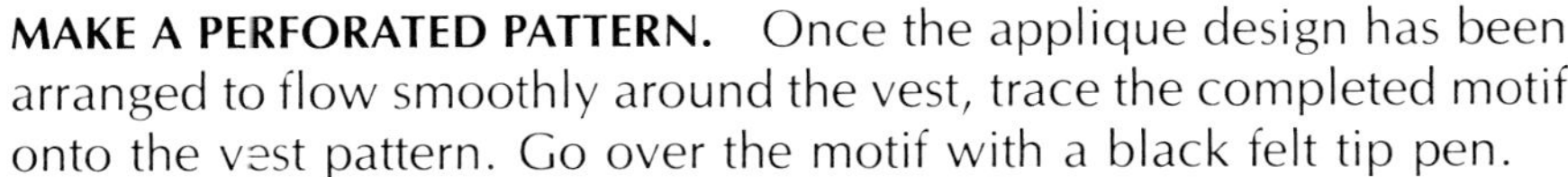

MAKE A PERFORATED PATTERN. Once the applique design has been arranged to flow smoothly around the vest, trace the completed motif onto the vest pattern. Go over the motif with a black felt tip pen.

Trace a copy of the vest front. Now you have a left front and a right front.

Perforate the applique motifs for all three vest sections. To do this, sew along the lines with an unthreaded sewing machine.

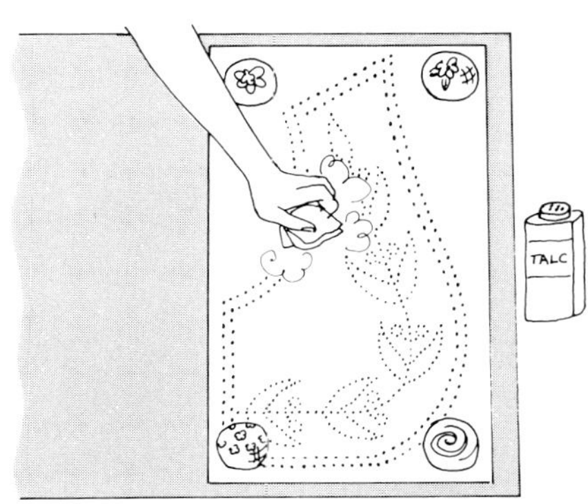

MARK THE VEST. Lay out the vest pattern pieces, placing them on the right side of the vest fabric. Secure the pattern pieces with weights. Stamp the perforated designs with stamping powder. If you are using a very light colored fabric, you may be able to lay the design *under* the fabric and then trace. If not, stamp the design, adding a bit of cinnamon or wood ash to your powder.

Immediately after stamping, draw along the stamped stem lines with a regular lead pencil. Do not draw in the leaves and berries. The stamped markings are all you need to position the appliques on the vest.

MARK AND CUT THE APPLIQUES. If you are using Wonder Under® to create iron-on fabric for your appliques, follow the manufacturer's directions for pressing it onto the back of the applique fabric.

Stamp the leaf and berry designs onto the red and green fabrics. Cut out the appliques, then position them on each vest section.

PRESS-BASTE THE APPLIQUES. Working with one vest section at a time, press-baste the appliques in position. If you are not using WonderUnder®, slide a few small pieces of fusible web under the edges of each applique, then press.

Before you put everything away, take the time to press-baste a sample swatch. Take a small scrap of applique fabric and press-baste it onto a scrap of vest fabric. This swatch will be used for testing your machine adjustment before appliqueing the vest.

PREPARE TO SEW. Press a piece of white freezer paper onto the back of each section to be appliqued. Thread the sewing machine with dark green thread and adjust settings for machine applique. Applique your test swatch, adjusting settings and tensions as needed.

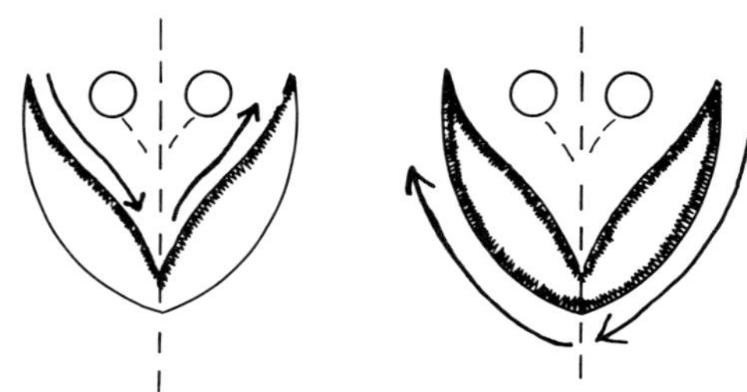

SEW THE APPLIQUES IN THIS ORDER. 1. Leaves. 2. Stems. 3. Berries.

Sew the leaf units in the direction shown in the illustration. When all appliques are sewn, remove the freezer paper backing. Tie off or bury any remaining thread ends. Lightly press each vest section.

MARK AND CUT OUT VEST, LINING AND BATTING. Mark both the cutting lines and the sewing lines on each vest section. Cut and mark vest lining. Cut out batting material.

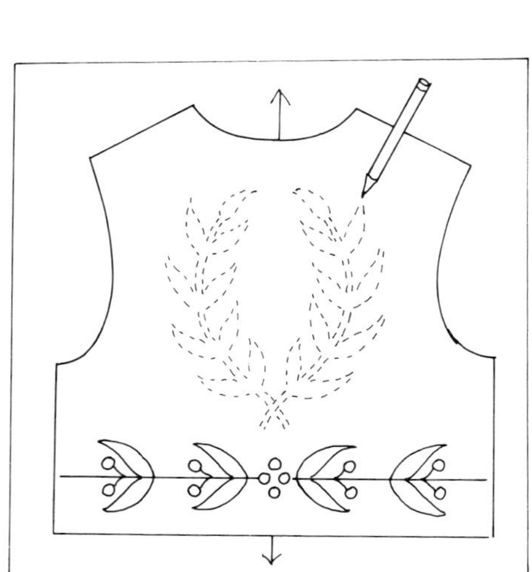

MARK THE QUILTING LINES. Using a lead pencil, trace the leaf "wreath" pattern onto the vest back. Use a ruler to mark the straight parallel quilting lines. It is only necessary to mark the intersections of the quilt lines. When you are ready to quilt, connect these marks with ¼" drafting tape, then quilt along one side of the tape.

SEW THE VEST TOGETHER. There are two methods for constructing a lined vest, the "turn through the side seams" method, and the "turn through the shoulders" method. Both are described in Chapter 4. If your appliques fall over the vest side seams, use the "through the shoulder" method. If not, either method is fine.

LEAVES AND BERRIES SKIRT

Construction Notes:

Hand quilting. Intermediate level.

"This feels so. . .cozy," said Sharon Ford. Sharon was all dressed up, with no place to go, waiting for her call to model the Leaves and Berries Skirt. "It feels like a nice lap robe." Quilted skirts *do* feel wonderful. They're very soft, weigh no more than a denim skirt, and rarely show wrinkles.

The Leaves and Berries Skirt is self-lined and completely quilted. Ordinarily, quilted skirts can be somewhat bulky, especially at the hips and waistline gathers. To reduce bulk, use a soft, thin batting that can be split into a half layer. We used Fairfield's Cotton Classic batting, which splits quite easily.

When choosing the fabric for this skirt, go for something that's soft and drapable, yet not too loosely woven. We used Stylecrest's 100% Rayon Challis for both the outer skirt and the lining layer. Other good choices would be silk broadcloth (self lined), silk noil (with a China silk lining) or lightweight wool flannel (silk or polyester lining). Our instructions call for hand quilting, but the project is easily adapted to machine quilting.

What You Will Need

4 yds. (36" wide) rayon challis (includes self lining)

Thin batting

Matching thread for quilting

Skirt zipper

Basic Skirt Pattern, adjusted for 60" finished bottom width

Very large size artist's tracing paper (tape sheets together if necessary)

¼" wide drafting tape

Stamping powder and felt pad

Lead pencil and/or white chalk pencil

2 yds. patternmaking cloth

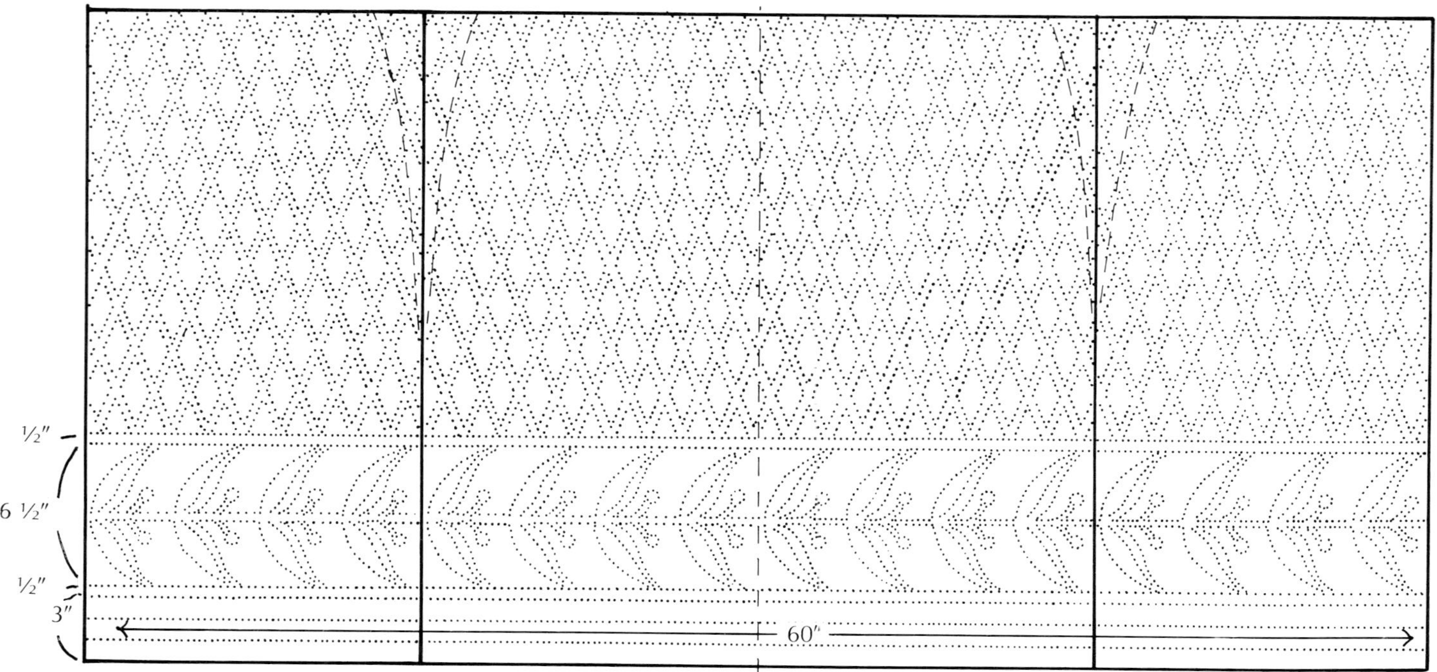

DIAGRAM: LEAVES AND BERRIES SKIRT

Directions

PREPARE THE MASTER PATTERN. Trace the basic skirt shape, one front piece and two back pieces, onto patternmaking cloth. Mark the hem line, adding only a ½″ seam allowance below the hemline. Draw in all horizontal border lines.

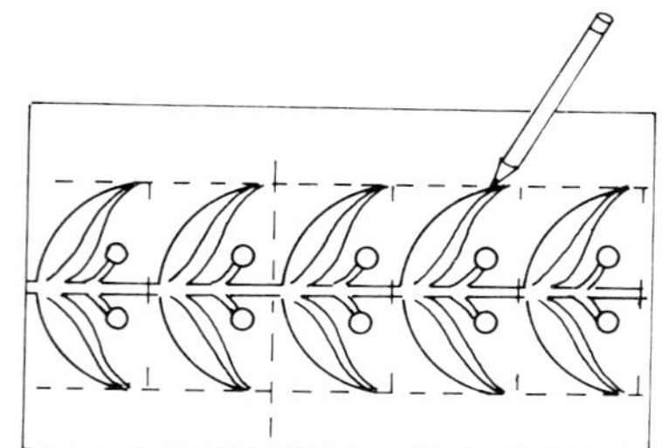

Trace the leaves and berries design onto a large sheet of artist's tracing paper. Try to make as long a repeat of this pattern as you can. Tape pieces of tracing paper together if necessary.

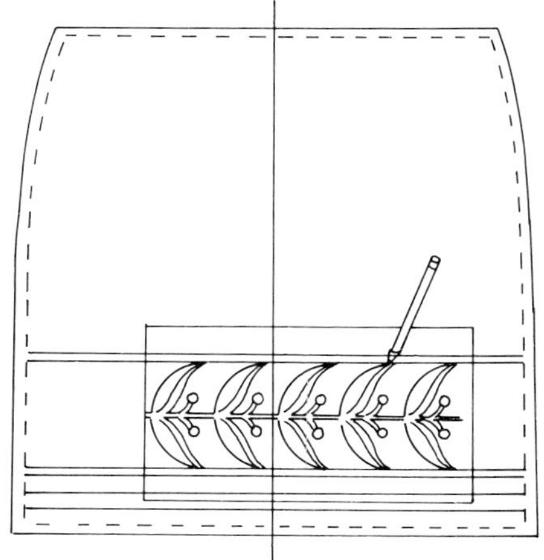

Position the leaves and berries tracing *under* the master pattern and trace the design onto the master skirt pattern.

PERFORATE THE PATTERN. Turn over the tracing paper copy of the Leaves and Berries design and perforate it with a hand needle or an unthreaded sewing machine.

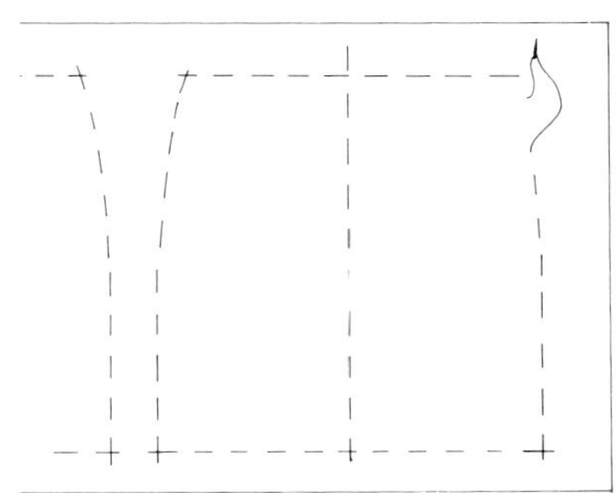

MARK THE SKIRT. Lay the skirt fabric right side up on a flat, smooth surface. Pin the skirt pattern pieces in place. If you plan to quilt each piece separately in a hoop, be sure to leave ample material between pattern pieces.

Mark all *cutting* lines with a chalk pencil or dressmaker's carbon. Pin mark the center front, all notches, and the hemline.

Hand baste, using long stitches, along these marked lines. As you quilt, you'll be handling these marks frequently. Many will simply rub off. By then, it will be too late to remark accurately, so don't skip this step.

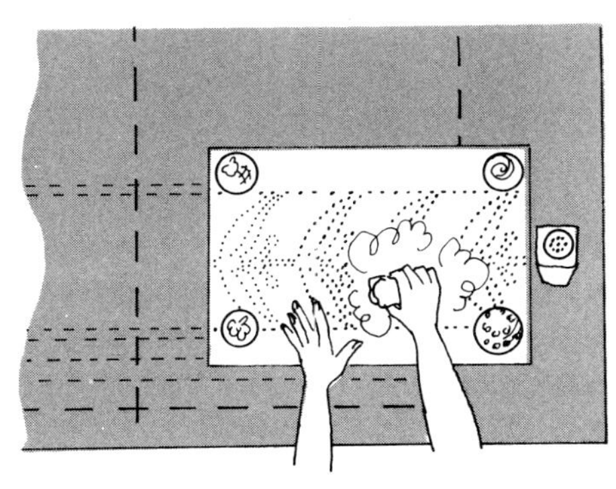

STAMP THE QUILTING DESIGN ONTO THE SKIRT. Following the measurements on your master pattern, draw all the horizontal lines of quilting on the skirt with a white chalk pencil or lead pencil. If your fabric tends to slide around as you mark, place a large sheet of fine sandpaper under the fabric.

After the horizontal lines are drawn, place the perforated Leaves and Berries pattern on the skirt. Hold the tracing paper with weights. Pat stamping powder through the perforations with a scrap of felt. Carefully remove the pattern and line it up further along the skirt section, or remove and place on next skirt piece. Be sure to align the design correctly. Repeat until the design is stamped all the way around the skirt sections.

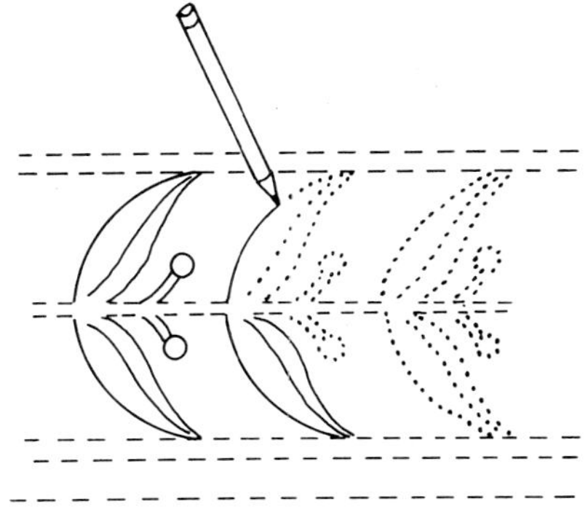

Stamped dots are only temporary. They brush off easily. So go over the powdered dots with a chalk or lead pencil.

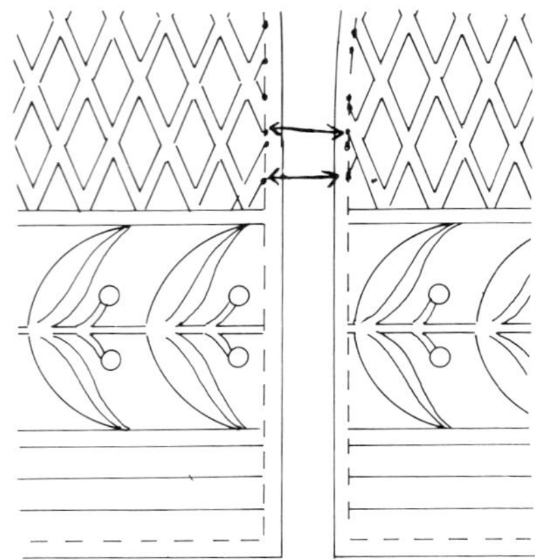

To mark the quilting lines on the upper portion of the skirt, the tracing, perforating and stamping method works well. An even simpler method is to mark these straight, regular lines with a ruler. Mark the skirt front first, then line up the side seams and continue the quilting lines at the same points on the back skirt sections. Matching these intersecting lines is a lot like matching checks or plaids.

PUT ALL THE LAYERS TOGETHER. Lay the lining face down on a smooth surface. Tape the fabric to the surface with drafting tape. Lay the batting on top. Place the marked skirt fabric (uncut, still in one piece of yardage) over the batting. Smooth out all the layers. Begin pinning all the layers together, working from the middle of the skirt toward the edges.

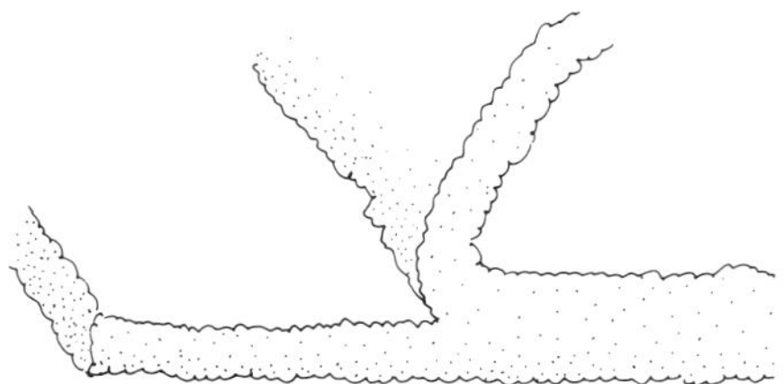

SPLIT THE BATTING. This is done to reduce bulk in the upper portion of the skirt. Fold back the upper third of the skirt fabric. Carefully peel the batting into two thin layers, stopping at about the hip line. Cut away the split half that is closer to the lining fabric. This leaves the more stable bonded side of the batting facing outward. Gently pull and feather out the cut edge of the batting. Fold back the top fabric and pin in place.

BASTE THE LAYERS TOGETHER. How much basting you need to do depends on the fabric you're working with and the quilting method you plan to use. Slippery fabrics like challis need lots of basting to prevent shifting. Hoop quilters will need to baste more securely than frame quilters.

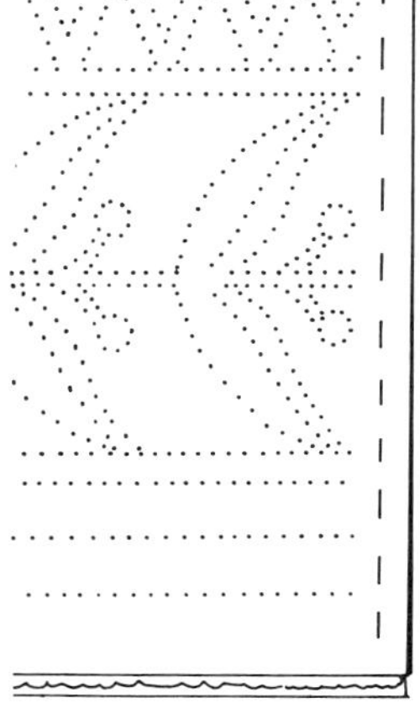

QUILT THE SKIRT SECTIONS. This design has lots of straight lines, which can make quilting quite easy. The simplest, and most accurate method for quilting straight lines is to use ¼″ drafting tape. Place the tape along the quilt lines, then quilt along one side of the tape. For double lines, quilt along both sides of the tape.

Be sure to stop all quilting about 1″ from the side, back, and hemline edges. These parts will be completed after the seams are joined.

ASSEMBLE THE SKIRT. In this step, you'll be assembling the skirt sections and blind-stitching the lining at the same time. If you've ever worked on a lap quilting project or a quilt-as-you-go project, these instructions will sound familiar.

Cut out the skirt pieces. Sew them together at the side and back seams, joining only the outer and batting layers, not the lining layer.

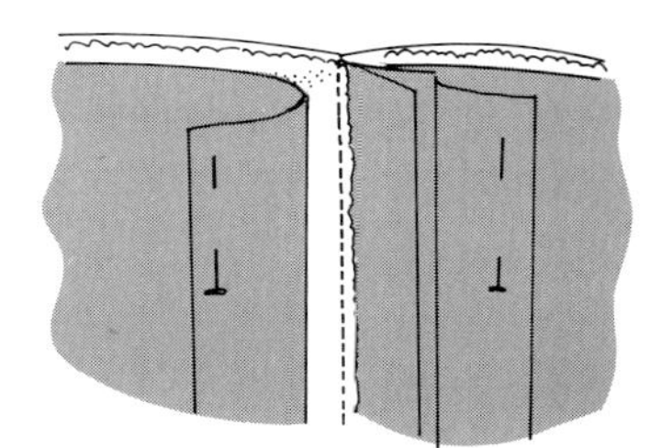

Trim the batting completely away from the seam allowance. You want as little bulk as possible.

Turn in the lining at the seam. Blind stitch in place.

For the hemline and zipper opening, trim the batting close to the seamline. Fold outer and lining layers so they face each other. Blindstitch the edges.

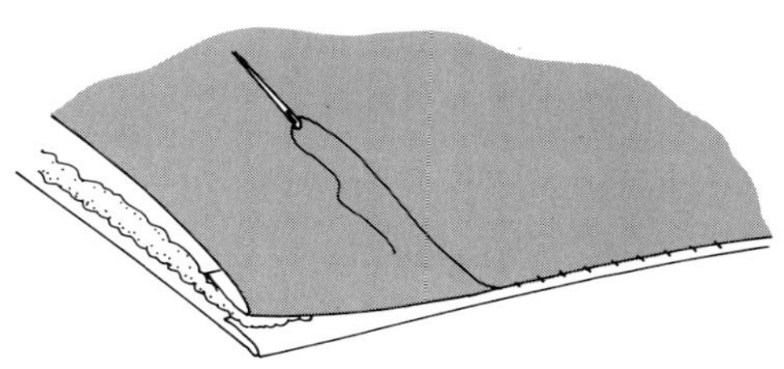

Finish quilting the long lines that were interrupted at the seam line.

Interface the waistband. Gather the skirt onto the waistband or, if your fabrics are very lightweight, arrange the fullness into soft, unpressed pleats.

Doritos
Ruffles
POTATO CHIPS
OATMEAL CAKE
WEIGHT WATCHERS
Cheetos
CRUNCHY

17
FLOATING TRIANGLES SKIRT

"You either sew or you clean house. I sew." Given a choice, Irma Keeney knows what's important. Quilting and sewing can put a strain on conventional housekeeping standards. When two or three projects are in various stages of completion, and the fabrics and sewing supplies for all three can't be put away without being lost forever, things can get a bit out of hand. Especially when the sewing room is also the dining room. Nevertheless, Irma's brick house (a farmhouse when it was built in the 1830s and now in the center of East Bank, West Virginia) is neat as a dressmaker's pin. Perhaps that's because her work in progress—folk art dolls for Cabin Creek's Charleston shops—blends beautifully with her collection of antique rugs, pictures and furniture.

Quilting is a hobby for compulsive collectors. And that includes people who can't bear to toss out even the tiniest scrap of fabric. They're the ones who understand that somebody might need that exact shade of green or lavender or whatever. . .someday.

Another way to justify fabric collecting is to think of it as creating a fabric bank, a closet full of fresh colors that you can draw from whenever you find yourself in a color rut and in need of inspiration. It's easy to get into a color rut. Some people tend to confine themselves to one or two favorites. Susan knows an art director who wears only black, white and occasionally when the two meet in a tweed, gray. This zebra-inspired wardrobe is her signature, but now that she's established her "look", it's time for the occasional jolt of color. Perhaps a pair of snappy red high heels.

The Amish have found their own way out of the dark-everything color rut. They pepper their dark neutrals with lively purples, fresh greens and shocking pink. For our dark toned Floating Triangles Skirt, we found all of these high volume brights in Diane's fabric bank.

Beige tones tend to trap people into color ruts too. It's tough to add colors to beige and come up with something really new. So for the light toned version of the Floating Triangles Skirt, we took a cue from the Amish again, and went with some color surprises. After many try-outs, we ended up combining taupe and beige with two tinted neutrals—a ripe peach and an unexpected lavender. If Diane hadn't saved that bit of lavender from a dress project, it might never have occurred to her to pick that shade. That's the value of having a wide selection of fabrics always on hand. Of course if she ever needs more lavenders, she'll have no trouble finding them. Somebody out there could be saving the perfect shade. In fact, it's probably in Irma Keeney's dining room, next to the soup tureen. Where else?

Construction Notes:

Hand or machine piecing. Beginner level.

To demonstrate the versatility of this design, we made the Floating Triangles Skirt twice—first an Amish-inspired version in blacks and brights, then a more subtle version in a rainbow of neutrals.

The fabric for both of the skirts shown here is available by mail order from Thai Silks in Los Altos, California. The Amish version uses a plain-woven silk noil, a very easy fabric to piece and sew. It comes in a wide range of colors. This skirt uses black with bright reds, blues and purples, plus a couple of light grays and off-whites.

The neutral version is made from a twill-weave noil. The main fabric is a light taupe, with whispery shades of beige, peach and lavender for the patchwork. Given a chance to make this skirt again in the same twill noil, we might think twice. Although twill noil is suitable for plain sewing, it's a bit difficult to piece. It's softer than most piecing fabrics, so bias-cut edges stretch easily. The twill is best reserved for experienced and patient piecers.

What You Will Need

2 yds. muslin

Silk Noil (36″ wide): 2½ yds. black (or other main skirt color) plus ⅛–¼ yds. each of 6–10 other colors

Thread to match main skirt color

Skirt zipper

Basic Skirt Pattern, 64″ at the hem

3 yds. patternmaking cloth

Graph paper

Artist's tracing paper

Template plastic

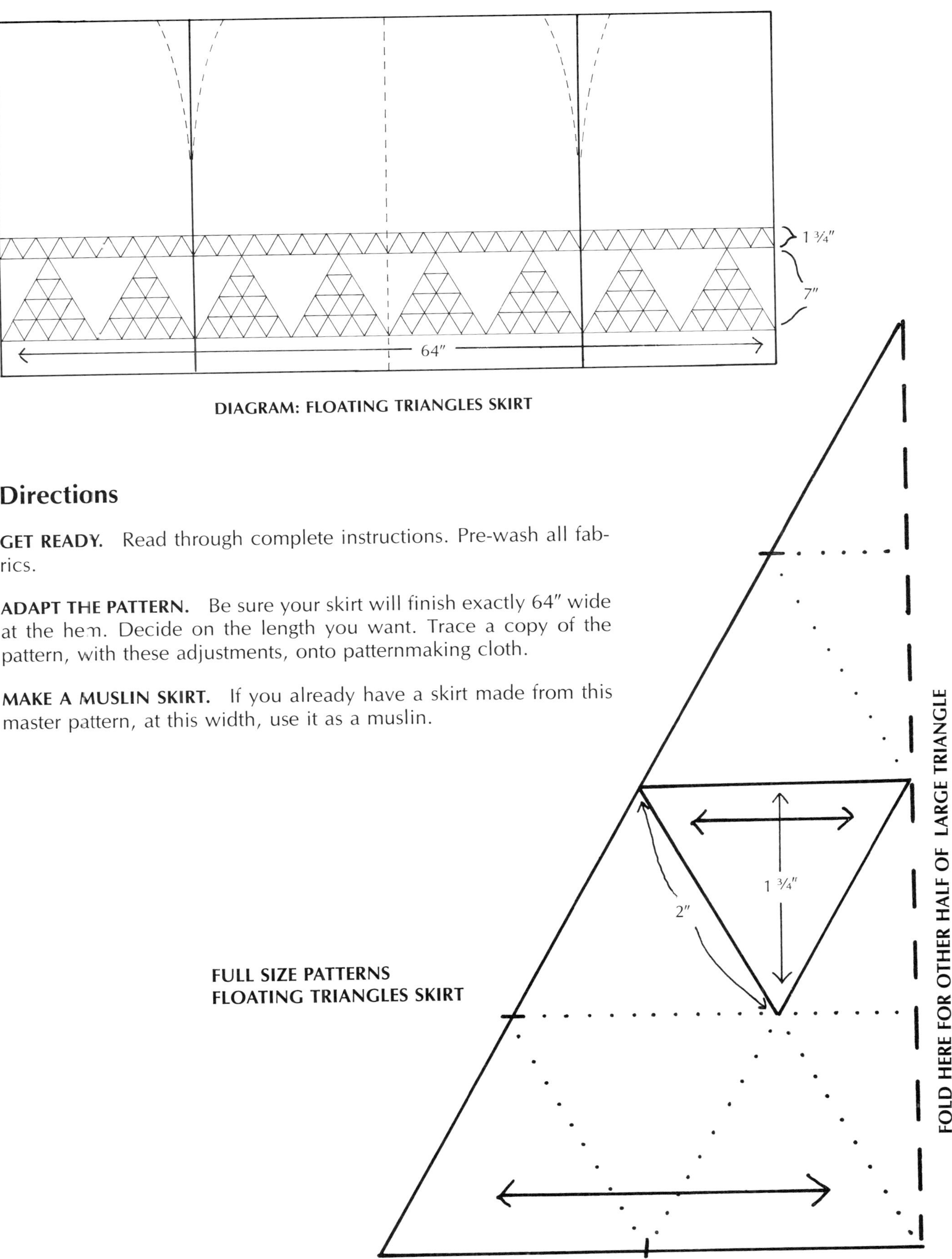

DIAGRAM: FLOATING TRIANGLES SKIRT

Directions

GET READY. Read through complete instructions. Pre-wash all fabrics.

ADAPT THE PATTERN. Be sure your skirt will finish exactly 64" wide at the hem. Decide on the length you want. Trace a copy of the pattern, with these adjustments, onto patternmaking cloth.

MAKE A MUSLIN SKIRT. If you already have a skirt made from this master pattern, at this width, use it as a muslin.

FULL SIZE PATTERNS
FLOATING TRIANGLES SKIRT

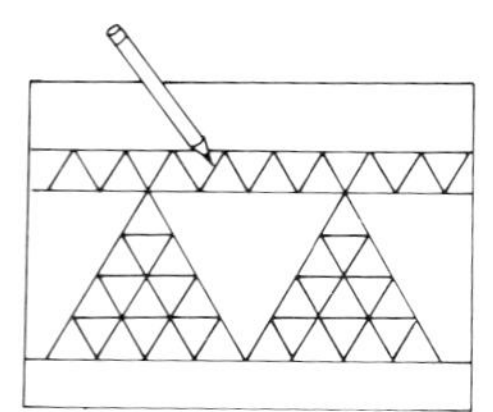

GRAPH OUT THE BORDER. Graph or trace at least part of the large and small borders onto graph paper or tracing paper.

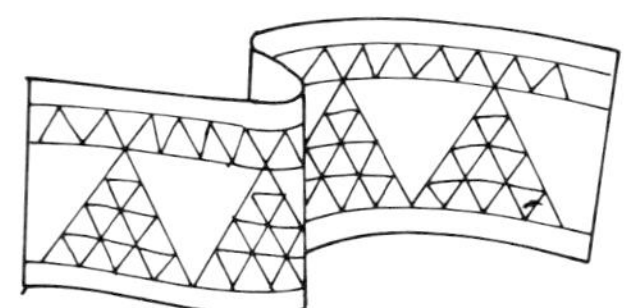

If you are not sure how you want the borders positioned on your skirt, trace out a facsimile of the border onto a strip of muslin as wide as the skirt hem.

Pin this muslin border to your muslin skirt. Try it on. Re-position if necessary.

TRACE THE PIECED BAND ONTO THE SKIRT PATTERN. To do this, refer to the diagram shown at the beginning of these instructions. There are four pieced triangles on the skirt front and two on each back half for a total of eight pieced triangles. You have now completed the master pattern.

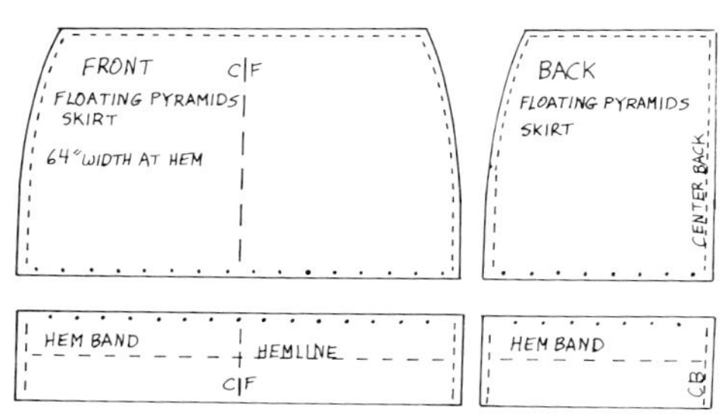

MAKE THE WORKING PATTERN. Retrace all of the separate parts for the skirt except the pieced bands. Add seam allowances and hems. Mark dots where the skirt sections will meet the pieced bands. These are the pattern pieces you will actually use to cut and mark the fabric.

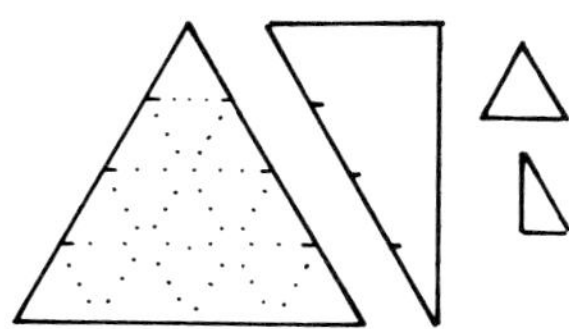

MAKE THE PATCHWORK TEMPLATES. Trace and cut out plastic templates of the small triangle and the large pieced triangle. You will also need a half-triangle of both sizes. Trace the patchwork pattern directly onto the template for the large pieced triangle.

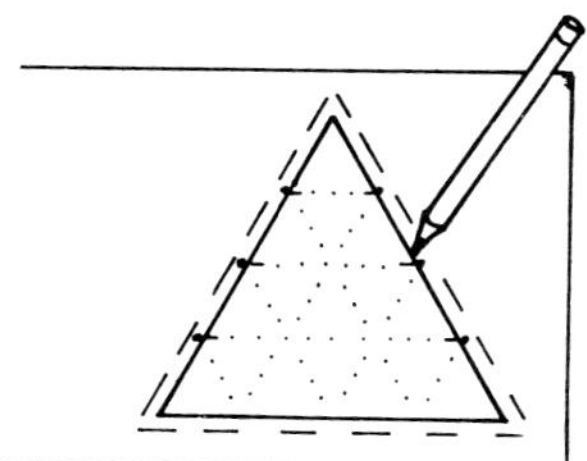

CUT OUT THE FABRIC. First cut out and mark the large skirt sections and the waistband. Set aside.

Mark and cut out the large and small triangles, adding ¼" seam allowances. One side should always be cut on the straight grain. You will need five large black triangles, six large black half triangles, 76 small black triangles, six small black half triangles and 112 assorted colored triangles.

LAY OUT THE TRIANGLES. Start by arranging one or two of the large pieced triangles. Place them so that all the straight grain sides run horizontally. All black triangles should point down, the colored ones point up. Play with the colors until you like your arrangement.

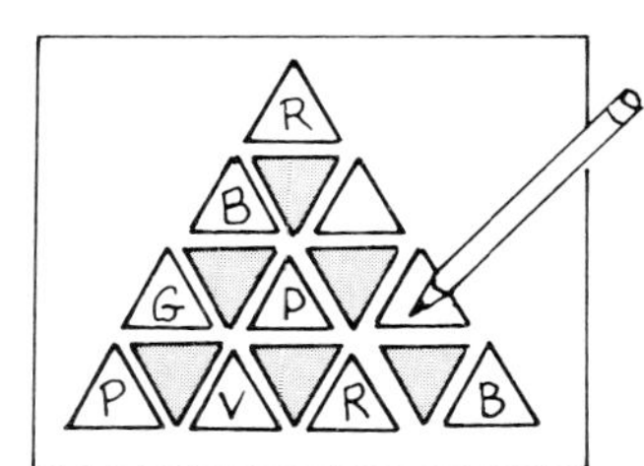

To prevent any confusion while sewing, draw a small diagram of the pieced triangle on a piece of paper. Note the color and position of each triangle. (Note: each large triangle need not, and should not, be pieced the same.) Refer to this diagram as you sew each triangle together. Make a notated diagram for each pieced triangle in the skirt.

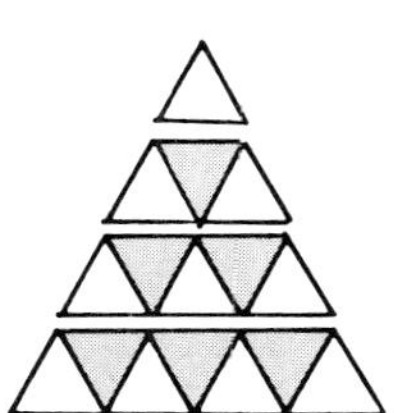

SEW THE LARGE PIECED TRIANGLES. Sew the small triangles into horizontal rows.

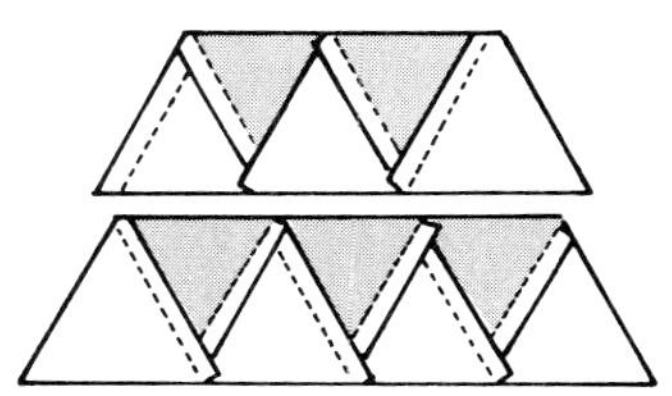

Press all the seams in each row in the same direction. *Alternate the pressing direction with each row.* This is the secret to ending up with perfect—not lumpy—points when the triangles are all sewn together.

Join the rows to form large triangles. Press. Usually such seams seem to want to be pressed upwards, but your fabric will tell you what it wants to go. Trim and grade the seams if necessary.

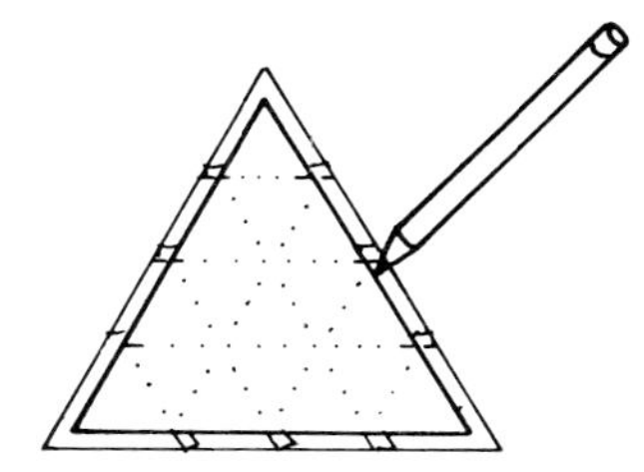

When the pieced triangles are completed, use the large template to mark the outside seam lines. Also use the template to check the accuracy of your piecing.

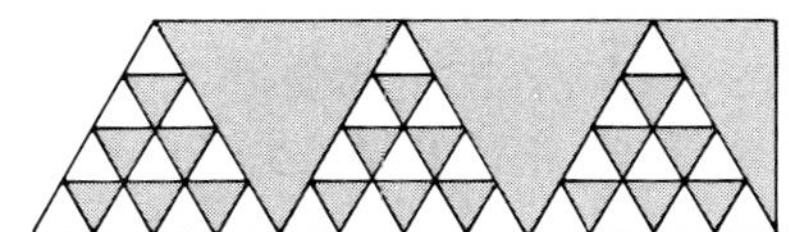

Referring to the diagram shown here, join the large pieced triangles to the large plain triangles, matching the dots to the seams. Remember to keep the grain of the plain triangles running horizontally.

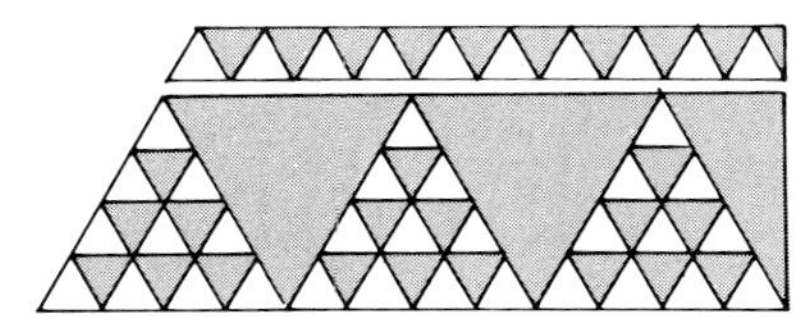

SEW THE SMALL BAND. Lay the wide band out on a flat surface. Place the triangles for the small band above it, arranging your colors so that two triangles of the same color will not end up touching. Draft a diagram or make a note of the colors to use as a sewing guide. Sew the band together, pressing all the seams in one direction.

JOIN THE BANDS. Match the dots on the large triangles to the seams on the small bands. Sew together.

ASSEMBLE THE SKIRT. Sew the upper skirt sections, hem bands and the pieced bands together. Sew side seams. Put in zipper. Gather or pleat the skirt onto the waistband. You may wish to make a full lining or to blindstitch a thin lining over the pieced borders. This is an especially good idea if your fabrics are likely to fray during cleaning.

18
PAISLEY GARDEN VEST

This traditional Indian pattern, named for the county seat of Renfrew, Scotland, is a simple pattern with a very busy past. At one time, it was both a threat to the British textile industry and a well-timed shot in the arm. Endorsed by a queen, then claimed by a generation of shop girls, paisleys are now a respectable Brooks Brothers staple. About once every 15 years, they become the latest fad. In fact, paisleys have been in and out of fashion so many times in the last two centuries, a few contradictions are only to be expected.

The paisley pattern is basically a curved, swirled abstract pattern derived from the palmette motif found in Persian rugs, classical moldings, frescoes and vase paintings. Although every paisley pattern starts out with a simple palmette motif, the use of repetitions, background colors, borders and stylized florals turns a simple form into a very exotic pattern.

In the 18th century, traders from the East India Company introduced the paisley pattern to English and American style setters in the form of cashmere shawls. For a very long time, the palmette pattern and the fine, soft, extremely lightweight kashmir wool on which it was woven or printed were inseparably linked. A cashmere shawl *was* a paisley shawl. Cashmere shawls were exotic and expensive and, therefore, fashionable. They were also quite practical. In the first few decades of the 1800s, when light, gauzy, shockingly bare empire-style gowns were the rage, cashmere shawls were a sensible, yet stylish alternative to contracting pneumonia. In upper crust country homes, shawls served the function of a sweater. Paintings from the period show paisley patterned cashmere shawls draped over the arms of elegantly dressed women, or casually arranged on a velvet chaise lounge.

It wasn't until much later, in the 1840s and '50s, that shawls came into use as outer garments. By then they were extremely long and very wide, almost blanket size. As skirts grew wider and more cumbersome, shawls were a fashionable way to provide warmth without adding even more to a woman's breadth. This is the point where Queen Victoria comes in. The British sovereign is often credited with launching a revival of the pattern. While the Queen's wardrobe was hardly known for its trend-setting qualities, she was interested in giving England's often troubled domestic textile industries an occasional benevolent nod. To assist the unemployed silk weavers of Spitalfields, the Queen and Prince Albert sponsored a lavish costume ball at Windsor Palace. This one night stand gave a much needed—if only temporary boost to a trade often threatened by foreign competition.

In the same spirit, the Queen is said to have established a "Buy British" dress code for the Prince of Wales' christening in 1842. All the ladies invited were asked to wear English lace rather than French or Battenburg lace. They were also asked to wear cashmere shawls produced by the woolen mills in Paisley, Scotland, rather than imports.

With time, Paisley-produced printed shawls were a grand success. They were warm, quite beautiful and less expensive than shawls imported from the east. In fact, they were so reasonably priced, it wasn't long before just about every woman owned at least one. Unfortunately, ubiquity can be a death sentence to a fashion trend. Though paisley lost its high-fashion cachet, it was only for a while. The pattern was destined to appear, fade, and be rediscovered so often, and with such reassuring regularity, that paisley has become one of the few fashions to be labeled both a fad and a classic, often at the same time. In the late 1960s, paisley was the battle standard of both the radical chic and the DAR. Today paisley prints are worn by silver-haired corporation presidents, purple-haired video artists and Ralph Lauren runway models. Proof that good design is more than just timeless. Its appeal is universal.

Construction notes:

Hand quilting. Beginner level.

Our vest is constructed from Stylecrest's Iridescent Twill Weave Pima Cotton, a smooth, lightweight cotton with subtle iridescence, an effect that is created when warp threads of one color are woven with weft threads of another color. This pretty iridescence is highlighted and enhanced by the three dimensional quality of decorative hand quilting.

What You Will Need

1⅞ yds. (36″ wide) pima cotton (yardage includes vest and self lining)

Quilting thread to match or contrast (we used a rusty-red shade)

Thin batting

Basic Vest Pattern (use shorter bolero length if vest is to be worn with Basic Dress)

Tracing paper

Pencils and black marking pen

Ruler

DIAGRAM: PAISLEY GARDEN VEST

Directions

GET READY. Pre-wash all fabrics. Read through instructions. Review "Quilting", Chapter 7.

PREPARE THE PATTERN. Trace your Basic Vest Pattern onto pattern-making cloth or large sheets of tracing paper. Trace each of the quilting motifs onto a separate sheet of tracing paper (use smaller size paper).

Following the diagram shown, arrange the quilting motifs in position *under* the vest pattern. Start with the large back medallion and align the center backs of vest pattern and quilting design.

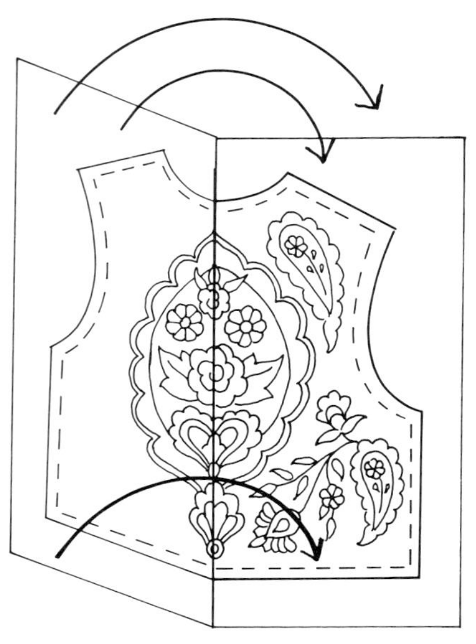

Then, working on only one half of the vest back, arrange the spacing of the other quilting motifs so that they fill the rest of the vest back. Working with each motif on a separate piece of paper allows you to adjust the spacing of the quilting pattern until it fits your particular vest size. When you like your arrangement and its spacing, trace the quilting motifs onto that half of the vest back. Now fold the vest pattern in half along the center back and trace the opposite side. Each side of the vest back is a mirror image of the other.

Follow the same procedure for the vest front, arranging the quilting motifs, then tracing them onto the front vest pattern. It is usually not necessary to draft left and right fronts. (The exception is if you are working with a very dark fabric and plan to use a perforated pattern.) To make the other front, simply flip the pattern over and it automatically becomes the other side.

TRACE THE QUILTING PATTERN ONTO THE VEST FABRIC. If your vest fabric is a light-to-medium color, tape the vest pattern to a light table or window. Place the fabric on top and trace all sewing and quilting lines directly onto the fabric with a pencil or water erasable marker.

If you are using a very dark color, perforate the vest pattern and stamp the design with stamping powder. Draw over the powdered lines with a white chalk pencil. When everything is marked, cut out the vest, lining and batting. Assemble the vest. (See Chapter 4, ''Assembling a Vest''.) Baste the vest layers together, then quilt.

RESOURCES

Fabric Sources

Thai Silks
252 State Street
Los Altos, CA 94022
(415)948-8611

This mail order company specializes in a wide variety of silks. Some cottons and woolens are also available. The silks include broadcloth, noil, shantung, crepe de chine and China silk. You may order color swatches for one particular type of fabric or a complete set of all available swatches for $20.00. If the swatches are returned within a month, all but $2 is refunded.

G Street Fabrics
11854 Rockville Pike
Rockville, MD 20852
(301)231-8998

This large fabric store near Washington, D.C., carries a wide selection of fabrics, notions, patterns and publications. The variety and quality are excellent. This is a good place to start, or turn to if you are searching for a hard-to-find fabric or are having trouble matching colors and textures. Ultrasuede® fabrics, J.B. Martin's Velvet, wool flannel, crepe, and gabardine, cotton batiks, Guatemalan cottons, imported lace yardage, glamorous evening fabrics and silks of every description are all here. G Street also carries a huge selection of ribbons, laces, braid, buttons, buckles and cords. They carry Kinkhame brand Japanese silk thread and DMC machine embroidery thread as well as a variety of other threads for sewing, topstitching and machine embroidery.

Anything in the store can be ordered through the mail. G Street's mail order department is quite different from most mail order fabric houses. It is a custom service. Perhaps you are looking for red wool crepe. They will send you swatches. Or you can send them a swatch of the blue tweed you've just made into a suit along with a request for a silk print for a coordinating blouse. They will send swatches and prices. It's also possible to order color cards for certain basic fabrics such as Ultrasuede®, wool flannel or wool crepe. The selection on these color cards usually includes 20 to 30 swatches of a given fabric.

An information packet describing G Street's custom services and a list of the fabrics that are generally available can be ordered by writing to the address shown above.

The Dorr Mill Store
P.O. Box 88
Guild, NH 03754-0088
(603)863-1197

The Dorr Mill Store started out as a supplier of pre-cut wool strips for rug hooking and rug braiding. Now they sell uncut yardage to quilters and fashion sewers. The wool, which is woven in Guild, New Hampshire, is 100% wool, 57″ wide and mothproofed. Two color charts are available. The first is a by-the-yard chart of 34 colors. A Potpourri chart, made of smaller swatches, covers 23 color ranges. Each color range is available in 6 shades. For example, the colors in the azure blue range vary from the palest blue to a dark navy. The set of two color charts is available for $3.00.

The following companies are manufacturers of fabrics. Their products are available in fine fabric stores throughout the country:

Stylecrest Fabrics, Ltd.
214 W. 39th Street
New York, NY 10018
(212)354-0123

Wholesale only. Stylecrest is a distributor of fine pima cotton dress fabrics as well as wool and rayon challis and fancy evening wear fabrics. Look for the Stylecrest name on fabric bolts.

Skinner Fabrics
Springs Industries, Inc.
1430 Broadway
New York, NY 10018

Wholesale only. Manufacturers and distributors of Ultrasuede® fabrics as well as other polyester and poly-blend fabrics.

J.B. Martin Co., Inc.
1290 Avenue of the Americas
New York, NY 10104

Wholesale only. Manufacturers of Matinee® Velvet.

Concord Fabrics
1359 Broadway
New York, NY 10018

Wholesale only. Manufacturer of high quality 100% cotton fabrics. Concord's solids and prints are classic quilting cottons. A good place to start when choosing and matching colors.

Notions and supplies

Silk Batting
Available from:
Marge Murphy's Heirloom Quilting Designs
P.O. Box 6306
Biloxi, MS 39532

Two packages are needed for a vest. One bag costs $3.00 plus $1.00 for shipping and handling (fifty cents for each additional item). Prices are subject to change.

Marlitt Rayon Embroidery Floss
Available in embroidery shops. Floss and color charts available from:
Home Needlework and Crafts
4647-T Highway 280 E., Suite 136
Birmingham, AL 35242
(205)991-2791

Send a self, addressed stamped envelope for price and ordering information.

Books and Magazines

Crazy Quilts
by Penny McMorris
© 1984 E.P. Dutton, Inc., publisher
2 Park Avenue
New York, NY 10016

The best book on this subject. Very interesting text. Study the pictures with a magnifying glass for lots of inspiration.

The Crazy Quilt Handbook
by Judith Montano
© 1986 C&T Publishing
P.O. Box 1450
Lafayette, CA 94549

Another highly useful idea book. A great place to browse for new stitches and piecing ideas. Has a color section showing crazy quilt garments and accessories.

Crazy Quilt Stitches
by Dorothy Bond
Self published
34707 Row River Road
Cottage Grove, OR 97424
$10.00 Plus $1.50 postage

Dorothy studied old Crazy Quilts and put together this spiral-bound book that clearly illustrates how to do hundreds of special, highly decorative stitches.

Baltimore Album Quilts
Published by the Baltimore Museum of Art in 1981, in conjunction with a special exhibition on Baltimore Album Quilts. An entertaining, authoritative resource that unfortunately is now out of print, but available in many public libraries. The Library of Congress catalogue number is 81-67526.

Treadleart
Magazine for Sewing Machine Enthusiasts
25834 Narbonne Avenue, Suite 1
Lomita, CA 90717
(213)534-5122
6 issues per year. $2 per issue, $12 one-year subscription, $1 catalogue

There are lots of magazines devoted to quilting and needlework, but this one is unique in that it focuses on machine work only. If you enjoy machine applique and machine quilting, you might want to send away for a sample issue ($2). Treadleart also publishes a 30-page mail order catalogue featuring a big selection of sewing machine supplies and attachments, notions that can be hard to find (for example, Teflon pressing sheets), specialized patterns and books.

Aardvark Adventures
P.O. Box 2449
Livermore, CA 94550

An entertaining, eclectic publication that's part quarterly newspaper, part catalogue. Full of hard-to-find sewing and craft items, plus articles, show notices, photos of loyal readers' completed projects and/or their pets. The merchandise includes Natesh rayon and Madeira metallic threads, Teflon pressing sheets, beads, books, fabric paints, belly dancer's finger cymbals, and giant inflatable crayons. Send $1 for a sample issue.

West Virginia Crafts

Cabin Creek Quilts
P.O. Box 383
Cabin Creek, WV 25035
(304)595-3928

Cabin Creek Quilts is a nonprofit, member-owned cooperative. Cabin Creek products, which include quilts, wall hangings, decorative housewares, clothing and toys, are available at the Co-op's retail store in downtown Charleston, West Virginia. In addition, Cabin Creek products are available in the State of Virginia, Dept. of Cultural Affairs Shops, located in Charleston and Wheeling.

Handmade Furniture

The rocking chair and two stools in our color photographs were created by David Barrett and were provided courtesy of the Cultural Center Shop. For further information, write:

The Cultural Center Shop
West Virginia Department of Culture and History
Capitol Complex
Charleston, WV 25305

David Barrett
Barretts Bottoms
Route 2, Box 231
Kearneysville, WV 25430

THANK YOU NOTES

Making this book happen took a lot of time, and lots of work. And for the extra help of some very special friends, we're eternally grateful.

Thanks to our friends in West Virginia. . .

Our friends at Cabin Creek Quilts helped make this book more than just a book about quilted clothing. It's also a book about quilters. The models for our photographs are all members of the Cabin Creek Quilt Co-op, a nonprofit corporation of professional quilters, all West Virginia residents.

Cabin Creek Quilts originally started as a Vista Project to help Appalachian craftspeople who might otherwise have no jobs at all. Some lived in very remote areas, far away from any kind of work. Others needed to give their families a hedge against the ups and downs of the mining industry.

Today, Cabin Creek Quilts is a member-owned cooperative. The quilters still work out of their homes, only occasionally coming into town to drop off finished quilts, pick up new fabric and perhaps get the details for a special-order project. Some quilters simply save up their completed work until someone from the Co-op gets the nerve to brave the twisted mountain roads that lead to their homesteads. Often, an entire family will participate in creating a quilt that carries the Cabin Creek label.

Working with the ladies from Cabin Creek was a lot of fun. We hope they enjoyed it as much as we did. Because we all live in different places, a lot of our planning work was done by long distance. Fortunately, Cabin Creek's Bonnie Masters and Judy Parcell are sharp cookies, and they kept us all organized. Thanks to their extra effort, our working vacation in West Virginia was practically a day at the beach.

Thanks to Lynn Payne, a terrific photographer's stylist and artist-in-her-own-right.

Thanks to our contributing artists. . .

To understand why we're beholden to all the quilters and sewers who helped us, take a close look at the workmanship of the garments in our photographs.

Coleen Walters quilted the Paisley Garden Vest, the Leaves and Berries Vest and constructed the Sawtooth Border Suit.

Etta McFarland stitched the Pinwheel Skirt, her first (and very successful) encounter with Facile®.

Hannelore Schultz took on the Fan Vest and the Floating Triangles Skirt.

Susan Reinsel pieced both the Sawtooth Border Suit and the Postage Stamp Dress.

Beverly Orbelo appliqued the Baltimore Bride's Vest.

Susan Stone made the quilted skirt and filled in with many hours of "grunt" sewing.

Rose Bailey quilted the Fan Vest and Baltimore Bride's Vest.

Jackie Isbell stepped in when we were getting down to the wire, helping us finish all the loose-end sewing.

Unfortunately, it is possible to have too much of a good thing. So when we were asked to make some page cuts, some of our favorite projects disappeared. But not forever. So stay tuned for next time around when we hope you'll get to see additional work by Rose Bailey, Roberta De Wire, Etta McFarland, and Beverly Orbelo.

And special thanks to. . .

Irene Wittig, Diane's next door neighbor and a perfect size 10, who patiently tried on muslins and half-finished garments. She never threatened to move away and her arms never fell asleep.

Our attorney, Rich Galler, who proved that one intimidating-looking letterhead can be worth a thousand lawsuits.

Rosemary Maceiras from *McCall's Needlework and Crafts Magazine.*

While this book often had us in a tizzy, occasionally it also had us in the doghouse. That's where our husbands are concerned. They were consistently helpful, and astonishingly patient. The word "saintly" comes to mind, although we have overheard muttered references to martyrdom.

Thanks to everyone who helped make it all look easy.

ABOUT THE AUTHORS

Diane Herbort is a fiber artist, designer and illustrator. Susan Greenhut is a writer. They share a love for quilts and skill for sewing. They also share the same early source of inspiration: their grandmother, Erma Daly, to whom this book is dedicated. Native Cincinnatians, they graduated from the University of Cincinnati; Diane in fashion design and Susan in broadcasting.

Diane worked several years in the fashion industry in New York, Philadelphia and Atlanta. Her clothing and quilts reflect a combination of this practical experience and her interest in the embellishment techniques used in antique clothing. She lives in Arlington, Virginia, where she designs projects for various needlework and crafts magazines. Diane teaches and lectures to quilting and embroidery groups around the country.

Susan lives in New York City. As an advertising copywriter, she has written about everything from cake mixes to hog slaughtering. In her spare time, she's an amateur historian, a hobby that leads quite naturally to an interest in quilting and other folk arts. Working on this book was a savvy career move for Susan; it forced her to learn how to make Flying Geese patchwork and how to use a word processor.